UNIVERSITY OF MAINE
NATIVE STUDIES SERIES

PENOBSCOT MAN

Newell Lion

PENOBSCOT MAN

THE LIFE HISTORY OF A FOREST TRIBE IN MAINE

by Frank G. Speck

The original 1940 University of Pennsylvania edition
with a new preface by David Sanger
and 30 additional photographs

THE UNIVERSITY OF MAINE PRESS
ORONO, MAINE 1997

To

JOHN DYNELEY PRINCE

Penobscot Man is an ethnographic classic written by an anthropologist
trained to reconstruct traditional native American, or Indian, lifeways.
When Frank Speck began his fieldwork early in the twentieth century, practitioners of the new field of anthropology witnessed the low
point of native populations. Once populous groups had vanished;
others were so decimated that only remnants of their traditional
behavior remained. The reconstruction of lifestyles, or cultures, prior
to the radical changes caused by European contact constituted a
major research goal. This book is a representative example of that
agenda. As such it has been widely cited as the authority for
Penobscot culture.

Speck's own Foreword recognized that scholars of the late 1930s
might find *Penobscot Man* antiquated and out of touch with the then
current research interests. Modern scholars regard research considered avant garde half a century ago quaint and even naive when
judged by current standards. Theories come and go, and with them
interpretations. Facts stand for all time, provided they do constitute
facts. Speck documented what he regarded as facts, although in the
area of social relations he recognized clearly the need for extreme
caution (see Chapter IV, p. 203). For the most part, Speck's information derived from native informants, people who remembered life as
it was in the nineteenth century. It is important to keep in mind that
Penobscot Man is not about a purely aboriginal lifestyle.

In the Postscript, written just prior to publication of the book,
Speck tells us how he regards his own efforts two decades after the
initial field work. This is a revealing chapter and the reader would do
well to consult it before diving into the descriptive body of the text.
Rather than an attempt to construct a pre-European contact Penobscot culture, Speck thinks of it as pertaining to "the latter half of the
nineteenth century." (p. 301). When Speck wrote the Postscript he
recognized how much had changed, and how the "Penobscot are in
reality an ethnic composite" (p. 301), the product of centuries of life

in the Northeast heavily impacted by French and then English culture. As Speck noted, "We cannot validly reconstruct the cultural
picture of an earlier period." (p. 311). This point is worth emphasizing; many have read and cited *Penobscot Man* as if its pages relate a
pre-European way of life, a recipe for reconstruction of a purely
Indian lifestyle.

Speck's vast knowledge of native peoples of the Northeast allowed
him to recognize that in 1936 Indian Island society was still very
much Indian. Although Penobscot language was fast disappearing as
a working language with the death of Elders, many traditional attitudes remained little changed. Speck speaks of the Penobscot sense of
humor. Ironically, a Penobscot Elder remembers how Speck was himself a target, and how, on occasion, he was deliberately fed false information to the merriment of on-lookers. Presumably Speck, an experienced student of Indian behavior, recognized a tall tale when he
heard one.

Speck would probably be surprised to find that, in 1990, the
Penobscot Nation numbered 1,954 people, of whom 425 lived on
Indian Island, the seat of tribal government and the center for traditional activities. Once linked to the mainland by boat or ice bridge,
a one-lane highway bridge built in 1951 connected Indian Island to
the Old Town shore. Recently, this bridge was replaced by a modern
two-lane concrete structure that removes the last vestiges of a physical barrier between the two communities. Social barriers continue,
however. During the 1970s, an event of major proportions forever
altered Penobscot society.

A highly acclaimed and successful Land Claim case raised public
awareness of the Wabanaki Indians of Maine—the Penobscot,
Passamaquoddy, Maliseet, and Micmac. The basis for the claim was
the contention on the part of the native peoples that various actions
by past individuals and governments had been illegal and in contra-
vention of the Indian Non-Intercourse Statute/Trade Act of 1790
which stipulated Congressional ratification of any treaties involving
aboriginal lands. A series of court decisions established that the
Penobscots and Passamaquoddies indeed had a valid case and that the
Federal government was obligated to act on behalf of the tribes.

Offering proof that the Penobscot and Passamaquoddy were resident in much of Maine in the mid-18th century, a law suit filed against the State of Maine in 1972 laid claim to 12.5 million acres of land, nearly two-thirds of the state. The ramifications horrified some state residents and elected officials who claimed the 1790 Non-Intercourse Act was not intended to apply to any of the original Thirteen States, but pertained only to the new territories of the then Western frontier. However, the wording of the Act does not exclude Maine (then part of Massachusetts), and in 1975 the courts rejected the State's claim. This opened the way for a potentially massive law suit, one that threatened the financial well-being of Maine.

In 1976, the Penobscots and Passamaquoddies offered to negotiate a settlement. The following year, President Jimmy Carter appointed a negotiating team which recommended terms for a settlement. On October 10, 1980, President Carter signed into law, with a symbolic feather pen, the Maine Indian Claims Settlement Act which transferred $81.5 million in Federal funds to the accounts of the two Maine tribes, together with the authority to purchase 300,000 acres of land for tribal use. In addition, a new relationship was established between the Bureau of Indian Affairs and the Maine tribes. Fiscally, and in terms of Federal recognition and services, a tremendous victory had been won. After 350 years of passive reaction to European and Euro-American policies, the tribes had taken a monumental step towards establishing their own agenda for the future and a measure of self-determination.

A decade after the land claims settlement, the impact has been significant. As might have been anticipated, life has gone on as usual for most of Maine's residents. Some property, most of it private timberland holdings and State land, has become tribal. But for some Penobscots and Passamaquoddies life changed abruptly and unalterably. Driving over the new concrete bridge from Old Town to Indian Island one enters the oldest part of the reservation—St. Ann's Church, the cemetery and a variety of older homes. Further on, the visitor arrives at the new section, mostly post land-claims settlement, with a complex of administrative buildings, a modern school, a tribal affairs and community center, and a multi-purpose arena. Beyond are several streets lined with modern homes that seem at first glance like any other middle-class American suburb. Investments have been made in various enterprises, and the Penobscots have entered into the world of high finance.

Despite the veneer of prosperity, things have not gone all that well. There are many on the reservations who feel that they did not get their "due" out of the settlement, that it was forced upon them, and that they should have held out for the terms of the original suit. The large sums of money have brought about claims of incompetence and illegal activities on the part of those who managed the funds. Lack of experience in business played a role in a series of financial disasters that have left the Penobscot coffers nearly empty a decade after the settlement.

On the reservations there are those who mourn the fast disappearing ethnic identity, the loss of being Indian, that formed the fabric of their unique society. For those concerned, the gains in material wealth cannot begin to compensate for the losses. And while attempts to stay the process will continue, for the Penobscots, at least, it will require a deep sense of appreciation for their heritage and formal programs to teach young tribal members what was once passed along from generation to generation within the family structure. Frank Speck and *Penobscot Man* must, and will be, a pivotal part of that heritage.

David Sanger
Orono, Maine, December, 1996

PHONETIC NOTE

THE characters used to represent sounds occurring in native terms are:[1]

Consonants

> *p* (*b*), *t* (*d*), *k* (*g*), *kʷ* (*k* followed by partial lip closure), *s* (*z*), *tc* (*dj*) similar to English *ch* in *chin;* voiceless lenes, between vowels varying between voiced and voiceless quality, depending upon the speaker. When voiced quality predominates they are written *b*, *d*, *g*, *z*, *dj*, *m*, *n*, *l*, relatively voiceless consonants, completely voiced between vowels. *h*, also written as ʻ, deep spirant or breath, always voiced. *w*, *y* semivowels.

Vowels

> *i*, high-front, unrounded; *e*, low-front, unrounded; *a*, low-back, unrounded; *α*, mid-open-back, unrounded, tongue tension similar to Maine English "*bur*"; *o*, high-back, rounded; *ə*, mid-mixed vowel, always short, like *a* in English *along*. Vowels (except *ə*) are long in open syllables and short in closed syllables. Vowels preceding nasal consonants, *m* and *n*, are usually weakly nasalized.

Accent

> ʹ, syllable stress accent written after or over vowel.

[1] Prepared in consultation with Drs. M. Swadesh and C. F. Voegelin.

FOREWORD

A FEW words of explanation seem to be called for at the beginning of a treatise conceived and carried to completion many years before its publication. The study to follow is the belated product of an undertaking that terminated about twenty-five years ago, both as respects the period of field work and the task of reducing it to writing. It shows in many places, I am sure, the anachronisms of a method in ethnology which was in vogue in the 'teens.

To those ardent and sincere critics—the frontier guardians of method in this type of research and publication before whom all earlier studies of American ethnology have been doomed to face the ordeal of judgment—I must plead for leniency. The moving reason for my action in releasing these records now lies in what they mean as documents of the thought and action of old Indians at a time when, as little more than a boy, I traveled and camped with them by day and by night, watched them and wrote down their verbal offerings drawn from experience and memory going back to their own youth and childhood. It is no wonder that certain aspects of this phase of ethnology of a northern people are not discussed in the fashion of the most modern approach and treatment. Ethnological investigation within the past ten years or so has indeed acquired a different technique from its forerunner, through influences brought to bear upon it by a much broader and deeper sophistication in the disciplines of social and psychological understanding. To incorporate the newer point of view, then, if this were possible for me, would mean to rewrite the volume from beginning to end. That has been made impossible under the existing circumstances.

I am furthermore perfectly aware by now that there will be some diversity of opinion among the many nature scientists and geographic historians who have become interested in the country and people of Maine, as concerns topics which the general nature of the book has obliged me to treat. It is not these points upon which I claim to lay stress but rather the data as the raw material which the people themselves enabled me to put upon record and what I myself observed. It is evident as we now view the material that the ensuing study will stand primarily as one which subsequent research may build upon as conditions of the future may dictate. The story of Penobscot life, we now realize, will never be completed!

F. G. S.

CONTENTS

CONTENTS   xiii

ILLUSTRATIONS

ADDITIONAL   PHOTOGRAPHS
(LOCATED   AT   THE   END   OF   THIS   VOLUME)

PROCLAMATION

GIVEN at the Council Chamber in Boston this third day of November 1755 in the twenty-ninth year of the Reign of our Sovereign Lord George the Second by the Grace of God of Great Britain, France, and Ireland, King Defender of the Faith.

By His Honour's command

J. WILLARD, Secry.

God Save the King.

Whereas the tribe of Penobscot Indians have repeatedly in a perfidious manner acted contrary to their solemn submission unto his Majesty long since made and frequently renewed.

I have, therefore, at the desire of the House of Representatives . . . thought fit to issue this Proclamation and to declare the Penobscot Tribe of Indians to be enemies, rebels and traitors to his Majesty. . . . And I do hereby require his Majesty's subjects of the Province to embrace all opportunities of pursuing, captivating, killing and destroying all and every of the aforesaid Indians.

And whereas the General Court of this Province have voted that a bounty . . . be granted and allowed to be paid out of the Province Treasury . . . the premiums of bounty following viz.:

For every scalp of a male Indian brought in as evidence of their being killed as aforesaid, forty pounds.

For every scalp of such female Indian or male Indian under the age of twelve years that shall be killed and brought in as evidence of their being killed as aforesaid, twenty pounds.

In the House of Representatives June 10, 1756.

. . . .

For every Indian enemy that they shall kill and produce the scalp to the Government and Council in evidence, the sum of three hundred pounds.

. . . .

Also, voted, that the same allowance be made to private persons who shall . . . kill any Indian enemy which is made to soldiers on the frontiers of the province.

INTRODUCTION

THROUGH personal and family associations in early life with eastern Algonkian woodland tribes, I was led by a renewal of interest in 1907 to begin a systematic attempt to investigate the long-neglected bands occupying territory in northern New England and eastern Canada. Attention was first directed to the Penobscot in northern Maine, the southernmost tribe of the Wabanaki group then retaining to any extent its original characteristics. Beginning with the summer of 1907, the succeeding summers through 1912 were spent mostly in contact with the people at home and in their summer camps; while during the intervening winters, on through 1918, periods of about a month sometimes divided into several visits were given to residence with them for participation in their winter home life. The partial results of my own share in the work are herewith submitted. Some of the material prepared during the course of the investigation has already appeared in print.

The investigation was first carried on in the interests of the University of Pennsylvania Museum, chiefly through the support of Dr. George G. Heye, for whom the ethnological collections were made. Penobscot material in the American Museum of Natural History in New York, the Peabody Museum in Cambridge, Massachusetts, and the Victoria Museum in Ottawa, Ontario, as well as various things retained in the possession of the Indians themselves, has also been used. Acknowledgments are due to the officials of the institutions mentioned above, and especially to Dr. Clark Wissler for aid in securing illustrations. I am under deep obligation to Dr. Boas for the inspiration of preparatory training with him, and occasional consultation on difficult points during the early progress of my work. Dr. A. A. Goldenweiser long ago also rendered me favors in consultation on the section dealing with social organization. I am also indebted to Mr. W. C. Orchard and to Dr. G. Herzog for contributing information and advice in handling technology, and to Dr. G. Herzog for reading and checking over the late Jacob Sapir's transcriptions of dance music. Mrs. Fannie H. Eckstorm of Brewer, Maine, has stimulated me exceptionally for several years past by reviving my earlier interest in Penobscot life, and has aided in checking data obtained from younger generations of informants with observations and notes on older phases of custom with which she is familiar. Although my opportunity to consult her came only within the past three years it enabled me to amend a number of statements recorded previously. For this I express appreciation. I shall refer frequently to her monograph on Penobscot industries.[1] Dr. Frank T. Siebert, Jr. has added to my work the benefit of his observations on certain topics of Penobscot linguistics and ethnology which are given as entries and footnotes. Dr. W. J. Phillips, of the University of Pennsylvania, Dr. Loren C. Eiseley of the University of Kansas, and Mr. Claude E. Schaeffer have been kind enough to give the manuscript critical readings. My colleagues, Dr. A. I. Hallowell and Dr. H. A. Wieschhoff, have aided and encouraged me with helpful suggestions and the reading of the text. To Miss Gladys Tantaquidgeon and Gladys McIntyre acknowledgments are due for secretarial aid. Mr. Robert Riggs and Mr. Charles T. Coiner, of Philadelphia, have generously given thought and talent to the make-up of the illustrations.

Through an appropriation in 1936 the Faculty Research Fund of the University of Pennsylvania made it possible for me to return to the Penobscot field to continue the collection of song records begun many years ago, and to refine certain sections of the manuscript. And finally come acknowledgments to the members of the Penobscot tribe, especially Gabriel Paul, Newell Lyon, Joe Hemlock, Charles Mitchell, Gov. Peter Nicolar, Frank Denis, Sarah Saul, Clara Neptune, Cecil Barker, Catherine Paul, Alice Swassion, Joe Solomon, Lola Coley, Gov. Sabattis Francis, Gov. Newell Francis, Buck Andrew, Roland Nelson (Needahbeh), Piel Sakus, John Bear, John Susup, John Attean, Mitchell Attean, Joe Francis,

[1] Fannie H. Eckstorm, *Handicrafts of the Modern Indians of Maine*, Bull. III, Abbe Museum, Bar Harbor, Me., 1932, pp. 1–72, Pls. I–XXVII.

FIG. 1

PENOBSCOT TYPES

Upper left, Labet Andrew
Upper right, Joe Solomon
Below, Buck Andrew

and the score of other members of the tribe—the hunters, guides, fishermen, shantymen, idlers, basketmakers, housewives, the majestic forest patriarchs and the struggling derelicts of the swift age of transition—whose coöperation made the work possible. Upon Needahbeh, my friend, I have in particular leaned heavily for aid and encouragement.

Despite considerable advancement in civilization of the rural American stamp, an undercurrent of conservatism resulting from insular location and the wilderness at their backs lurks in the minds of these Indians. Until about 1870 they lived in an atmosphere practically unchanged by European influence, except for the changes wrought by Christian conversion. Even in living and working among them when I did, it took a long period of contact to overcome their reticence. Until forty years ago it was common belief in the tribe that the legendary culture hero, *Gluska'be*, was still busy manufacturing stone arrowpoints in his mythical abode, for the day when he should return and expel the whites from the country. This conservatism is mentioned to anticipate the possible query, which may be raised by some who are not intimately acquainted with local conditions, as to the validity of native tradition concerning things supposed to be aboriginal which survive among a people who have been in fairly close contact with Europeans for a hundred years.

A short chapter of history lying behind the preparation of this research remains yet to be added. The main investigation of Penobscot general ethnology begun in 1907 closed in 1914, with my concentration of effort transferred to the field of the Montagnais-Naskapi of the Labrador peninsula.

From 1914 to 1918, when occasion permitted, attention was focused upon the recording of myth texts and religious beliefs, shamanism, social organization, and decorative art, with the coöperation of Newell Lion, who proved to be a most capable informant. He froze to death in the woods in 1918. I then began to bring out some papers and monographs on phases of Penobscot culture, embodying the results of the later research. Thus several studies were carved out of the accumulated material and dealt with somewhat comparatively, knowledge being used which was acquired meanwhile through field research among other Wabanaki bands and the more primitive Algonkian nomads north of the River and Gulf of St. Lawrence. The topics covered in these reports have been omitted from the following study, and therefore should be consulted independently in connection with Penobscot life. They are listed chronologically in the list of sources given in the bibliography at the end of the volume (page 316).

Exceptionally attractive inducements lurk at every turn in the treatment of Wabanaki material culture, tempting one to pause for discussion of comparative and distributional traits. My decision, however, has been to refrain from that at present, considering the incomplete state of our knowledge of the northeast. Much remains to be determined of the extent of culture-stimulation brought upon the early Algonkian by the Iroquois and Huron, and the probable displacement of the Algonkian tribes formerly about the eastern Great Lakes region and the upper St. Lawrence. That there have been epochs of culture change in Algonkian history no one would be inclined to deny, although perhaps not all would agree with the suggestions of those who have written variously explaining it (Brinton, Dixon, Sapir, Birket-Smith, Schmidt, Prince, Eckstorm, Krickeberg, Jenness, Barbeau, Parker, Ritchie, Wissler, and Skinner among others). From century to century, the Wabanaki have been subjected to changing conditions invading their southern and western borders from distant centers of development. The temptation is strong to theorize upon the possibility of a migration bearing easterly from an earlier location—a later separate existence as a group sprung from a common source with the eastern Ojibwa-Algonquin cultural phylae. But hold: without yet having before us the knowledge to come when projected research in the area has been completed, we may better postpone theories until later. My restricted purpose is at present to offer chapters on the composite and historic cultural life of an integral group.

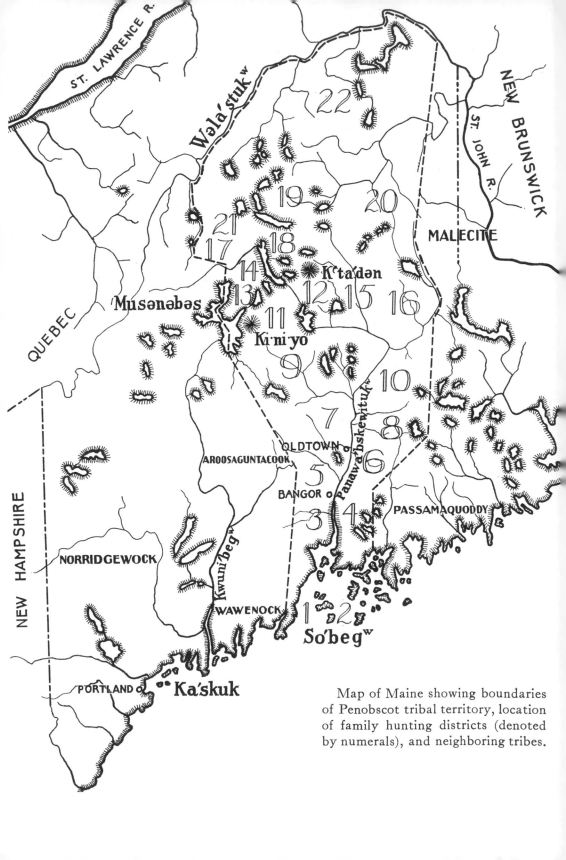

Map of Maine showing boundaries of Penobscot tribal territory, location of family hunting districts (denoted by numerals), and neighboring tribes.

I

TRIBAL NAME AND HABITAT

THE Penobscot Indians refer to themselves as *Pa'nawamp-ske'wi·ak*, "People of the white rocks (country)," or "People of where the river broadens out." The masculine of the name is *Pana'wampsk'ewi;* the feminine *Pa'nawampske'wis-kwe''su. Pana'wampskik*, "Place of the white rocks," or also "Place where the river broadens out" (*Pana'wapskik*), denotes the tribal habitat, and even the tribe itself. The name is evidently a very old one, for which many and varied interpretations have been attempted by both Indian and white authorities. Further than to give the interpretation most generally agreed upon by the old men of the tribe would, I fear, hardly be warrantable, for the term comes down to us in a more or less stereotyped form.[1] It is also the name of the principal village at Oldtown.

The territory occupied by the tribe had no very well defined limits owing to its wide extent and the paucity of native population. The loose tribal organization characterizing the people of the whole northeastern region, indeed, did not tend to develop very strict land distinctions outside of the family hunting territories. Close ethnic relationship, furthermore, made their contact easier and less liable to intertribal constraint. Generally speaking, however, the tribal hunting territory was the valley of the Penobscot River and its tributaries. Beginning at Penobscot Bay, it extended a short distance back from both shores and spread out, going up-river, reaching almost as far as the upper St. John River. The northern tracts were, we learn, not definitely appropriated by any people, the same being true in general of some unclaimed stretches of wilderness lying between the river systems occupied by adjacent tribes. Thus nearly all the Penosbcot villages were on the Penobscot River, and their hunting grounds bordered it. The bounds were less sharply defined

[1] Cf. article on Penobscot in *Handbook of American Indians*, Bulletin 30, Bureau of Amer. Ethnology, Wash., D. C. See also Godfrey, p. 85.

FIG. 2

PENOBSCOT TYPES AND ACTIVITIES

Upper left, Man Scraping Sealskin
Upper right, Playing Dice and Bowl Game
Lower left, Lola Coley
Lower right, Boy of Attean Family

as the distance increased until the recognized outlying territory of some neighboring tribe was reached, and eventually, in
proceeding farther, the river upon which were its villages.
So the Penobscot, of the eighteenth century at least, had the
Norridgewock west of them on the Kennebec River, the
Malecite northeast of them on St. John River, and the Passamaquoddy as their immediate neighbors on the southeast
along the coast to the St. Croix River and Passamaquoddy
Bay. The Passamaquoddy hunted over and occupied country close to Penobscot Bay on the east, including Mt. Desert
Island, which was consequently not in Penobscot territory,
the same being true of Union River just east of the Penobscot.
It seems probable, as Mrs. Eckstorm thinks, that their earlier
occupancy extended still farther west on the coast, under the
collective group name Etchemins as given in the narratives.
To the northeast, however, the Penobscot occupied the Mattawamkeag and Passadumkeag River systems spreading eastward, the Piscataquis and Penobscot systems extending westward to beyond the Katahdin country and the watershed of
the Allagash and St. John. From what can be learned, the
territory beyond this seems not to have been definitely appropriated in later times by any natives in particular.

The accompanying territorial map shows an attempt to
delineate the main locations in the country of the Penobscot
and the situation of the neighboring tribes in the period upon
which the ensuing study of culture is based.

Concerning the land itself the Penobscot country is con-
sciously beautiful in the eyes of its aborigines. From the
deeply indented bays of the rock-lined coast the land slopes
upward in rolling well-watered tracts. The tidal movement
reaches as far inland as Bangor, above which the river narrows
and becomes shallow. Below Bangor, the river, though narrow in places, becomes deep enough for navigation, with high
shores even bordered by mountains near its embouchure into
the bay. The tilt of the country northward gradually leads
to a range of mountains, some hundred miles or so from salt
water. Here, at a point about midway from the ocean, rises
Mt. Katahdin (Ktaadn), almost alone, like a peak above

the seemingly level, densely forested plateau surrounding it
(Fig. 3).

This impressive landmark justly commands us to pause
for attention through the importance it acquires in native
geography and legend. The following historical observations
are quoted from an illustrated article by Dr. E. S. C. Smith,
of Union College, and P. W. K. Sweet, appearing in the
Geographical Review.

FIG. 3

MOUNT KATAHDIN (KTAADN)

From Daicey Pond, Piscataquis County, Maine
Penobscot Tribal Landmark

Numerous excursions took place in those earlier days, and there
is much of historical interest attaching to Ktaadn in this connection.
In fact, a volume might be written concerning those pioneer ascents,
and it may be well to review some of the outstanding ones. The
earliest recorded ascent of the mountain was made in 1804 by
Charles Turner Jr. and party. Turner was engaged in duties as a
land surveyor. It appears that the Indians of the vicinity, Penobscots and Abenakis, believed the mountain the lair of an evil spirit
whom they called Pamola; and never would an Indian ascend higher
than the tree limit for fear of this monster. Nevertheless, the

Indian guides of Turner's party went to the top, apparently will-
ingly, after they found the white men determined to go. The
name Pamola is at present applied to one of the lesser peaks of
Ktaadn. During the northeastern boundary controversy we find
that the mountain was ascended in 1819 by Colin Campbell, one
of the Surveyors employed by the British Government. In 1836
Prof. F. W. Bailey of West Point and Professors Keely and Barnes
of Waterville (now Colby) College visited the mountain. The
following year Dr. Chas. T. Jackson with a party climbed Ktaadn
in a snow-storm while performing his duties as first State Geologist
of Maine. In 1847 an ascent was made by the Rev. Marcus R.
Keep. . . .. It was he who accompanied Chas. H. Hitchcock about
Ktaadn in 1861 at the time of the Second Geological Survey of the
State. In the summers of 1873 and 1874 Merritt C. Fernald, at
one time President of the University of Maine, made expeditions to
Ktaadn which resulted in the first reliable determination of its
height, previously believed to be much over a mile. Fernald's
determinations gave about 5215 feet as the altitude. Subsequent
measurements show the true elevation as 5273 feet. It was the
privilege of the writers to visit this region in August 1923 and carry
out a study of the bed rock geology.[2]

Eastward beyond Union River and also westward in the
Moosehead region are still other mountains. The pitch of
the land is so gentle that comparatively few places occur in
the paths of the streams flowing into the Penobscot to produce
rapids rough enough to require portages in canoe travel. At
the time these studies were made, a dense forest of mixed
evergreens and deciduous trees, mainly consisting of red and
white spruce, pine, hemlock, fir, white cedar, canoe birch,
elm, maple, black and white ash, still mantled practically
the entire region. Some fertile land had been settled and
cultivated along the main river, but for the most part the
country was yet wild, with few roads. It is interesting to
know that Rosier, with Weymouth, as early as 1605, encountered and recorded oak, ash, elm, and hemlock. On the
eminences were dense beech, maple, birch, and hornbeam
while the swamps had fir and spruce.

[2] *Geographical Review*, Vol. XIV, No. 3, July 1924. For further treatment of
topography of Ktaadn the authors quote C. E. Hamlin, *Bulletin*, Museum of Comparative Zoölogy (Harvard Univ.), Vol. 7 (1880-4), pp. 189–224, and R. S. Tarr,
Bulletin, Geological Society of America, Vol. 11 (1900), pp. 433–48.

The climate is characterized by long and very cold winters, the rivers and lakes freezing generally in December and remaining so until about the first of April. The snowfall is also great, some drifts in the dense evergreen thickets of the up-country near Ktaadn lasting until the middle of April. The approach of spring and summer is sudden. The summer season, though short, comprising June, July, and August, is fairly warm, with cool nights and many clear, crisp, windy days. The autumn, in September and October, is surpassingly beautiful and, it behooves us to know, its charm is thoroughly appreciated by the Indians. They also love the snow. Game of various kinds is abundant, especially moose, deer, hare, muskrats, and partridges. Bear, lynx, and the smaller carnivores are more common farther north. The caribou, some thirty years ago, deserted this region for unknown reasons.[3]

Native fish are abundant, and add considerably to the sustenance of the people. The chief food varieties are salmon, shad, frost fish, pickerel, eels, white perch, and trout.

Water everywhere, snow in winter, firewood of best quality within reach of hand, game and fish in abundance. It was winter that brought them misery—the incessant cold, and the withdrawal of animals either by migration, hibernation, or through seeking protection against predators beneath snow and ice.

HISTORICAL SKETCH

A brief and cursory perspective of contact history relating to Indians and Europeans in the Penobscot region reveals some well-known events in the annals of Maine and Massachusetts.[4] Some confusion exists in reference to the names of tribes and local subdivisions; unspecified inclusion under the names Tarratine and Etchemin of tribal bands which were later assigned proper names such as Norridgewock, Aroosagunticook, Kanibas, Sakoki, Wawenock, Sagadahock,

---

[3] The investigator in this field of Algonkian ecology may be referred to the dissertation of Dr. Ralph Palmer, of Cornell University, for the summarization of zoölogical data.

[4] See the following authors listed in the Bibliography: Sullivan, Davies, Dillingham, Eckstorm, Hallowell, Leger, Maurault, Rosier, Vetromile.

Penobscot, Passamaquoddy, and Malecite. Closer historical discriminations may be hoped for through Mrs. Eckstorm's insight into the question.

Champlain in 1605 first visited the Penobscot River territory and wrote of its native inhabitants. Weymouth at about the same time (1605) encountered in Penobscot Bay people who if not Penobscot were Wawenock, and he left some few observations on the country. Another, traveler, James Davies, shortly afterward (1607–8) went into the same region and recorded some facts concerning it.

During 1615–16 a conflict is supposed to have arisen between the Penobscot (Etchemin or Tarratine) and the tribes (Abenaki) west of them, after which an epidemic of sickness occurred—the historic "plague" that nearly annihilated the natives of the northern New England coasts.[5] Likewise for many years (1647) the Penobscot were involved with the bands east of them (Malecite) as a result of partisanship with French leaders who had conflicting interests on the Penobscot and St. John rivers. Again, according to the records, a devastating struggle was carried on from 1662 to 1669 with the Mohawk, in which the Penosbcot suffered severely. Hostilities, however, in this direction must have been more or less constant before and after this period, though not specifically recorded. From this time (1669) the village at Oldtown became the chief Penobscot settlement. In 1687 the Catholic church under Abbé L. P. Thury first founded at Castine a mission which has been maintained interruptedly until the present time. As early as 1719–20, near what is now Thomaston, a trading post and blockhouse which subsequently became St. George, the scene of many skirmishes between the whites and the Indians, were erected on the Georges River. By 1722 affairs had developed into a general war, during which two hundred Indians attacked Fort St. George and attempted to undermine and blow up the ramparts. This campaign engaged fighting men from a number of the eastern tribes, and was known as Lovewell's War. French interests dominated the Indians.

[5] See the essay on the medical history and analysis of this interesting epidemic by H. V. Williams: *The Epidemic of the Indians of New England 1616–1620 with Remarks on Native American Infections.* Johns Hopkins Hospital Bull. 20: 340–349 (1909).

In 1723 Colonel Westbrook attacked and destroyed the Penobscot stronghold at Oldtown which he found temporarily deserted. He describes a fort seventy yards in length and fifty in width, with a stockade fourteen feet high enclosing twenty-three wigwams. In 1745 the Penobscot, who for a short time previous to this had held back from joining hostilities opened by the eastern tribes against the English, becoming exasperated over the French defeat at Louisburg, again precipitated action by falling upon Fort St. George. These attacks were repeated in 1746 and 1747. The English about this time offered bounties of four hundred pounds to volunteers and one hundred pounds to enlisted men for Indian scalps and captives; the scalp bounties being continued for at least ten years thereafter.

Matters having grown intolerable to both sides, in 1749 the eastern tribes entered into a general treaty of peace which terminated organized hostilities on the part of the Penobscot toward the English. Again, in 1752, at a meeting of all the eastern tribes except the Micmac and the St. Francis Abenaki, with four commissioners from Massachusetts, another treaty was drawn up, in which it was stipulated that the English should not settle above the tidewater or sell whiskey to the Indians. In 1753 another similar treaty, at which thirty chiefs were present, and at which a great dance took place, was made at Fort St. George.

With the breaking out of the French and Indian War in 1755, this whole region was severely affected, the Aroosaguntacook and their allies being chiefly embroiled. The Penobscot, however, were supposed to have been excepted from the English declaration of war. After this and largely on account of it, the rupture between the Penobscot and the tribes to the westward grew wider, and the Aroosaguntacook, Norridgewock, and their allies retired to Canada, leaving the Penobscot resident in Maine. After the fall of Quebec and the decline of French power in Canada, a general treaty of peace was concluded at Boston on April 13, 1760, between Massachusetts and the Indians remaining in Maine.

During the Revolutionary War (1776–1781), the Penobscot served the Colonial cause. In 1786 the Penobscot ceded to Massachusetts all the lands in the Penobscot Valley from tidewater to the mouth of the Piscataquis on the west, and to the Mattawamkeag on the east, reserving for themselves Indian Island and all the islands above it. Much inland territory was quitted in 1818 and still more in 1833. The tribe still retains, it is stated, 146 islands in the Penobscot River amounting to 4,481 acres, this land being allotted to families. Since 1838 the State of Maine has paid a bounty on agriculture, although the Indians do not engage in it extensively.

The Penobscot now enjoy an independent government, paternally subject to the legislature of the State of Maine, though having no formal relations with the United States. They govern themselves by two political bodies, known as the Old Party and the New Party, each having an alternate term of two years and each electing its own Governor, Lieutenant Governor, Representative to the State Legislature, Constable, and Council as well as the other minor officers. The tribe does not adopt others, but allows Indians of other tribes to marry in without sharing in the Penobscot funds. While the emigration from Indian Island is great, the birth rate keeps high; enough, in fact, to warrant the impression that the Penobscot are not doomed to total decay as some writers who evidently aim to enhance the interest of their essays by emphasizing the moribund condition of the natives, would have us think.[6] Enumerations show 387 (1900), 410 (1910), 580 (1939).

The Penobscot people of 1915 formed the third generation descended from a band of semi-nomadic hunters comprising twenty-two families. The present population includes a large number of the offspring of neighboring Wabanaki peoples and Europeans. From a summary of marriages contracted within the tribe itself and with outsiders, a strange conclusion may be drawn. During a period of about seventy-five years (1840–1915) fifty-three marriages took place between parties both of whom were Penobscot, and fifty-two between Penobscot

[6] For example, cf. Prince, *American Anthropologist*, N.S. vol. XI, no. 4 (1909), p. 626: ". . . in all probability, fifty or sixty years hence, nothing will be left of this picturesque remnant of our eastern Algonquian stock." As early as 1795 Sullivan expected a similar fate to befall the Penobscot remnant of less than three hundred "within a few years" (Sullivan, p. 96).

and other Indians of the Wabanaki division; of the latter thirty being with Passamaquoddy, fourteen with Malecite. Such statements have a significant bearing upon the racial make-up of small tribes. The constituency of the tribe is so blended with other Wabanaki communities through extensive intermarriage that the tribal groups can be little more than social or dialectic units.

NEIGHBORS AND ETHNIC RELATIONSHIPS

A stretch of country on the west some three hundred miles across separated the Penobscot from the Mohawk whom they called *Me'gwak* (singular *Me'gwe*), derived, it is said by some, from *me''kwe*, "red." This is also the name for the Iroquois in general. Related terms denote the dreaded members of the Iroquois League in Algonkian tongues as far as the Delaware, the synonyms limited, however, to territories south of the St. Lawrence. As will be seen subsequently, the Penobscot, allied with other eastern Algonkian, were intermittently in strife with the Iroquois until some time after the general Indian peace of 1749. The territory lying between the two groups was regarded as being too dangerous for permanent occupancy by the Penobscot, who, after the withdrawal of the Aroosaguntacook and their allies to Canada, were left exposed to the Iroquois on their western and northwestern frontiers.

The Iroquois at Lake of Two Mountains, near Montreal, are known to the Penobscot as *Kana'sada'giak* or *Kan''sada'-kiak* from their own name *Kanasata'ke*, "at the hillside."[7] The Caughnawaga Mohawk know the eastern Indians, including the Penobscot, as *Ronats'a'gana*, "stutterers," expressive of their esteem of Algonkian. Though the Penobscot respect the Mohawk, they do not in any sense esteem them as their superiors. Even now very little social intercourse takes place between the two peoples.

With the Malecite, their neighbors on the northeast and east, the Penobscot are on most intimate terms, there being, as formerly, many intermarriages between the two tribes. The Penobscot, however, as a tribe, hold themselves somewhat above the latter. The Malecite are known as *Wəla'stukwiak*,

---

[7] Cf. *Handbook of American Indians*, Vol. 2, Article Oka.

"people of the beautiful river," taking their name from the St. John River, called *Wəla'stegukʷ*, "Beautiful River," in Penobscot. They in turn call the Penobscot *Panawa'pskik* or *Pana'pskik*, which they translate variously as "Rock people" or "At the widening of the river."

The Passamaquoddy, occupying the coast east of the Penobscot as far as and beyond Passamaquoddy Bay, are designated as *Pestamoka'diak*, "Place of the undertow people," as some Penobscot explain the term, referring to the great undertow caused by the excessive tides in Passamaquoddy Bay. The name, however, is supposedly borrowed from the Passamaquoddy themselves. Another derivation for this name is "plenty of pollock." They call the Penobscot *Panawa'pskik* as do the Malecite. The Penobscot and the Passamaquoddy have always maintained a close relationship, and frequent intermarriages have taken place. The Penobscot are correctly aware of the dialectic similarity between Malecite and Passamaquoddy, attributing it to the fact that the latter are an offshoot from the former, their separation dating back several hundred years to a division of the Malecite at a breaking up of their main village *E'kpohak* near Spring Hill on St. John River. Those who migrated southward settled at Passamaquoddy Bay and founded the tribe, it is said, and there seems to be other evidence to support the truth of the idea. With the Passamaquoddy, the Malecite, and the Micmac, the Penobscot were joined in early times in a loose alliance for protection against the Iroquois. These friendly relations are remembered now, though formal meetings have not been held since about 1840.[8]

The Micmac, *Mi'k'makik* (singular *Mi'k'ma*), are well known to the Penobscot, who regard them as large strong people, but poor and inclined to be mean. The name *Mi'k'ma* is evidently, though obscurely, related to the term *Mi'kamwe's* referring to a class of dwarf-like supernaturally gifted human creatures who inhabit the dense woods. The connection between these names is brought out more clearly through the Malecite *Mi·k'am*, "Micmac," or "Wood Spirit."

[8] Cf. Speck, "The Eastern Algonkian Wabanaki Confederacy," *Amer. Anth.*, Vol. XVII, no. 3, 1915.

The Micmac know the Penobscot as *Gani'bax* [9] (*Gani'-biwatc*, singular). They in turn consider the Penobscot very much their inferiors. The feeling is manifested in a statement which I heard a Micmac woman make to the effect that the Penobscot used to eat people. Persons from Prince Edward Island, both Micmac Indian and white, are collectively called *Enigwi''tak*, "Blue Noses," by the Penobscot. In early times a war between the Penobscot and Micmac is said to have taken place, in which the Micmac claim the Penobscot were defeated. The Prince Edward Island Micmac are called *Mala'mkiak*, "People of the white sandy country."

Directly west of the Penobscot, and closely related to them in language and culture, formerly dwelt the Norridgewock, *Nali'djɔwagiak*, "People of the swift water," inhabiting the valley of the Kennebec; and still further away, the Aroosaguntacook, *Alsega'ntegwiak*, "River abounding in shell fish people" [10] (St. Francis dialect). The people on the lower Kennebec and Androscoggin rivers were called *saŋgɔdɔla'wiak*, "Mouth of the river people"; they formed a subdivision of the preceding. The *Sak'o'kiak*, "People of the difficult river," (?) dwelt still further westward in the White Mountains on the Saco River, which was considered difficult to ascend on account of its rocky bed. Penobscot tradition fails to mention the people who have gone down in New England history as Pennacook and Pigwacket, tribes famous in New Hampshire colonial times. Pennacook, however, may be rendered *Pena'nki·ak*, "those (living) down hill"; and Pigwacket may be a form of *bigwa''kik*, "abundant game country," as suggested by Newell Lion.

These tribes are known to the Penobscot only by tradition, because they removed to Canada after being defeated by the English, and there, amalgamating with other New England Algonkian refugees, notably Scatticook and probably Mohican and Wampanoag, formed the band and tribe known thenceforth as the St. Francis Abenaki at Pierreville, P. Q. The

[9] x denotes a guttural spirant. This name may be derived from Kennebek, "at the long water reach," a local tribe name of the Norridgewock.
[10] Laurent, p. 206.

Penobscot think that the dialect of the St. Francis Abenaki people sounds like a child's talk.[11] The St. Francis Abenaki are still known to the Penobscot under the old name of *Alsega'ntegwiak*, and they call the Penobscot *Panawo'ⁿbska'iak*, "People of the steep rocky place."

A small and unimportant tribe formerly dwelling on the coast, near Georges River, immediately west of Penobscot Bay, was known as *Walina'ʿki·a'k* (or *Wa'linak*) "Cove (or little bay) people." These people are recorded in the historical accounts as Wawenock.[12] While supposed to be extinct or to be scattered among other tribes of the east, being remembered only by name among the Penobscot, some of their descendants are still to be found with the latter.[13]

The Hurons of Lorette are called *Pǝma'dnayak*, "Hill people," on account of their proximity to the Laurentian Mountains. They are known to have ethnic affinities with the Mohawk.

Other people known as *Osa'gene'wiɑk* (*Osa'gene'wi*, singular) are remembered by the Penobscot as having lived far to the northeast of them. The name is said by some to be applicable to the Montagnais (Saguenay), but we have reason to think that it may be a form of the name by which the Beothuk of Newfoundland referred to themselves, and which in an analogous form spread among the other northeastern tribes.[14]

Some significance rests in the fact, as Willoughby has independently suggested through his archaeological researches in Maine,[15] that this extinct tribe may originally have occupied the coast far to the south of its last known habitat in Newfoundland. Some of the more distinctive negative and positive ethnic traits of the Penobscot and the related tribes of

[11] Comparisons based on linguistic and ethnological material collected by the writer in 1908 among these people.

[12] Cf. Name in *Handbook of American Indians*.

[13] An independent study of the group at Becancour, P. Q., was made by the writer in 1914, published in the Forty-Third Annual Report, Bureau of American Ethnology, Wash., 1928, pp. 167–97.

[14] Information on the Beothuk, called by themselves, and also by the Micmac, *Osa'ganna*, and by the Malecite *Osa'genik* (pl.), obtained from *Santu*, a half-Micmac, half-Beothuk woman of Newfoundland, has since been published by the writer. Cf. *Beothuk and Micmac*, Indian Notes and Monographs, Museum of the American Indian, Heye Foundation, N. Y., 1922.

[15] Cf. Willoughby, ref. 4.

the Wabanaki group may have been derived from contact with these mysterious aborigines, if one favor the supposition, which indeed has something to support it, that the Wabanaki were immigrants into their present habitat in comparatively late prehistoric times, either incorporating or destroying other aboriginal occupants of the coast.

Other peoples known by name or traditional hearsay to the Penobscot are the *Aski'mowak*,[16] "raw meat eaters," Eskimo; the *Ebaga'təba'djik*, "Flat Heads," possibly the Têtes de Boule on the upper St. Maurice River, P. Q.; the *Oda'wag*, Ottawa of the Ottawa and Gatineau rivers, Ontario and Quebec, also known as *Kəmusu'msna'wak*, "our grandfathers," which has some significance as a historical memory *referring to the west*. The *Mo'ta'neyak* (Indianized "Montagnais") are nowadays chiefly heard of through the Malecite. The Ojibwa are called *Tci'pwesag*. The Têtes de Boule, as we suppose, are definitely spoken of in local tradition. A small stream near the village at Oldtown is named ·"Flat Head Brook" (*Ebagateba'duk*) after one of this tribe killed there while trying to approach the village. Various tribes southwest beyond the Saco River, in what is now New Hampshire and Massachusetts, are also vaguely remembered by name; the *Mala'mekwiak*, "Lazy-fish (togue) people," on Merrimac River, the *Gowe'siak*, "Pine people," dwelling at Cohasset, and the *Mohiga'niak* (*molhi'gan*, "river with steep banks" (?)),[17]

---

[16] *Ski·ha'o*, "raw food"; *ski·'po*, "one person who eats raw victuals."

[17] There seems to be little doubt that the name *Molhigan* is a variant of the *Malingan* or *Amalingan* recorded in the narratives of Maine late in the seventeenth century as the title of a group of Indians known to the Penobscot. Newell Lion did better than he thought in recalling this interesting form of the proper name. It unlocks the identity of the old references in the Rasles letters (1697) to the establishment of a nation of "Amalingan savages" near his mission on the Norridgewock.

It seems, furthermore, to substantiate the idea conceived by Mrs. Eckstorm that an influx of Indians from the defeated tribes of southern New England (Massachusetts and Connecticut) took place into the southwestern frontiers of the Wabanaki. Mrs. Eckstorm's conclusions communicated to me in recent correspondence (Jan. 16, 1939, excerpting from her forthcoming article announced as being in press) point to acceptance of the fact that the penetration of the southern invaders into the hunting territories of the Wabanaki led to difficulties in adjustment of territorial claims among the conflicting groups, and that certain influences of alien nature were introduced into the Wabanaki culture area. That further effects may be traced to these events one may only as yet surmise. Mrs. Eckstorm promises to bring out her notes on this subject in a paper in course of preparation. (See Bibliography, Eckstorm 4, pp. 219–20 and Hallowell, 2, p. 99.)

the Mohegan of Connecticut. Speculations upon the former relationships of the Penobscot with these peoples are ready to open up some discussions among the historians of Maine.

The whites in general are called *awe'notcwak* (singular *awe'notc*), *aweno''s·ak* old form, "People from whence, People coming from yonder" (?), and also *wəbala'gikʷs*, "white eyes." The early animosity between the races has now nearly been forgotten, although they, like other Indians, attribute most of their present ills to white intrusion and interference. The *average* white people they consider as inferiors; their low esteem is manifested in behavior toward them. A Frenchman is called *Pla'ndjəman;* an Irishman, *I'lisman* (corruptions of the English proper names); the English, *Agle'ziau;* a Jew, *Leswi'p* from French *les Juïfs.*

Indians in general are known as *a'lnabak* (singular *alna'be*), "people." With other Indians the Penobscot sympathetically recognize the bond of race relationship.

Negroes, *e'tsit*, "colored," and *Sawana'ke'djik*, "Coming from the south," are regarded indifferently. Another name for the Negro is *bla''kman* (English, black man). A story accounts for the Negro's black skin and constant laughter. He is said to be descended from a child who showed extreme disrespect for his parents by continually laughing at them. As a punishment for this fault, "he laughed himself black in the face, and is now always laughing and showing his teeth."

The culture of the Penobscot is typical of the tribes east of the Piscataqua or the Saco River, and south of the St. Lawrence, which constitute the ethnic group known as the northeastern Algonkian or Wabanaki. Dependence upon hunting and fishing for subsistence amid extensive and well-watered tracts of forest, upon birch bark and wood for economic material characterize the area. Passing from west to east the tribes of this grouping include the present St. Francis Abenaki (formerly Norridgewock, Aroosaguntacook, Sokoki, and other remnants), the Wawenock, the Penobscot, the Malecite, the Passamaquoddy, and marginally the Micmac. Culturally these six tribes have many common attributes, though differences are numerous and marked when details are considered, and the same is true in regard to dialect. They are known among both Indians and Europeans as Wabanaki, a name derived from the native generic term *Wabana'kiak*, "eastern (daybreak) land people," a convenient designation, now accepted in ethnographical usage. While, at the present writing, only cursory investigations among these tribes have been made to serve as the basis for comparative judgment, I may venture nevertheless to present the following observations. Excluding the Micmac, who are at present the least known and the most distinct, the phenomena of social culture become more complex as we go westward, the St. Francis composite group being first in complexity, the Penobscot following, with the Malecite and Passamaquoddy showing a still more simple cultural configuration. Similar gradations exist in dialectic complexity. This is especially noticeable in the shortening of endings and the contraction of terms, with eliminated vowels in Malecite and Passamaquoddy.[18] The dialectic relationship between Micmac and the other idioms of this group has not yet been conclusively worked out. Nor has the problem of relationship between the Central dialects and Labrador Algonkian with Wabanaki as a whole been treated, except by Michelson using a limited series of tests.[19]

[18] A point relating to tribal classification on the basis of language that I should like to mention here is the assumption by Professor Prince that the Penobscot and the St. Francis Abenaki are only very recent offshoots from the same parental group. He says, "It will thus be seen, in examining the Penobscot and Abenaki idioms, that we have to deal with a dialectic differentiation which must have taken place within a period of two hundred and twenty-two years; i.e. from 1679 to 1901. It should be added that the similarity which is still so evident between these dialects precludes the supposition that they were linguistically apart at the time of the Indian flight to Canada (circa 1679). Probably nowhere among American languages, therefore, has the philologist so favorable an opportunity as he has here of determining the *exact* extent and period of time necessary for linguistic differentiation." Cf. J. D. Prince, *The Differentiation Between the Penobscot and Canadian Abenaki Dialects, American Anthropologist*, N.S. Vol. 4 (1902), p. 18. My own conclusions, based upon historical, linguistic, and ethnological comparative data, do not agree with this. It is most probable, on the contrary, that the Penobscot of the Penobscot River valley, and the Aroosaguntacook (later the St. Francis Abenaki) of the adjoining river valleys westward were, at the time designated (1679) and earlier, distinguished by the graded differences in language and culture that we find characterizing the succeeding tribes occupying the river valleys eastward, the Malecite, Passamaquoddy, and Micmac. It would be unsafe for students to accept Professor Prince's conclusions at face value, because the differences between the two are too fundamental to be ascribed to such a recent separation. This will come out more clearly later when material from the Abenaki is published.

[19] Truman Michelson, *Preliminary Report on the Linguistic Classification of Algonquian Tribes*, Twenty-Ninth Annual Report, Bureau American Ethnology, Wash., 1913.

Speaking, however, from what we know internally of the northeastern group, it seems that cultural complexity decreases with each succeeding tribe to the eastward. Whether this can be attributed to Iroquois proximity on the west, or whether it is due to the migration of the Wabanaki enclaves from west to east moving south of the St. Lawrence seems to remain the local question.

There is, furthermore, reason to believe that the tribes of the Wabanaki group came southward into New England, supposedly having crossed the St. Lawrence, and reached the coast where they settled, later branching off into bands which turned their faces farther eastward.[20] To support this it is also true that a break is found in the sequence of culture between the Wabanaki and the tribes south of them on the Massachusetts coast and that the two groups were in early colonial times politically quite disassociated.

The testimony of the natives themselves is interesting in regard to the question of precedence. Said Captain Francis of the Penobscot some years ago, "All the tribes between the Saco and River St. John were brothers: that the eldest lived on the Saco: that each tribe was younger as we passed eastward."[21]

In the matter of external relationships we have here some interesting problems right at our doors. It remains to determine just how much or just how little, outside of political matters, had been borrowed from the highly advanced Iroquois on the west. And again we have the difficult question of a possible prehistoric contact with people related to the Beothuk, or the Eskimo, as astonishing as it may first seem.[22] There is some reason to think that the former may have been a source of influence for many of the northeastern Algonkian. While to a definitive type of mind such allusions may be of some significance in determining the culture relationships and trend of migration of the Wabanaki tribal groups, they seem to lack conclusiveness. Mentioning them tentatively, it

[20] These theories are broached in the various works on the region, listed in the Bibliography, particularly Vetromile, Maurault, Dixon, *Handbook of American Indians*, etc.

[21] Dillingham, P. 1. P. 50.

[22] Willoughby (ref. 4) discusses the archaeological evidences for this supposition.

seems that we shall have to await more complete investigation of all the constituent tribes and neighboring Algonkian.

The Penobscot, and we may also include the related Algonkian of the northeast, present a uniform type of culture, the material side of which is practically shared by tribes of the Canadian area from the Great Lakes to the Atlantic. In subjective matters, more individuality, though equally simplified, appears for instance in the specialization of art motives, wood carvings, hunting groups, and the limited range of fundamental religious ideas and rites. Located in a geographical corner, the Wabanaki tribes had little or no influence upon their neighbors, but have shown only lately some receptivity in adopting from outside new activities and institutions where practical in their mode of life. What there remains of local distinctiveness in the life of the northeastern group has evidently developed out of the comparative isolation of their habitat, away from paths of culture transmission.

Again, with the Algonkian north of the St. Lawrence, the Penobscot present close similarities both in positive and negative respects; particularly noteworthy in social organization, religion, decorative art, shamanism, artifacts, and economic forms. To be more precise, the differences between the Wabanaki and the Labradorean group are greater than those that prevail between the tribes within the Wabanaki group itself. The Labrador Algonkian, to be sure, present a greater simplicity of culture than their Cree and Ojibwa relatives from whom they have supposedly branched off. Here also they present a problem quite analogous to that of the Wabanaki and Penobscot in their supposed contact with coastwise predecessors. Can it be that both groups have had similar historical experiences and have undergone similar mixing processes in migrating eastward from earlier seats of the Algonkian?

In presenting these discussions I am more anxious to offer suggestions to those interested in the ethnological problems of the Eastern Algonkian than to lay down theories prematurely.

VILLAGES

The three present villages of the Penobscot are believed to rest upon old sites. Other locations on the lower river and

bay are also spoken of, but no opportunity has occurred to
determine their location definitely beyond the archaeological
surveys projected during past years. The present villages,
which represent the only permanent locations of the tribe,
are as follows:

(1) *Panawa'bskik* is the oldest known center of the tribe,
from which it takes its name. Various translations of the
term have appeared, but the most satisfactory are "At the
rocks," or "The white rocks place," and "Where the river
broadens out." [23] These and other names of places, however,
are archaic, and translators do not agree among themselves.
This village is on Indian Island opposite Oldtown. In colonial
times there was a palisaded village here, and the first Catholic
mission was also founded at the same place. The population
in 1914 was something over four hundred including Indians
of other Wabanaki tribes. All of the villages are prettily
situated on rather high land, preferably at the southern ends
of the islands in the river. Both the settlements at Olemon
and Lincoln are, however, on the eastern side of the island,
surrounded by clearings.

(2) *Welama'nes·uk*, (English form Olemon), is some twelve
miles up the river above the first-mentioned village. This
settlement is on the eastern shore of an island, the population
being limited to four or five families. It is so named from
the fact that in the olden times they used to obtain there
supplies of red ochre for paint. (3) *Matna'gak*, "Long Island,"
the most northerly permanent settlement, is located also on
a large island about thirty-six miles above Oldtown, opposite
Lincoln. There were seven families here in 1912. This location has become unpopular in recent years, because the Indians
consider it to be too far from civilization. It is two days'
journey up the river from Oldtown by canoe, and the descent
to it from the nearest town upstream requires one day. In
their material life the people of this island are somewhat
more conservative than their relatives nearer civilization,

[23] *Pena'ps* meaning "rock,"—*kik* locative. The element *wab* "white" possibly
being included. The Indians, some of them Malecite, vary considerably in their
interpretations. Among numerous essays which discuss the etymology of this proper
name may be mentioned, J. E. Godfrey, "The Ancient Penobscot or Panawanskik,"
Historical Magazine, Feb. 1872, Vol. 1, No. 11, New Ser. pp. 85–92.

though many pass back and forth either bound northward on hunting trips or returning to Oldtown for social reunions. In former times *Matnagak* was much exposed to the attacks of the Mohawks, and many war incidents center round about it. Other large camps, possibly villages, are known to have been situated on the Penobscot river at the south of the Mattawamkeag river, that of the Passadumkeag, and at Castine on the eastern shore of Penobscot Bay.

The former settlements and more important camps of the tribe, beginning at the bay and going northward are, as well as can now be remembered, *E'sik*, "Clam place," Stockton; *Madji'bigwa·'dos*, "Bad supply of game," Castine; *Kɑde'skik*, "Place of overgrown eels," Oldtown; *Pɔske'tɔgwe'suk*, Piscataquis, *Pesadɑ'm'kik*, "Sand bar point place," Passadumkeag; *Madawɑ'm'ikik*, "Where the current makes a sand bar at the mouth of the stream," Mattawamkeag; and *Tcimski'tɔguk*ʷ, "Big dead-water," Kingman. The settlement at Castine is mentioned in history under the name of Penobscot or (*Panawa'mpskik*), from which was derived Pentagouet, a former tribal synonym.

Within this stretch of country the Penobscot used to divide their time somewhat regularly, spending the summer months (June, July, August) in the lower coast or salt-water region, then ascending the river to the family hunting territories for the fall hunting (October, November, December), and finally returning to the tribal rendezvous at the main headquarters at Oldtown for the dead of winter (January, February, March). The early spring months (April, May) were spent in drifting down toward the ocean and hunting through the neighboring streams and in the main river for eels. This, it should be understood, is only a general outline of the movements of the people; many of them would spend longer periods in the interior, while some "lazy" families would remain most of the time at salt water, gaining an easy though monotonous living from the sea. Particular designations of the seasons and months in this connection will appear under the topic Division of Time.

II

MATERIAL LIFE

SHELTER

THE dwellings of the Penobscot were of several major and minor types, only one at all permanent, composed of birch bark (occasionally elm, evergreen, hemlock, or spruce bark) coverings and supporting poles. The usual dwelling was (I) the conical birch-bark wigwam, *wi'gwom*, "camp (habitation)" also *bɔdɑ'gwigan*, "round habitation." Its correspondent, destined more particularly for winter use, having a log understructure (II), is called *dagwɑ'kswi·gamik*, "autumn, or finished, habitation," because it was built in the fall to serve through the wintertime. A circular or ovate, rounded-top camp (III) was also known, its covering elm or evergreen bark sheets, and another (IV) flat-topped lean-to, *aba'gikɑn*, "flat habitation," besides a form of the conical wigwam for transient occupancy (V) with a covering of spruce, balsam, or hemlock boughs entire laid over the poles, and known as *wulge'ski·gan*, "hemlock habitation," or *sidi'k·an*, "bough house."

Descriptions of these house-types follow, arranged from studies by Mr. Orchard, whose published notes [1] together with the observations given by Mrs. Eckstorm in her paper [2] I have combined with notes that I made on camp construction. Native house-types have been a thing of the past here for three generations; hence their description rests upon tradition and memory; my reasons for presenting it in a condensed abstract.

(I) Conical shelter; approximately eight to ten feet in height at peak and ten in diameter at ground, framework of nine, sometimes ten, peeled cedar or spruce poles supporting bark cover, another series of poles or unpeeled lengths placed outside over bark to hold it in position. Supporting or foundation poles, two inches in

---

[1] W. C. Orchard, "Penobscot Houses," *American Anthropologist*, Vol. 11, no. 4, 1909, pp. 601–6.

[2] Eckstorm, 1, pp. 65–7.

diameter at butt and about twelve feet long.   In process of erection,
four poles are tied together with a cedar bark thong at point about
two feet from their tops, laid in pairs one atop the other.   When
moving camp the poles were left in place and the birch-bark sheets
rolled up to be transported in the canoe.

To erect the lodge, the four poles tied together are stood up and
spread apart, as shown in figure.   [See Fig. 4 for crude example.]
Nos. 1, 2, 3, and 4 are the poles fastened together; 5 and 6 are two

FIG. 4

TEMPORARY BIRCH–BARK WIGWAM

(Malecite, St. John River, N. B.)

poles placed between 1 and 2 to form door posts; 7, 8, and 9, placed
between 1 and 3, 3 and 4, 4 and 2, complete the circle of foundation
poles.   A short pole is tied between 5 and 6, about six feet from
the ground, forming a lintel.   A hoop of some flexible wood is
fastened to the inner side of the poles, about seven or seven and
one-half feet from the ground, to give additional strength, also to
support sticks laid across for drying clothing.   The inside hoop is
characteristic of wigwams in the Wabanaki and Montagnais area.

The covering consists of sheets of heavy winter birch bark about
3½ feet wide lapped and sewed together with split spruce root,

forming long strips stretched over the poles. Temporary camps were made without sewing the bark, the sheets being laid over the framework, other poles laid on pressing them down. Width of the bark sheets about ⅓ the height of the lodge, consequently three tiers are necessary to complete the covering. The two lower tiers made in two sections each to facilitate handling in transportation. One section suffices for the uppermost tier. Sheets are joined so that seams are vertical. Ends and joinings of bark sheets are strengthened by inch strips of cedar bound with wrappings of spruce root to stiffen and prevent fraying. The covering of the framework begins with a section of the lower tier at one of the doorposts. If the ends of bark sheets did not have stiffening strips they were bent around the door pole and fastened with spruce root binding. The sheet then stretched around to middle pole at back. The second tier is put on in the same way, its lower edge overlapping the first tier. The third or upper tier is started from middle pole at back, fastened to it through its upper edge, and not bent around front poles as are lower tiers, but carried around until one end overlaps like a collar and made fast. An opening between the top edge of covering and the intersection of the poles is the smoke-hole. Outside poles about ten feet long are laid over covering to weight it down, their lower ends driven into the ground a few inches, the upper ends tied to the corresponding poles inside with withes just above the edge of top tier of bark.

The door (*kla′gan; ksa′dan*, "door-flap"), facing to south or east, is a tanned moose-hide laced to a pole at upper and one at lower end, the upper tied to door lintel; in foul weather lower end tied by thong or cedar-bark rope to door pole or stake in ground.

Interior furnishings consist of three bed spaces (*abu′n*) and a fireplace. Beds are carpets of evenly laid spruce or fir boughs covered with tanned skins, separated into spaces on floor by three logs bounding the center space (fireplace, *madatwa′gan*). Space at left of door (A) was occupied by the owner, that at back of house behind fire (B) occupied by wife, also place of honor, that at right of door (C) was for others of family and visitors. Fireplace was within the rectangular space formed by the three boundary logs which protected bedding and floor material from taking fire, the longer logs laid lengthwise of the space and on top of two shorter logs of enclosure. Cooking pots suspended over fire from pole resting upon hoop inside wigwam framework, or on cross stick supported by crotched uprights driven into ground. Pot hooks of twisted withe with loop at upper end to slide along cross stick

and crotch at lower end. Outside stone fireplace for hot weather
is three-sided enclosure about four feet long, one side open. Pots
and kettles suspended here as on inside or from pole thrust into
ground extending over fire and adjusted for elevation by stone
at base.

The conical camp was at times covered simply with shingle-like
slabs of bark peeled from elm, spruce, or hemlock according to
available sources *en voyage*, and again the pole framework would
be thickly overlaid with hemlock boughs, tips pointing downward
to shed snow and rain. The specifications given above apply to
these cruder structures in approximate terms.

(II) For more permanent use than the conical lodge, and also
for better protection in winter, a square (or rectangular) wigwam
was erected. The lower part consisted of four or five tiers of
logs, built up in the usual method employed for log cabins, the
upper part a roof of birch bark supported by poles. The minimum
size was ten feet square and ten feet high at the apex, and larger
according to the number of persons accommodated. A variation
of this type of camp was common when intended for several families
also. In this the bark covering extended to the ground, there being
no log part. It amounts to about the same as two lean-to camps
facing each other. This will be described a few pages farther on.
The log structure was built from three to four feet high, and on the
side facing the warmest quarter sections of two or three of the
upper logs were cut out to make a door opening from two and a
half to three feet wide, the lower logs left entire to keep snow from
drifting in. Roof of four main poles about twelve feet long, tied
together in the same manner as the poles for a circular lodge. The
poles were spread apart, one brought to each corner of the log
structure, notched into the intersections, and tied with spruce-root
or cedar-bark cords. At the opening left for the door, two poles
were notched into the ends of the logs and carried up to the point
where the main poles crossed. A short lintel was tied across,
about six feet from the ground. The three remaining sides were
filled in with poles, one from the center of the log to the apex, and
the spaces on either side with shorter poles, at right angles to the
logs, reaching to the main pole and tied at that point with spruce-
root or cedar-bark cord. The birch-bark covering was fitted and
laid on in tiers, the upper overlapping the lower, and tied to the
supporting poles as described for circular lodge. Outside poles held
the bark more securely. The arrangement of bedding and the
fireplace corresponded with that of the circular lodge.

The crevices between the logs and between the bark and the top of the log structure were packed tightly with moss, to keep out cold winds, and for further protection the walls were banked outside with moss and leaves, covered with earth. The usual moose-hide door and method fastening were employed.[3]

(III) Mrs. Eckstorm (*op. cit.*, pp. 66–67) gives a description of the round-topped circular camp as follows: It was made of "slender poles, lapped by each other, in pairs, far enough to be tied several times, thus stiffening them to support the heavy strips of elm, hemlock or spruce bark used for covering. The bark was laid on outside uppermost and fastened down by poles to keep it from warping. The upper strips lay across the top of the camp, hanging down on each side. In rains this was not as good as the conical camp; but it was warmer in cold, snowy weather and it could be built in places where birch trees did not grow. The fire was in or near the center, the smoke hole above it."

Some further notations seem important in respect to house equipment.

A wind and rain flap of birch bark was frequently placed over the smoke hole of the shelter in windy and rainy weather. This is called *likhi'gan*.[4] I was also told of an interior lining of deerskin between the inner poles and the back covering for additional protection during the coldest weather. Between this and the bark, quantities of fir boughs were packed. In winter camps, besides earth piled about the edges, fir boughs were leaned against the outside. The chief labor of erecting the camp and arranging the surroundings was attended to by men. Women here are not expected to do much heavy labor.

The interior of the habitation was lighted by the fire at night, or for special need a torch was made of birch bark in a cleft stick, similar to that used in night-fishing. A location having good water, plenty of wood, and accessible by canoe is required for a camp, which is called *wi'gi·*. In the old days in the villages, no particular order of arrangement of the wigwams was followed, the head of each family choosing his

---

[3] That the same fundamental idea was well known to the aborigines of other parts of the northeastern area, if not throughout it, is shown by the detailed account given by Cartwright (1798) of Beothuk lodges in Newfoundland, in which both the log structure and moss chinking were essentially the same as here. Cf. Lloyd, pp. 23–25

[4] It also denotes a sail.

own spot. Clumps of bushes nearby furnished a place for depositing refuse and offal, whence the term applied to the modern privy, *bəzədi'k·ɑnsis,* "little dark bough shelter."

Particular attention is called to the distinctive element of the Penobscot house, namely, the hoop or ring tied inside the frame halfway up from the ground. This not only rendered the structure firm but also served, as mentioned, to support cross poles upon which clothing and other property were hung to dry. A pot hook suspended from this pole dangled directly over the fire (Fig. 5).

FIG. 5

Suspension Hook for Pot

During cold weather in the lodge, or out of doors, the people slept rolled up in blankets with their feet toward the fire. Sometimes, when traveling, they did not bother to erect a shelter, but merely rose at intervals between a few moments snatched for sleep to replenish the fire during the night.

A most ingenious device for warming the wigwam was in vogue during some of the almost unbearably cold nights of the region. I learned of it from an old man who with his companion had been saved from freezing by employing it when driven to camp on an island in Penobscot Bay one cold winter's night. A big fire was made and quantities of large stones were heaped upon it. Then when the stones were hot they were carried by means of green sticks inside the tent and piled in the center. Thus the interior was kept as warm during the night as though heated by a furnace, and the occupants slept comfortably rolled in their blankets.

A temporary shelter of the original type, one still used by hunters and others in making short camps, is known locally as the "lean-to" (IV). It consists simply of a sloping flat roof, either of slabs of birch bark, or spruce boughs piled thickly with the twig ends down, supported on several pairs of crotched supports bearing crosspieces tied on, upon which the roofing is laid. The two sides and the back are filled in similarly, but the high front side is left open and the fire is

built before it. Under this sloping shelter the blankets are
made into beds, and the provisions are kept. Exactly the
same thing occurs among the Montagnais, and the other
northern Algonkian all seem to know it. Its size, of course,
varies according to the occasion and the number of occupants;
commonly five feet high at the front opening and about six
feet wide, the depth being about six or seven feet to where
the roof slopes to the ground at the rear. The "lean-to" is
called *abagi'k·an*, "flat camp."

The conical wigwam was often made of balsam fir boughs
laid upon the poles, tips downward (V). By placing a thick
layer of boughs on in this way and weighting them in place
by other poles leaned upon them, a camp of sufficient protection was afforded for several months. The fir-bough wigwam
is called *sidi'kan*, "bough house."

Referring again to a variation of the long, rectangular-
based winter camp mentioned previously, we have further
information, as this style of camp is still occasionally made
by hunters. It amounts practically to two lean-to camps
facing each other with a fire between. Two pairs of crotched
uprights a little more than head-high, according to the plans
of the party, are placed a few feet apart, and at a distance
from each other sufficient for the demands of the camp—
about ten or twelve feet. A horizontal pole is laid across the
long space between each pair of supports, and against these
are leaned poles reaching to the ground. Then the bark
sheets are fastened, as in the lean-to, upon this framework,
leaving the long space between the two poles open for the
exit of smoke. The entrances then are at each end, and one
may be kept closed according to the direction of the wind.
The sheets of bark here, as in the other wigwams, are either
held in place by being tied to the framework, or are pressed
down by outside poles, the method depending upon the whim
of the maker.

Before concluding treatment of shelter constructions I may
mention the rectangular single-room log house with gable
roof of modern materials, yet one which has a wide distribution in the Indian northeast. I have seen it among the Newfoundland Micmac with a door but no windows, and even in

1936 one was inhabited by a Penobscot family on Orson Island. In its construction the logs are placed upright from ground to gables, and the spaces between filled with moss. Mrs. Eckstorm calls them "earlier log camps" (*op. cit.*, p. 67) of an English form and gives a reference to their occurrence on Kennebec River in 1719, as shown on a map by Captain Joseph Heath.

Shelters of a still more improvised form occur: a simple windbreak of evergreen boughs, head-high, long enough to shelter the party, erected on the windward side of the fire, cleared away and banked with snow in winter; and then the inverted canoe under which a couple of hunters may bivouac, sheltered from frost or rain. Of the latter, Cartier (1534) made mention as being the only dwellings of Indians he met.

HUNTING

The hunt had an inconceivably prominent place in native life of the region. It put the indelible stamp of northern Algonkian identity upon Penobscot ethnology. No other regular activity occupied spirit, mind, and body so incessantly. It furnished the dominant food supply. Moose, deer, caribou, beaver, bear, muskrat, hare, porcupine, partridge were sought in the forest, seal and wild fowl on the coast, of importance in the order given. These sources provided fresh meat for immediate use and to be smoke-dried and stored away in birch-bark receptacles until needed. In the old days, the Penobscot divided their time regularly between a winter hunt, separated in family camps far off in their hunting territories, and a summer gathering at the various villages and camps along the Penobscot River. Within limits quasi-nomadic, they moved in "primary family" groups, remaining for a time at the village to attend festivities, then going up the remote preëmpted streams to hunt and replenish their supply of meat, fish, hides, bark, and other necessities. The division of the tribal territory into family hunting districts, their "rivers" as they denoted them, is to be dealt with under "Social Characteristics." Some hunting customs are still in practice, and the following observations are offered. Occasion was taken by the writer whenever possible to observe methods at first hand by accompanying hunters and trappers as a helper on their excursions into the woods.

Of paramount importance in native life of the region is the orderly progress of seasonal occupation through the year, in which hunting assumes the chief rôle. The annual economic cycle of activities as it existed in Penobscot culture until half a century ago is given in the following summary showing the six regional and occupational movements. Considerable emphasis should be given to these facts.

The divisions and their descriptive terms were assembled with some difficulty from the recesses of memory of two or three of the aged Penobscot hunters in 1914. During that winter, I obtained from some Malecite informants a fuller but similar chronology which suggests that, with local variations, it was common to the area.

kpo't'hadin, "still-hunting, stalking": From about the first of February until the break-up of the ice on the lakes and rivers of the interior, the Penobscot engaged in their winter hunt. During this period they began with moose killing, following with beaver taking and trapping for fur in general. They obtained the winter supply of meat. It was with the break-up in spring that they descended the main river to the village.

ma'kwa'n hadin, "maple sugar gathering": About the first of April, the different families went out from the main villages into the neighboring "sugar-bush" groves, which, as we shall learn, were inherited properties of families. Here they began the sugar-making operations separately described.

ki'khadin, "planting": With the termination of sugar making, generally about the end of April, the families came down to the main villages and planted their corn, staying there until sometime in July, when the crop could be taken up.

*noda'ki'k*ʷ *hadin*, "hunting seal": Sometime in July, and continuing through August, they left the villages again and went down to the coast to occupy chosen locations bordering salt-water bays and the islands to hunt seals for the much-needed supply of sealskins and blubber for cooking purposes.

*wla'k*ʷ*han*, "still-hunting at night in canoe," or *kim'ska''-soldin*, "going about to find something": In September the families scattered through the country as they worked back into the forest toward their proper hunting territories. During this time, the moose, deer, and caribou are driven to seek refuge from the flies that molest them, by resorting to the lakes and rivers. Here the hunters in canoes sought and killed them.

nadie'lin, "hunting" (*giz məde'ʿkwezəwag mo'zuk*, "calling moose"): From the middle of September until about the middle of November, the season for moose calling is in full swing, as described. This is the most exciting period of the fall hunt. At its conclusion the families returned for a while to the villages, or packed themselves down in their winter quarters to begin the regular winter hunt as circumstances decided for them.[5]

Hunting, designated by the terms *gado'nʿke* and *nadie'lu*, had its religious aspects. These I have treated in a separate report (see Bibliography, Penobscot Religious Beliefs).

The implements of hunting consisted of a bow, a simple five-foot stave, and arrows, supplemented by a lance and knife. By 1675 the New England Indians were as expert in the use of the musket as the white people (Sullivan, p. 255). The bows and arrows are described under a special heading (page 113). Hunting lances were of several types, depending upon their functions. The beaver lances, for instance, were similar to fish leisters, one kind having two wooden side prongs and a metal point, another having a barbed head like that of a harpoon. After the coming of Europeans

---

[5] I add Mrs. Eckstorm's excellent summary of seasonal activities. "In spring our Penobscots stayed by the rivers to take the alewives, shad, salmon and sturgeon when they ran up the streams to spawn. Then they planted their corn and beans and a few potatoes. About the first of June the black-flies and mosquitoes drove them out of the woods, and they went to the seashore for seal and porpoise, to get the oil and the skins; also, in earlier years, to get the eggs and nestlings of seabirds. They also dried quantities of clams and lobsters which they stored for winter use. In September, they went up river to harvest their crops. In October they moved on into the big woods and prepared their lines of traps for the fall fur-hunt. Before Christmas they came back to their villages and feasted for not less than two weeks. Then they went into the woods again, moose-hunting in the deep snow and trapping. Before the ice broke up, in March or April, they made their spring catch of otter and beaver, and when the rivers were clear, they came down in bark or skin canoes to the villages again, ready for the spring catch of muskrat and the fisheries and planting. The seasonal migrations of the tribes as a whole depended upon the climatic conditions which governed the fish and game they lived upon." What a picture of abundance to regale the senses of the primitivist!

these were of iron; before then no one is able to tell what form they took, except that the heads were of stone. The hunting knife, originally also a stone article, was of iron in historic times. Some are hafted in wood, some in antler (Fig. 6). The aboriginal hunter's outfit included, moreover, a game

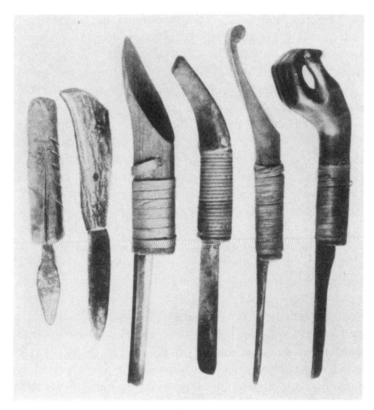

FIG. 6

TYPES OF KNIVES

Two on left, Wood and Antler Handles, for Slitting and Cutting
Others, Men's Crooked Knives

bag of harbor-seal skin, fire-tool pouch of an entire woodchuck skin, knife case, decoy head coverings, and in later times when guns came into use, a gun-case of sealskin, as well as other articles of convenience in traveling through the woods, such as snowshoes, toboggan, sled, pack baskets, and men's articles.

Moose hunting was, and is, perhaps, the most developed
activity among the Wabanaki, who live in a favored region
where the animals abound.   Moose are hunted by different
methods in different seasons.   In the summer they are seldom
molested, for their qualities both in hide and flesh are then
poorest.   In former times, however, when encountered within
range, a moose was taken at any time if his substance were
needed.   In the winter moose were hunted on the snow,
their clumsy movements in floundering through the snow,
different from those of the caribou, rendering them easy prey
to a hunter on snowshoes.   In the springtime the chase was
generally desultory, since the pursuit of muskrats, bears,
deer, and other game claimed much time.   In the fall of the
year, however, when the voice of the hyla is heard in the cool
woods giving forth his message that "moose-calling time has
come," regular moose-hunting trips were, and are, made to
provide meat to be smoked and preserved.   However, deer
and caribou, as well as other desirable game, are never ignored
at any time.   By the middle of September the moose are
thought to be in their prime, the bulls being in their rutting
mood, and the cows fattest.   Advantage is taken of the bull's
autumnal passion by the hunters in luring him within range.
During the fall twilight, evening, and early morning, the
cows from some solitary thicket bellow their call abroad to
attract a mate.   Some bull who hears this answers and proceeds to the spot, deviously and noisily, in order to frighten
away or, contrariwise, to challenge a possible rival who may
be bent on the same objective.   It may be several hours
before the bull reaches the cow, on account of his jealous
passion.   It is this responsiveness that the hunter uses to
his own advantage, imitating with a cone of rolled birch bark
the luring call of the cow and shooting the bull when he
approaches.   The Indians become crafty and skillful in employing this call, and the methods present a lively and interesting topic of investigation.

Let me attempt to describe a few typical occasions, not
forgetting that many fine passages from able pens of sportsmen have detailed the art of moose-calling.   To begin with,
moose or deer hunting which is begun at evening or late

afternoon is called *wlu'k'ʷhat*.   In a region where large bulls
are known to range, a camp is made at evening, and everything is kept quiet.   After midnight, about two o'clock,
several long, loud, and tremulous calls are given on the
moose-call, or "horn" as it is called, *muswi'kwi·m'ɑt*, consisting of a sheet of birch bark rolled into the shape of a
megaphone, and fastened either with a couple of wooden pins,
or by sewing if the horn is a permanent possession, or sometimes merely wrapped around with a
strip of root, splint, or a moccasin
string.   The Penobscot birch-bark
moose-calls (Figs. 7, 8), are about
fourteen inches long with the opening
wide enough to admit the palm of the
hand.   Some of the hunters prize their
horns and have them ornamented.

FIG. 7

Birch-bark Moose Call

The first long call, lasting sometimes nearly half a minute,
is to signal the district.   During this call the horn is revolved
several times in the air in a circle, then the call brought to a
close, mouth downwaid.   If a bull is within hearing he will
proceed to answer and approach.   When an answer is received, a luring call is again given, after which all is kept
quiet until a few hours before sunrise.   The bull is, during
this time, approaching cautiously from a point possibly several
miles away.   Just before daybreak, about four o'clock, another encouraging call may be given, with the horn held
straight out, and then turned down.   About daybreak the
final trial is made to bring the bull within range.   The delay
is made purposely until enough light comes to see to aim.
Between the periods of calling the hunters sometimes enjoy a
nap.   In making the last calls, the operator spreads out a
little flat space on the dead leaves and holds his call within
six or eight inches of it, the mouth pointing directly downward.   More of a squealing tone is incorporated into these
calls, representing moose-passion, to hurry the bull's approach.
By this time he may be heard trampling down the bushes and
thrashing the thickets with his antlers in impassioned rage.
The hunters make ready, and a few whispered words of warning precede the last call, which is meant to bring the bull into

FIG. 8 HUNTER DEMONSTRATING METHODS OF USING MOOSE CALL

sight. When his huge form appears in the dim light, he is shot. With shouts the hunters dash to the spot where he stood, and if there is light enough examine the traces of blood. If it is still too early to see, they stick a twig in the ground at the spot and wait till there is light. If the blood is dark, the bull has been mortally wounded and may be looked for not far away. If, on the other hand, the color is light, the hunters decide how severe the wound may have been, and whether it is worth while to track the animal.

Let us imagine ourselves under somewhat different circumstances, accompanying the same hunters after moose in a canoe, upon some lake or river. Here the time chosen is also early morning or around dusk. The canoe is paddled noiselessly along near the shore where the game is known to come. At frequent intervals the bow man gives a call with the bark horn pointed up into the woods lining the banks. When he gets an answer he puts an appealing note into the call. Paddling is stopped. So is the bull lured to the bank where he thinks a cow is feeding. Now the operator takes a canoe bailer, or his bark horn, and dips up some water, pouring it out to make a sound like a cow raising her dripping mouth from the stream, or better to imitate her urinating. The bull, seeing the shadowy form of the canoe and hearing the splashing noise, comes out. Now the man paddling in the stern backs the canoe away from the spot and the bow man gets ready to shoot. When the big bull has reached the place he finds that his quarry has retreated from him, and becomes furious. Here while he stands deep in the water the marksman shoots him. Keeping the canoe at a safe distance the hunters wait till he succumbs, or paddle ashore to follow him if he takes flight. The Indians, of course, in both cases have to take into consideration the direction of the wind, and many other details which mean much to the success of the hunt. In ability the different hunters range from experts to novices. The details of preparation, and the length, quality, and timing of the calls vary considerably, depending upon skill and experience.

When still-hunting moose, or other game, the hunter carries a shorter and smaller call, about nine inches long and three wide at the flaring end. Through this he grunts at intervals as he goes through the woods, so as to deceive moose, and formerly caribou, that might be in the neighborhood. The crackling twigs and occasional grunts sound innocently like another moose moving through the woods. This trick is also used at "carries" or portages, in order not to alarm game that may be started up. It also served as a definite call for caribou; a few short grunts being the signal. In the old days when a moose, deer, or caribou was shot with an arrow they say that it was not necessary for the shot to be fatal at first because if the arrow penetrated almost anywhere between the ribs the animal would lie down after he had run awhile and roll on the arrow to dislodge it, so driving it in farther until it would result fatally.

Some interesting beliefs are current concerning the history of game in their territory. Three times in the life of one old man did he remember the caribou leaving the region. Another remembered how, forty years before, the deer left and for four or five years hardly any were seen. The wolves also left the country, it was supposed, going north to Canada. Then, after a few years, deer tracks were found heading southward, and the deer soon became plentiful again, but the wolves never returned with them, and are not now found in Maine. The gray squirrel is said also not to have been found until lately in the north central woods. And the raccoon is relatively scarce.

Deer are hunted in their runways, or by stalking—no such deer-calling devices being known to the Wabanaki as those among the tribes of the South. The caribou, which were formerly abundant in the Penobscot region, have in the last generation totally disappeared. Dr. Ralph Palmer places the last date for authentic record of the animal in Maine as being about 1908.[6] They were stalked or killed along the streams, in much the same manner as deer. Both, however, were snared, as will be shortly seen, and killed in their "yards," as the hunters of the north designate the beaten runways

[6] Palmer, p. 37. In consideration of Dr. Palmer's thoroughgoing study of the mammals of Maine, still unpublished so far as I know, I shall have to reiterate an earlier statement to the effect that my remarks are largely records of native beliefs in natural history; not scientific.

where the cervines resort for shelter and food in times of heavy snow. The "yard" is called *awusɔnu'di*, "enclosure." "Torching," or luring deer within gunshot by means of a light in the bow of a canoe was also practised, called *awa's anɑ*, though it is now forbidden by law.

An important feature of hunting to be discussed later under the topic of the "Pure Men or Runners" is the aboriginal custom of running down and killing game by fleet-footed young men, who formed a semi-esoteric, bachelor age-group regulated by prohibitions of conduct. Stories of this feat show that formerly it was no very uncommon thing for a hunter to chase a moose for days and days before killing him.

Bears are said to come out of their dens in spring when the chipmunk is first seen. A smaller fat variety was considered very good, while the large lanky bear ("racer") of these regions is much feared and seldom molested unless needed. It is said that before the days of firearms there was a rule among the hunters when they were confronted by one of these bears, which are "very savage," to await the beast's approach with a thick fir branch or some similar object, and to throw it into his arms the moment the bear rose on his hind feet. When the animal hugged and mangled this, which took his attention for an instant, the hunter had an opportunity to strike him on the head with his ax. Some observances of a semi-religious nature concerned with the killing and disposition of the bear have appeared in a previous monograph (see Bibliography, Penobscot Religious Beliefs).

In taking beaver, whose flesh formed no small part of the diet of the Wabanaki a generation or so ago, the usual practices of stalking, chiseling, and driving the animals beneath the ice of the lakes or ponds were in vogue. The protective law in Maine has, however, put an end to Indian beaver hunting, for which reason we have only some general notes on killing to record and some picturesque beliefs attesting to the deep sagacity which the Indians accredit to the beaver. Several times I visited beaver colonies with Indians, in the remote bush of the Aroostook country far from the ordinary hunting precincts of the present generation of woodsmen.

Nothing was done on these occasions beyond wistfully regarding the possibilities of plunder, and describing in terms already familiar to us the older methods of breaking in the cabins and spearing its inmates. Such occasions, however, bring out interesting talk. And I heard, forthwith, that the adult beaver sleeps upon a platform built just above the water-line within the "cabin." He allows his tail to hang over into the water. Thus, should a hunter break open the dam, the lowering of the water would be perceptible to the beaver through the senses in its tail and would cause alarm. Another observation by the Indians here, believed to be true like the foregoing, is that the female bears her pups one at a time and at periods far enough apart so that when one is born the other is weaned and driven forth to seek a territory and pond of its own. The native designations for the young are interesting; *piwe''so*, the elder of the pups, and *nidja'nsis* the younger. The latter term corresponds in derivation with the human kinship term for brother and uncle. In the term denoting the beaver cabin, *gwabitewəzə's*, "beaver nest," an interesting synonym occurs; the animal being denoted by the term in common use for beaver among the neighboring bands, namely *gwa'bit'*, "red tooth." It is also said that if the female has two pups at once she kills one as being superfluous.

The beaver was thought to be sensitive to the mention of his death. When the hunter returned from beaver killing he did not tell how many he had taken, but silently threw chips of wood, corresponding to the number of animals killed, to his wife or companion to inform of his success.

Starvation may occasionally have been the fate of hunters and their families in remote times. This is indicated in the tales. It is evident, however, that none of the Wabanaki peoples were menaced by death from want to the extent that we learn of among the tribes north of the St. Lawrence. Some idea of hard times in the woods about 1850 is conveyed by the short narrative of experience by Hemlock Joe, the oldest man in the tribe in 1922.

I started for the woods with only a rifle; Charley Denis with an ax. There were no deer here then, only some moose. But there were many caribou and many wolves. The wolves were going in packs. At a place I told Charley to stop, and he went over to a ridge to look for tracks. We had European clothing at that time and a toboggan pulled with a basswood pack-strap. I found the tracks of four moose and went over to Charley, told him to stay there, make camp, and come on after me the next day. Then I chased those moose for two days, keeping on until it was so late at night that I could only drop down to sleep at night under the shelter of a big cedar trunk that had fallen. At last my dog chased two of the moose to me and I killed them with my old rifle. The next day it snowed and I got lost. Charley did not come up to me, as he went back after giving me up. And it was another day before I reached home and got something to eat. No, I did not eat any of the moose meat, because I had no matches with which to make a fire.

FIG. 9

HUNTER'S DECOY CAPE

Representing Owl, for Approaching Deer in Winter

The hunting cap, serving both as a disguise and a protection from the cold, was until recent times used by hunters. The general form of this article (Fig. 9) is similar to that employed by many northern Algonkian and Athapaskan tribes. Description is hardly necessary; it is squared across the top with the two ear-like flaps, and comes down narrowly along the sides of the face and hangs well over the neck and shoulders. The whole construction represents, as the Penobscot say, the cat-owl, the deception augmented by a piece of red flannel sewed over the forehead and the red ears that carry out the imitative effect. The specimen figured is of brown cloth, and was intended for fowl hunting; the red and brown is thought not to alarm ducks or geese. A similar decoy headdress, gray in color, was used in approaching deer. It is called *wezǝmu'sɑk*, "horns."

Muskrat hunting is quite important. They are hunted and trapped in the spring and fall; their pelts are sold, and every portion of their flesh is eaten with great relish by the Indians, who esteem muskrat meat most highly. An interesting instrument is found in use as a muskrat-call (Fig. 10). It consists of two pieces of wood two and a half or three inches long, mortised together, and between them an opening with a shred of birch bark between. Blowing through this

FIG. 10

Muskrat Call

produces a resonant buzzing which resembles the call of the muskrat. The instrument is called *mǝde'kwe'zudi*, "calling tube." The same sound can be produced by drawing the lips tightly and sucking through one corner in short jerks. By paddling along the banks of the river near deadwater, where muskrats are plentiful, the animals can be lured out to the canoe by manipulating the calls. When they are near enough they are hit with the paddle. It is not unusual for the muskrat to be so deceived that he tries to clamber up on to the canoe, evidently taking it to be a log.

According to old authorities among the Penobscot, a sling-stone attached to a leather line about three feet long was used to knock over water fowl. These slingstones were, it is claimed, carried in the canoe ready to be thrown at birds or other small animals when espied on the water. The plummet-shaped stones found commonly throughout New England and numerous also in the Penobscot valley are identified by the Indians as the slingstones. Several were obtained, one having been fixed to a thong to illustrate the complete object. They average from two and three-quarters to three inches long, and one and a quarter to one and three-quarters wide. The pear-shaped stones, or slingstones, as they probably were, must have formed part of the paraphernalia of almost every man, for Willoughby found them present in nearly every grave, together with other stone tools.[7] They are common in northern New England. The Indians also claim that some of the smaller of the pear-shaped stones were likewise employed as ear and nose pendants. Various wild fowl are decoyed by imitative cries, in the production of which some of the hunters are very clever. Mention at least should be made here of the ceremony of rejoicing, to be presented subsequently, which is performed upon the safe return of the hunters (page 300).

Rules existed for the distribution of game. The first man of the season to kill a deer or moose, even nowadays, must divide the meat among the villagers as far as it will go. He does not eat of this himself, or he would damage his luck. Likewise, two hunters traveling in company give each other their first kill, whatever it may be, before keeping either meat or pelts of their own. This is called $\alpha d\alpha'b\partial gw\partial h\alpha'$, "gift."

The first game a boy kills must be shared by the camp. Should he eat of it himself he would never get any more. When a little boy, for instance, kills and brings home his first squirrel or rabbit, he is praised, the meat is cooked, and people are invited in to eat it up for him.

The idea of sharing game was so strong that it is said to have been the custom formerly for practically all game brought into the village to be given away. This practice seems to have survived from the old period, to be referred to

[7] Willoughby, ref. 4, and Pennypacker, 142–4.

later, when the runners, or "Pure Men," ran down and killed game for the community.

We should also note that before embarking on the hunt for big game, the man indulged in the sweat-bath as a protective medicinal rite. This is described with details under another heading. And there was also a hunter's rejoicing dance.

Traps

The different animals, large and small, were trapped by native devices, some of which are widely known among northern Indians, while others seem to be more distinctively Penobscot.

Fig. 11

COMMON SNARE SET IN RUNWAYS FOR HARES

The common snare (*pia'nis*) and drag (Fig. 11), consisting of a rawhide or leather noose attached to a tough stick about three feet long, is set in runways of rabbits or other small animals. This stick, supported on two forked uprights, or in any way convenient to the situation, holds the noose above the ground high enough to allow the animal to insert its head when passing through. A small forked twig may be needed to steady the loop. When the victim has caught the noose over his neck, he dashes off, only to be brought to a sudden stop and choked by the drag catching upon some obstruction. Such snares are used for all kinds of animals: rabbits, wildcats, and formerly for deer, caribou, and partridges.

The spring snare is also used for small mammals and birds, and is as widely known as the preceding. In this, the slipping noose is attached to a springy, bent-over sapling, which is released by a slight disturbance of the noose, jerking the animal into the air, where it is safe from molestation by foxes or other prowling scavengers.

Both these snares may be surrounded by upright sticks forming an enclosure called *biziaz'u*, "fence," inside of which is some bait; or they may simply be set in runways, as more convenient during snow time. One sees numbers of these snares, from which many families get their fresh rabbit meat, set on the islands above the village.

In former days of greater abundance of the spruce grouse (Canachites canadensis canace, Linn.) in the northern districts of Maine the pole snare was used for its capture. This was a noose of hide fastened to a long pole by which the bird was caught by the neck as it sat unsuspectingly on a branch.

The Penobscot deadfall, intended chiefly for mink, otter, sable, fisher, bear, and other predacious fur-bearing mammals, was studied by Mr. W. C. Orchard of the Museum of the American Indian, Heye Foundation, who has contributed the following account and sketches of this and another ingeniously simple device.

That common crushing trap (Fig. 12), generally known as the dead-fall, and found from the Pacific to the Atlantic, was used by the Penobscot for securing all kinds of game and fur animals. The

FIG. 12

Gravity Fall Trap for Fur-bearers

trap consisted of a crushing beam, which is supported by an unstable prop, resting on a trigger holding the bait.[8] The slightest disturb-

[8] This is the trigger release termed "samson-post" by Dr. Cooper in his recent monograph on Algonkian traps cited in the Bibliography.

ance of the trigger by the animal in an attempt to secure the bait causes the prop to fall out of position, and allows the crushing beam to descend and kill the victim. To prevent the animals from getting the bait without reaching under the beam, an enclosure was built around the back and sides and sometimes roofed over. When setting the trap for small animals, the enclosure might be built of small slabs of split wood driven into the ground, or even birch bark. For large game, the enclosure would be made of poles driven into the ground, and the crushing beam would be weighted by resting other logs on it.

A very interesting trap for small animals, particularly for mink, is made by boring a horizontal hole in a standing tree (see Fig. 13).

Fig. 13

Device for Catch-ing Fur-Bearing Carnivores

The hole is about three inches in diameter, and six or eight inches deep, and just high enough from the ground to make the animals climb up to investigate. Two sharpened hardwood sticks are driven through the lower edge of the hole, pointing upward and inward. The bait is set just beyond the points. The inquisitive animal, during investigation, is tempted to reach over the points to secure the dainty morsel, after which it proceeds to drop to the ground, but the pointed sticks catch in the animal's throat. Its frantic struggles to back out of the hole drive the points still farther into its throat, causing death. This trap is said to be irresistible to mink where others fail (unpublished MS).

The subject of traps and snares is only casually treated in the preceding paragraphs. It awaits a thoroughgoing review at the hands of a field investigator who shall carry it forward by participating in trapping excursions in the woods among the tribes of Maine. Mr. Orchard's notes serve to introduce the trap forms in common use at the time of his visit to the Penobscot. The cage-fall trap, I may add, is unknown.

The Indian trappers all believe strongly in the efficacy of beaver "castoreum" as a scent for traps. The trapper pro-vides himself with a small vial or bottle, formerly made of birch bark, containing beaver or hog testicles, raw or pre-served in alcohol. This is smeared on traps after they are set. The castoreum may also be drawn over the ground by a string from some distance away leading toward the trap, as a lure for a passing animal. The scent vial or bottle is carried attached to a button or cross-stick toggle to be inserted under the hunter's belt leaving his hands free while the bottle hangs safe and handy.

By way of discussion, a little may be said in explanation of animal names. According to native natural history, there seems to be no generic classification of animals. Many of the terms do not submit to satisfactory analysis. The names appear to be divided between onomatopoetic forms and descriptive terms, the clarity of which has been lost in some developmental stage of the language. An interesting point brought out is the lack of specific differentiation in the genera. One gathers that different closely related species are only varieties of the same beast. So we find, for instance, that the two varieties of fox are covered by the one name; the same holds true for the red and gray and black squirrels, and also with many birds, such as the hawks, herons, gulls, and finches, and the insects. Some of the families, however, the ducks, for instance, appear to be more minutely classified.

There are two forms of bears recognized: the small, fat, harmless one known locally as "hog bear," and the larger, lanker one known as "ranger bear." The former builds himself a regular den for the winter, with the entrance closed, while the ranger bear roves about till winter drives him to hibernate fully exposed until covered with snowdrifts in whatever unprotected spot he may be, often only in a tree cavity or along a rocky ledge.

A peculiar faculty of scenting deer or moose is claimed as a possession by the hunters. When the animals jump up alarmed from their retreats, they emit a scent which attracts the hunters' attention. The sources of this lie in two tufts of hair (metatarsal glands) between the hind knees. When they urinate, the animals rub their hind legs together, rubbing the urine into this hair. This the Penobscot say is a provision for man's benefit, so that the game may be scented out by him. Further information on the habits of animals, and beliefs regarding them, have been presented in the essay on religion.[8a]

[8a] See Bibliography, No. 19, p. 317.

A few brief extracts from the myths regarding the transformation of animals and the bestowal of their characteristics
by the culture hero may be pertinent here. Gluskabe, the
culture hero, it seems, prepared the world for the advent of
human beings by modifying some of the ferocious creatures
who would menace them. Among these was the squirrel,
then of monstrous size, which was dwarfed by Gluskabe's
hand, for threatening and bragging of what he would do to
man. Another monster we hear of (identified by the Indians
with the elephant and mastodon, strangely enough) had long
teeth. He was destroyed.[8a] The moose, incidentally, escaped
alteration, despite his size, by professing humility and inno-
cent intentions toward man.

The animals, moreover, are responsible among themselves
for many transformations by their own deeds, by pranks
played upon each other, and by events which befall them in
their careers. Among the incidents are found those of how
the muskrat loses his fine flat tail to the beaver; how the
rabbit loses his tail and gets his flanks lengthened in trying
to help a friend; how the kingfisher gets his sharp beak; how
the wolverine has an inverted membrum; how the partridge
fed his family from the flesh of his legs and so developed bony
thighs; how the woodchuck, Gluskabe's grandmother, pulled
so much hair from her belly to make him a pouch that she
has very little hair there now; how the loon originated from a
man who incestuously married his cousin. Another interesting story relates how one time in the mythical period a big
whale was washed ashore, and Gluskabe portioned his carcass
off among the different creatures, some of them deriving their
permanent characteristics from the event. The ant, for instance, was given the whale's skull. In this he made his nest
and nibbled the bones clean, so that nowadays the ant builds
in the fields his many-tunneled nest like a whale's skull and
clean bones. The spider was given the whale's cavity to
live in. There he spun his web across the openings and
snared other insects that came for plunder; and so the spider,

[8a] For discussion of the tale as a Pleistocene memory among Indians, see W. D.
Strong, pp. 81–88, and Speck, 21, pp. 159–63.

"spinning ant," still finds a broad orifice, and there spreads his mesh.

The passion for living in the solitudes of the forest where game exists in abundance is but a memory with the younger generation of Wabanaki. The old Penobscot hunters with sighs lament the change. One stormy January night, while talking over the good old hunting days before the settlement of the country, I noted the remark, "It was as easy for the Indians to pick up berries, game, and fish as it is for them to pick up snow outside tonight."

Use of Dogs

The associations between man and dog in the northeastern region are significant enough to call for some attention in connection with practices of hunting and travel. Dogs figured in mythical associations as the companions of man from the transformation period. In the myth of distribution of animal traits, the text runs that Gluskabe assembled the animals before him and sounded their future intentions in respect to mankind whom, he told them, he was about to create. Most of them declared their intentions to be hostile toward man-to-be. The dog, however, elected himself to be man's companion, associate, and helper, and so it was. When man appeared the dog went and lay down at his side. There are tales of dogs conversing with the hunters, their masters: tales of communication in dreams by which dogs instructed their masters how to succeed in life, that is, in the hunt. There are also implications in social history of human-canine miscegenation, even with fertile offspring.

The status of dogs in the living cultural sphere is that of hunting associates. In the common interests of the chase a system of communication has developed, in illustration of which a few examples of signals, address, naming, and interdependence will shortly be given. They explain the fitness of the term a'ləmus, "domestic creature," which designates the dog.

It should be noted however that there is no indication whatever that dogs were harnessed to sleds or toboggans by the Penobscot or any of the Wabanaki peoples. Neither is it known that dogs were employed here as pack-bearers. The St. Lawrence River seems to be the southern frontier of dog driving in the northeast, since both Montagnais and Naskapi have learned to train dogs for this purpose. The latter have apparently acquired their sled-dog breed and the equipment of driving from the French-Canadians, while the Naskapi seem to have acquired theirs from association with Eskimo. In both cases the acquisition bears evidence of historical lateness. The Penobscot have even shown a disposition to disregard the advantages of dog driving deliberately during the time of my contact with them. Upon several occasions when traveling in the bush in winter, I attempted to induce my hunting companions to harness the dogs running free in the retinue of toboggans, putting them to helpful service, as I had observed the Montagnais to do. They saw and admitted the worth of the idea as a relief to the sweating and plodding progress through the deep snow, but nothing ever happened toward the adoption of the idea, though it was urged repeatedly for several years. Among some Indians, innovations seem slow to be acquired. The primary function of dogs here lies in their service in tracking game and bringing it to a stand. It is rare for a hunter to embark for an up-river hunting trip without one or two dogs. They are admirably trained to take their place in the loaded canoe and lie still, curbing their inclinations to move about. They are made to lie down behind the middle thwart of the canoe, resting on the pack of woods equipment. After a few words or blows a dog will remain quiet in his place for hours at a time, though he is always glad to jump out and stretch his legs when a landing is made. The proximity of game is overtly betrayed by every action of the animal, which the hunters well understand. In the summer time, when the Indians make their exodus to the salt water for the basket trade and the enjoyment of a change of life from the interior, the families who move down to the sea usually leave their dogs behind to shift for themselves upon Indian Island. Here they will voluntarily remain. During this season they may be observed roaming in troops along the shores of the island, romping, fighting, and foraging for whatever refuse turns up.

It would be interesting to know something of the degree of old native canine blood which these animals may possess. There is, however, nothing in their appearance or pedigree to indicate difference from the usual breeds of mongrel hunting dogs of the region. Some of the older people assert that a wolf strain runs in their dogs, there having been one animal as late as 1912 which was half wolf by definite statement.

The signals of address to dogs, which are generally well obeyed, especially if backed by kicks or blows, are the following—*gɔs·ha'*, "Get out"; *gɔs dama'lɔs·in*, "Go lie down somewhere!" ordered when a hunter wants to prevent his dog from chewing the game he has just shot; *gɔs·*, "Lie down!," *tcuwi's tcwis*, "Watch out!, Hark!, Stop!" *na'udjo'se*, "Come here" (accompanied by the usual chirping), *su + su + gwi·la'we* (whispered) "Go fetch it"; *su + baga'le* (whispered) "Go bite him." By the last two signals the dogs recognize the direction indicated by pointing with the hand when ordered to fetch something or to run game.

The animals are often petted with long caressing tones: *wuli·ges·u"alamu's·is*, "Good creature, doggie." And furthermore, individual names are given to most of them, of which the following list is typical. Some are derived from the Malecite and Passamaquoddy.

Awɑ's·is	Baby	Di'ktɑgli	"Cat" Owl (Barred Owl)
Pi'nsis	Little pin	Awe's·us	Bear
Sawɑnhi'gan	Sauce (lit. "that which bitters")		
Pabe"tciman	Ask him.	Ezɔba'nɔs	Raccoon
Agwe'djiman	Try him.	Tekne'bɔs	Monkey
Awe'n	Who?	Bi'ksi	Pork (lit. "pigs")
Dano'wa	Where's that?	Tcigwa'lus	Frog
Kokokha's	Hoot Owl	Ma'lsɔm	Wolf
Djabu'tdes	Clown	Adjagwa'l	Perch

By final judgment it seems that the status of dogs is one of close living association with people; a status not far below the human level. The dog is distinctly a companion in the esteem of the Penobscot by contrast with the Montagnais attitude toward the creature.[9]

TRAVEL AND TRANSPORTATION

Owing to the constant necessity of getting over large tracts of country in quest of game both in summer and winter, devices for transportation came to be highly developed. The main Penobscot River was the artery of travel, with numerous smaller streams leading into it like a network over the country, winding down from remote valleys or discharging from lakes or chains of lakes, making practically every part of the Penobscot territory accessible by canoe; and this, too, without many portages. Several of the large systems of lakes and rivers are almost joined at their sources, so that by ascending one the hunter can pass by a short portage or carry into another which ultimately conducts him into a different watershed. So, for instance, by ascending the Penobscot to the East Branch, and by this to Webster Brook and Lake, the passage is open, after a short carry, to Telos Lake, Chamberlain Lake, and Eagle Lake, leading to the Allagash River, and so down the St. John to the Bay of Fundy through the country of the Malecite. Another short carry from Cut Lake, at the head of Nolopsemic Stream, connects Seboeis River with Umcolcus Stream, leading into the Aroostook, which flows to Tobique, the Malecite village on St. John River.

The Penobscot River was, and is, the highway of movement, traversible by canoe in summer and sled in winter. From the principal village at Indian Island (Oldtown), a two days' journey, with an overnight stop near Bucksport, brings the canoeman to Penobscot Bay, where former camps were numerous on the different islands. Seal and porpoise hunting, oysters and other shellfish and salt-water fish, besides the need of sweetgrass for basketry, led them continually in this direction. Northward from Oldtown were innumerable rivers and lakes, teeming with fish, in districts where deer, moose, caribou, and the other creatures abounded, accessible from the main river or by branching off into the Piscataquis,

[9] F. G. Speck, "Dogs of the Labrador Indians," *Natural History*, Vol. XXV, No. 1, 1925, pp. 58–64.

Mattawamkeag, Passadumkeag, Seboois, and others. The largest lakes, too, lie near or directly in the course of the Penobscot.

The annual hunt was the chief event in the round of Penobscot life. As mentioned before, the different family groups traversed their hunting territories continually, spending only part of the year in the permanent village locations on the main river. This constant dependence upon watercraft and schemes of transportation developed the faculty of travel to an extreme. So we find such articles as canoes, toboggans, sleds, snowshoes, pack-baskets, carrying and dragging devices, and other equipment indispensable on the voyage, constructed with care and much practical ingenuity. The manufacture of these objects, in fact the whole science of travel, is the concern of the men who go hunting alone, or, as was more customary in former times, who embarked on hunting trips with their families to be gone from the settled villages for months at a time.

Canoes

The birch-bark canoe, *u'l*, "boat" (modern form from Passamaquoddy or Malecite *agwi'den*, "floater"), another old name being *igwa'wal*, is the most complex and intricate product of native mechanical genius in the north. Two sizes in general are recognized by them, small and large, the former from twelve to sixteen feet long, the latter from sixteen to twenty. Fig. 14 shows a typical large canoe with the peculiarities of Penobscot construction. The types made by the neighboring Malecite and Passamaquoddy, while fundamentally the same, differ in details of proportion. These differences are apparent to the eye of one experienced in lines. The Penobscot canoe rides rather low in the water; at the waist it has incurved sides, and not a very high up-turn at the ends. Moreover, the brown and white triangular decoration along the bark insert at the waist is considered a Penobscot mark of distinction, as also the series of double-curve ornaments etched on the bark flaps at the peaks. Sometimes, in addition, one sees triangles or double curves painted just below the gunwale all around.

Gluskabe, the culture hero, is accredited with having introduced the canoe among Indians and with having instructed them how to make it.

FIG. 14

BIRCH–BARK CANOES

Showing Characteristic Curve Designs at Ends and Middle

The construction of canoes [10] is a most important procedure. This description is based upon personal observation of the method. Two men usually require about a week to build a bark canoe.

[10] Since this craft is now a thing of the past at Penobscot, I may make the most of our resources of knowledge of its details by referring to the excellent description given by Mrs. Eckstorm (*op. cit.*, pp. 55–63).

The birch-bark covering is usually in one large piece, the white outside surface being placed inside. The canoe-builder uses as tools an axe, a crooked knife, and an awl. In beginning he lays his sheet of bark, white outer side up, after having shaved off inequalities with his knife, upon the ground, or, as in later times, often upon a board foundation. Warm weather is preferred for the work, as the bark is more pliable when warm. Beneath some fine shady tree is the spot chosen for the work. Two false gunwales, just the size of the canoe gunwales, are laid upon the bark, and the whole central space of the bark is then covered with stones to weight it down and to hold it flat and firm to earth. Then the workman bends up the sides and drives around the periphery a series of upright stakes with inside pieces clamped at the top projecting downwards inside the bark, thus fixing it in the shape of the craft. These stakes commonly number fifteen. A rail is

Fig. 15

BIRCH–BARK CANOE OF LAST CENTURY
AND BUILDER, LOUIS PIELSAK

sometimes run inside and outside the bark between it and the stakes. As the bark is bent up at the sides it becomes necessary to slit it in several places along each side to allow for the upward bend of the bow and stern. The main rails of the gunwale are next put in place, after which the clamp stakes are removed, the ends of the rails having been fastened with pegging and a sewing of spruce root. The two rails, one coming inside and the other outside the bark, are fitted over the upper edge of the bark and the edge is trimmed off even with them. The measuring stick, which has been cut and notched beforehand, is used for getting this gunwale at the right elevation all along, and giving it the right spread where the thwarts are to come. One old-fashioned way of fixing the overlapping edge of the bark along the gunwale was to bend it inwards, wrapping around the inside rail.

Next the bow and stern are cut into shape. A length of bark about six inches wide and three feet in length is needed on each side to piece out. This section of bark, called *abaha'dαgan*, "piece spliced in," is sewed in place with spruce root. Now a curved piece of cedar, bent to give the bow and stern their shapes, is put in place from where the end curve commences curving up to the rails. This is called *skwala''kwen*, "bow wood." The thwarts, five in number, one in the center, two halfway toward the ends and two more beyond them, are sewed and mortised to the inside rail. The thwarts of ash are called *pska''teguk*, "spreaders," or *mitsimənak*, "cross bars." In some canoes the middle thwart is ornamentally carved at the extremities. The two end thwarts, which have to serve as seats, are flat and several inches wide. Now the inside and outside rails are made fast to the bark by sewing with spruce root or by pegging or nailing. When they are sewn, wrappings of root over a space of an inch and a half and the same distance apart extend all the way down both sides. The inside rail of the gunwale is called *wi'bodagan*, the outside rail, *pi'gwalsagan*. Where the bark has been slit on the sides to accommodate the bend, another small piece of bark is sewed on, extending down from beneath the rails to serve as a backing for the seam.

When the bow and stern are sewed up, the canoe begins to assume some form. By this time most of the rocks have been removed from the inside of the construction because the bark has taken its shape. A bulkhead of cedar, shutting off the extreme ends, is now cut and put in place at bow and stern, the lower end fitting into a notch in the "bow wood," the upper end fitting into the place where the rails converge. This bulkhead is called *wuni'gesu*, "carrier," or "old woman" for some reason. In good canoes it forms a watertight compartment at each end and is sometimes filled with shavings.

An oval piece of bark like a flap has also been put over each end, reaching along the top of the bark from where the rails meet, right out to the end, and projecting over and down the sides for several inches. This is a reinforcement for the ends and prevents water from entering at the bow and stern when the canoe bow dips in rough water. It is figuratively termed *wule'ge*, "diaper," "breech-cloth." Its flaps are commonly decorated with etchings, cross-hatchings, double-curve designs, or floral figures, some examples of which may be seen in the plates. The builder at this point looks over his hull to piece out and sew up any rents or openings which may have occurred beneath the gunwale. The slits on the sides are now also sewn together, and the canoe is ready for its lining and ribs. Before putting these into place a thin coating of pitch, balsam or pine, is smeared over the inside as a sizing. The canoe builder has in the meantime been making his ribs and lining which are of cedar (arbor vitae).

The lining, *mane'ʻkanak*, "bedding," is made of thin cedar strips four or five feet long, several inches wide, and not more than a quarter of an inch thick, which have been shaved down with the crooked knife. The whole inside of the canoe must be covered tightly with these between the bark and the ribs. One of the cedar lining strips is first made to run lengthwise down the middle of the bottom from end to end, and on each side of this, beginning at the bow, outer pieces are laid, somewhat irregularly, while the first ribs are placed and hammered fast in the same end. The process of placing the lining and fitting in the ribs goes on simultaneously, as the one holds the other.

The ribs themselves, *magina'k*, are of cedar and number from forty to fifty-five according to the size of the craft. They are about two inches broad and not quite one-half inch thick, and are generally placed an inch apart. While the builder has been working on his bark, he has at odd times been preparing his ribs and has bent them properly, keeping them in shape by tying them with a strip of cedar bark, four or six in each bundle, like leaves of a metal spring. Now as he needs them, while putting in the lining, he unties them and fits them in place with the canoe mallet, *pagama'ʿkwagan*, "pounder," a spatula-shaped implement (Fig. 16), spreading

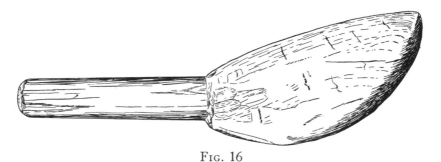

FIG. 16

WOODEN MALLET FOR SETTING CANOE RIBS

each one so that the ends poke under the gunwales, thus holding the rib fast without pegging or nailing. An interesting and ingenious device is used for spreading the ribs and getting their ends under the rails. This consists of a piece of cedar, stepped or notched, and several square-ended cedar rods. By putting one end of this "key" inside one end of a rib set in place and fitting an end of the rod into a notch while the other reaches to the opposite end of the rib an upward pull on the handle pokes its end beneath the gunwale. Fig. 17 shows how this is applied, the arrows indicating the thrust. The lower arrow shows where the operator's hand exerts its pressure. By using a shorter or longer lever stick, different distances may be reached. Working from both ends, and placing the filling while he sets the ribs, the operator after a few hours' work brings the interior to completion. A tool shaped like a small spade, called *wuligakska''sudi*, "fix cedar tool," about eight inches long is used to even up the lining under the ribs while they are being placed. This tool is used with the mallet as one would use a punch, to slide the ribs up or down a little. This part

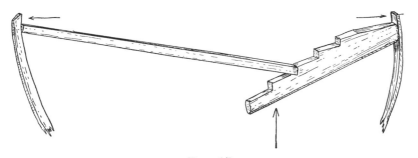

FIG. 17

SPREADER OR "KEY" FOR FORCING CANOE RIBS
INTO PLACE UNDER GUNWALES

Arrows Denote Direction of Force when Lever is Raised

of the work requires careful watching, and the builder is constantly trimming and fitting the ribs, pounding here and there, and measuring to keep an even shape in the rounding-out of the canoe bottom, and to have everything smooth and firm on the inside. A notched stick, *ebe'skwodi'gan*," halver," is often used to measure the middle depth beneath the middle thwart. This distance is in all Penobscot canoes either ten or twelve inches. The final operation is generally to peg on the top rail of the gunwale, *wuskida''kwabidj'ik*, "top (?)."

With the ribs all finally in place, the canoe is practically finished, except for pitching up the outside seams and ends with fir or spruce pitch, with which sometimes a little tallow is mixed to make it elastic. To test the covering for leaks, the canoe is put upon a couple of logs and the inside partly filled with water. Where water trickles through, the leak is patched with pitch. The stitches in sewing the bark, and other details of handling the bark will be treated separately later on. During the sewing the spruce-root threads are kept in a vessel of water to preserve their softness.

I give below a list of canoe measurements of Penobscot specimens which were available.[11] The measuring stick referred to before has three notches on one side giving the inside height of the three different-sized thwarts from the bottom of the canoe, while the full length of the stick and the two notches on the other side give the inside length of the respective thwarts. These notches are made upon specifications worked out independently by each builder.

As to canoe outfit and travel more data is at hand, for there has been little change in this since early times. The paddle, *toha'ngan*, is of maple or spruce with a flattened grip (Fig. 30). The stern man uses a paddle about six, the bow man one about five feet long. The blades at the widest part average six inches. Every canoe party on a journey needs the pole, *gika'mkwahan*, "prodding under the water," a stout staff about ten feet long, often shod with iron nowadays, used in poling up-stream in swift water. The pole also is useful in many ways about camp as a tent pole, or pot supporter. Originally the canoe was provided with fawn skins on the bottom for the man's knees, as the position was to kneel, buttocks resting against the thwart. Of late years, however, the Indians prefer sitting in the canoe, the stern man sitting on the thwart, the bow man on the bottom, leaning his back on the thwart. The canoe bailer is a piece of folded birch bark, sometimes set in a notched stick, sometimes not, and resembling the improvised eating spoon. Another article of importance in the canoe is the dish of pitch generally tucked out of the way in the end. This is a plain folded bark receptacle containing hardened pitch to be melted and applied immediately over a rent in case of accident to the

[11] The dimensions are inside measurements in feet and inches. To get over-all dimensions, add 1½ inches for each gunwale and 1 inch for each thwart.

Specimen	Length	Width, middle thwart	Width, second thwart	Width, end thwart	Depth at middle thwart	Depth where gunwales join	Height of bend from ground	No. of ribs
1. S. Francis	16′ 5″	29″	20½″	11″	10″	13½″	19″	46
2. Francis	16′ 4″	29″	20½″	11″	10″	13½″	19″	46
3. F. G. S.	19′ 1″	30″	23½″	12″	10½″	17″	24½″	52
4. Peabody Museum	18′ 11″	35″	26½″	15″	10″	15½″	22¾″	51

(Dimensions of 4 furnished by Mr. C. C. Willoughby, Harvard University.)

bark. This pitch, *agwe'dəni'kʷ*, "canoe gum," is usually from pine. The anchor, *tca'upəna'pskwagan*, "throw overboard stone implement," as the name implies, consists of a good-sized stone, battered so as to be narrow around the middle, tied with a long rawhide line.

The canoemen have an ingenious way of getting a drink of water without halting. They raise the blade of the paddle in the air, and when the water runs down the handle hold the mouth against it to catch the drip. This done three or four times provides enough for a drink. Indians sway their bodies noticeably with each stroke of the paddle. When alone, they frequently paddle standing up. One man paddling alone in a canoe, is expressed by a special term *sila'mebie'*, one now obsolete. When more than one are paddling, the best man stations himself in the stern and steers the canoe.

Parties in canoes always keep close to the shore, where, in ascending, the current is not so strong. This also gives an advantage in landing quickly should game be seen, and in former times sheltered the canoes from the gaze of a possible enemy near the river. In making camp, while on a canoe journey, the canoe is often turned upside down and used as a shelter. Parties traveling in canoes have songs for different occasions. One of these intended for use in rough weather is given on page 168.

As long ago as Rosier's time it was recorded—"Their canoes are made . . . of the bark of a birch tree, strengthened within with ribs and hoopes of wood, in so good a fashion, with such excellent ingenious art, as they are able to bear seven or eight persons." [12] In running rapids where sharp rocks would be likely to gash the canoe, or in dragging or poling up through such places, they frequently make four or five thin cedar planks to be lashed to each side of the bottom of the canoe as a protection.

A canoe of another kind was the moose-hide canoe, *muso'lakʷ*, or *musa'wal*, "moose craft." [13] In spring, when

[12] Rosier, page 368.

[13] *Memoirs of Odd Adventures, Strange Deliverance, etc. in the Captivity of John Giles*, 1689 (Cincinnati, 1869), p. 20, gives some particulars of this interesting type of native craft among the Malecite.

the ice broke up, the hunters in former times regularly came down the river in these craft made of two moose skins tanned waterproof with grease. The skins were sewed together head to tail, and the seams were covered with moose tallow boiled with pitch. About a dozen ribs, the keel, thwarts, and gunwales, over which the skin covering was stretched, completed the framework. The returning hunters could then load their craft with moose meat and peltries from the winter hunt and drift down to the village. The canoe could finally be taken apart and the hides used otherwise, for moccasins or cut up for rawhide thongs or babiche.

FIG. 18

MOOSE–HIDE CANOE

One of these canoes (Fig. 18) I observed under construction. A whole day and part of the next were required for it. Formerly, when in the woods, the hunters who made these canoes to return home with their loads took two days ordinarily in building the framework and preparing the hide covering, employing the second night in drying the craft by suspending it from trees over a fire.

In building the canoe mentioned, two men were employed. One started by soaking two whole moose skins, then shaving the hair from them. With awl and babiche thongs he then sewed them together, the neck of one to the rear of the other. Sometimes, in making larger boats, three skins would be sewed together side by side. Meanwhile, the other man had split a cedar log and begun cutting out ribs and linings, rather roughly and about three inches wide. These he shaved down and smoothed sufficiently. The day before in the woods nearby, some elm poles had been cut, long enough to make gunwales and keel. When the material was ready, the skins were spread on the ground and sewed up the bow and stern with the proper curve, determined by a bent stick, to conform with the framework. The skin covering, kept wet, was then complete and ready to be put on as soon as the frame was finished. Very soon the workmen had tied the gunwale sticks end to end and spread them with three thwarts of elm bent over the gunwale and lashed back on themselves, one large one in the middle and two smaller ones at the ends. To this gunwale and deck, as it were, the keel of white birch was bent and fastened by lashing at the ends. At this stage the frame appeared as in Fig. 18. Now the skins were placed over the frame and sewed fast at stern and stem, and the overlapping parts along the gunwale were turned over the gunwale and roughly sewed taut along the edge. The canoe then had its outline but lacked ribbing and its final shape. Next, both men working together placed in the ribs and the lining strips, using their feet to press the ribs, which had been steamed a little, into their curve, and employing the ordinary canoe mallet to hammer them vertical. By using their judgment the builders finally got the thing properly rounded and bellied on the bottom and firm all over. The ends of the ribs coming under the gunwale held the overlapping part of the skin fast all around.

The skin canoe then required pitching and greasing to make it water-tight. Some pitch was melted and a little melted moose tallow was poured in to make it less brittle. The seam in the middle was then thoroughly pitched, as were the seams at the ends, and all were allowed to dry. Then a quantity of moose tallow was daubed on the entire skin with a rag. This, when soaked in, was followed by another coat to prevent the hides from soaking up water. After being suspended over a fire for a night this craft was complete. Its measurements were as follows: Length, 10 feet 7 inches; beam, 31 inches, depth at middle 15 inches, number of ribs, 17, lining slats 10, thwarts 3. This boat was judged capable of carrying two men or a load of about 400 pounds. With a pole, two paddles, a dish of pitch for repairing, it was considered a good, practical, temporary canoe by all the Indians who saw it, though hardly a thing of beauty.

Another type of craft formerly used was the spruce-bark canoe, the particulars of which, however, are lacking.

Snowshoes [14]

Snowshoes, *a'gamak*, next to the canoe are the most essential means of travel in the Penobscot country. The specimens in Fig. 19 represent the Penobscot type. The frame is perfectly flat, with no upturn at the toe, and from 4 to $4\frac{1}{2}$ feet long and about 18 inches wide. Women's snowshoes sometimes have the up-curved head part when intended for use in the level spaces about the camps. The rather sharply rounded toe and lengthened tail show proportions differing slightly from Malecite and Abenaki forms. In other respects, however, the type of snowshoe of the whole region occupied by Wabanaki tribes is about the same, in having a one-piece frame, two bars, and deer or moose rawhide (babiche) filling with similar qualities of weave and fastenings. Through observation of a number of specimens it would seem, if anything, that the only noticeable peculiarity in the weave of the Penobscot snowshoe is a rather uniformly wide spacing between the frame and the network proper, especially at the toe and heel sections. The outside of the frame is usually ornamented with little tufts of colored yarn, moose hair, or leather fringe, inserted under the countersunk fastenings. In the three specimens figured, the one at the left has leather fringe, the middle one moose hair, and the other the yarn tassels. As to the lashings, where oftentimes one finds tribal distinctions, the Penobscot insert the toe under the strip of thong intended for this purpose, then bring the loose thongs over the heel, forward to where they are wrapped with a half hitch once over the first length and tied, the knot generally coming at the heel. This is left permanently tied so as to be ready for use. By slipping the foot in and twisting the heel thongs once or twice if they are loose, the lashings may be quickly and tightly adjusted.

A rough account of snowshoe construction is as follows: The frames are made of ash, cut down and curved over the

---

[14] The extended discussion and description of snowshoes given by Mrs. Eckstorm will supply valuable additional details (*op. cit.*, pp. 52–5). See also D. S. Davidson, *Snowshoes*, Memoirs of the American Philosophical Society, Vol. VIII, 1936.

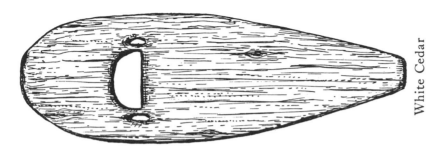

White Cedar

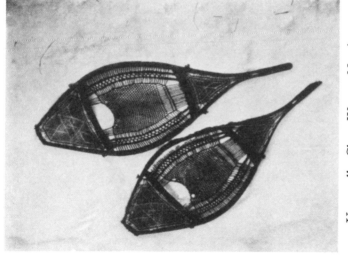

Unusually Close Woven Netting

FIG. 19
SNOWSHOES

workman's knee, then bent over the cross bars which are mortised in, and fastened together by rivet at the tail. A babiche runner is strung inside the toe and heel spaces through holes in the frame. The toe and heel filling is put in, then the center, the weave being the hexagonal twill. The snow-shoe needle (Fig. 20) is sized according to the fineness of the mesh. The diagonal warps are strung in first, passing under a runner just inside the frame, then they cross horizontally. The final shaping is given by the wooden or bone punch with

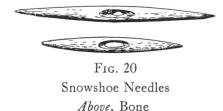

FIG. 20

Snowshoe Needles

Above, Bone

Below, Wood

which the mesh is jabbed rapidly to even it. The snowshoe is then hung up indoors to dry slowly.

The snowshoe needle, *tcama'gwis*, is usually made of wood (Fig. 20), though occasionally of bone and recently of iron and copper, and is between three and four inches long and about one-half inch wide. An elongated hole in the center forms the eye through which the thong of rawhide is passed. This needle serves only the one purpose. Those who make snowshoes usually have a number of needles in assorted sizes, some even as large as six or seven inches for very coarse snowshoe netting, though this size is unusual. It is claimed that a wooden needle has the advantage over one of bone in not being so slippery, though the Montagnais prefer them of bone exclusively.

The other implement necessary in making the snowshoe complete is the mesh punch, *wli'gwihi'gan*, "evening or fixing tool." This is a smooth tapering piece of hardwood about seven inches long. The specimen figured has a loop to hang by and some notches as property marks. Holding the snowshoe frame freshly netted in his lap or arms, the operator punches the holes of the mesh vigorously with the punch, making them regular and even. Like the Huron and Algonkian north of the St. Lawrence, the Penobscot some-times used a moose or deer leg-bone for this purpose.

While not all typical of the ordinary modern snowshoes of the Penobscot, the remarkable specimen shown in Fig. 19 is an example of the finer work of some former snowshoe artist-craftsman. The pair was owned by Newell Francis, ex-Governor of the tribe, and is very old. The babiche filling is of extremely finely cut caribou skin, and the geometric openwork figures (*sibosimone'tɑdjik*, "laced end") are brought out by wrapping the woofs about the warps. The workmanship is as fine and complex as is found on the best of the much-admired snowshoes of the Montagnais and Naskapi, showing the wide distribution of talent in weaving. The almost square forward end of this specimen illustrates the type described in Penobscot tradition as the one in vogue several generations ago—one bringing the original snowshoe pattern into closer conformity with that of the Ojibwa. The Penobscot are also acquainted with the more rounded and broader shoe known as the "bear paw" model, having only one foot-bar, for use in mountainous districts. Such, however, are not ordinarily made in the tribe.

Another old form is the "codfish" type, having a broader, rounder head, though its other proportions are usual. In the so-called "pollywog" snowshoe pattern, the head section is still shorter and smaller (Fig. 30).

A still more interesting variation in snowshoe types is the wooden plank-sandal, one extemporized for use in slush by hunters who are caught in the distant woods during a thaw. These are made of cedar [15] (Fig. 19). Something over three feet in length and nine inches wide, they have the foot opening cut out and the tying thongs run through holes at each side. The rough finish is given with the crooked knife. These shoes require only an hour for their completion.

To summarize the information on snowshoe types with their appropriate terms we observe the following:

temskwa'dəbɑ'djik, "squared head," the earliest form remembered

[15] Cf. the wooden snowshoes similarly found by Turner among the Whale River Naskapi, Turner, page 311, fig. 131. Specimens from various Algonquin bands of the Ottawa Valley are common.

eskwɑ'hɑdəbɑdjik, "pointed head," the commonest pattern for hunting

kwe'nuskwɑdəbɑdjik, "long pointed head," a variation from the preceding

kwɑlɑ'gʷdjiswɑ'dəbɑdjik, "tadpole head," the short rounded form

Sleds

The sled, *sohe'wik*, is a construction of wood about six feet long and two and a half wide (Fig. 21). Two flat slabs form the sides, connected by eight cross bars inserted in

FIG. 21

DRAG SLED FOR BIG GAME

With Shoving Sticks and Snowshoes

holes. A set of wooden runners nailed or pegged on the bottom, and a drag strap which passes over the chest or forehead of the traveler, complete the sled. It is simple, strong and serviceable in transporting firewood, meat, or household effects, and seems to have taken the place of the toboggan. Its origin is a matter of question among the Penobscot. Some say it is a native article; a few say it is not. Similar articles, it may be noted, are common among

all the northeastern Algonkian, including the distant Naskapi.
The Penobscot use the sled continually upon the frozen river,
where a well-defined winter road marks the path, leading
northward from Indian Island to the forests beyond, taken
by those who travel up and down with sleds. They are
propelled by a pair of pokers, *ala'mkwetauzo'dial* (plural),
shod with iron, sometimes with a cross bar to improve the
grip. Sitting or kneeling on the rear of the sled, a man
can travel swiftly on the ice, especially if the wind favors
him. Dogs were never used as draught animals. The indifference throughout of the Wabanaki to the patent advantages of driving dogs, by contrast with the Montagnais-
Naskapi, is a phenomenon of some significance in the history
of diffusion and the matter of native attitude toward innovations. It may be observed also that the whites of Maine do
not drive dogs in winter, while north of the St. Lawrence
they do.

The toboggan, *tciba'gan*, has now gone out of use.

Burden and Drag Straps

Burden and drag straps for carrying baskets or packs,
dragging sleds or toboggans, are indispensable articles of the
trail. These the Penobscot women made either of a strip of
moose skin or of woven cedar bark or basswood inner bark.
Burden or drag straps are in general called *wɔskwa'bi*, "head
strap or cord." A short burden strap is sometimes specially
designated as *pemo'wa'kagan*, "carrier."

Several types of straps are shown in Fig. 22. The plain
strip of moose hide about five feet long broadened to three
inches in the middle portion needs no further description.
Like the rest, it can be used either on the chest or across
the forehead. More remarkable in construction, however,
are the others figured. The short one is used in the same
manner as the skin strap, for carrying burdens on the back,
the tying thongs passing through the loops of the burden
strap. The longer are for dragging sleds or toboggans or
can be used as the others by wrapping the bundle with
the longer ends and carrying it with the broad section across
chest or forehead. They are all woven in the same manner

in different degrees of fineness, depending upon the skill and fancy of the makers. The process, described in detail further on, consists in boiling the inner bark of the basswood in wood ashes, then dyeing it the desired colors (see

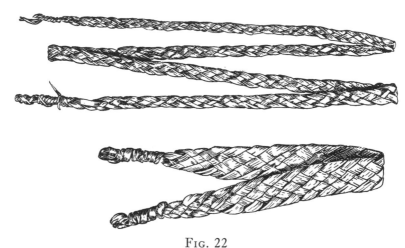

FIG. 22

Upper, Drag Strap for Toboggan
Lower, Braided Basswood Burden Strap

page 137), and stripping it first with a knife, then over a hand stone (see page 135) to smooth and soften it. The weaving then is commenced. This is an elaborate braiding process. The fine drag strap shown in Fig. 22 is nearly fifteen feet long, and a remarkable example. The woven head-band section is nearly three feet long and two and three-quarters inches wide. The lines are braided first, then braided again, and finally twisted like a rope. It approaches to some extent the extraordinary articles made by the Iroquois, of wild hemp with a false embroidery in colored moose hair.[16] Designs in Penobscot pack straps possess no intentional motives; they are simply the technical result of using varicolored strands.

Pack Baskets

The Penobscot pack basket, *towɑla'gan*, has an average height of a foot and a half and a width of several feet, the open-

[16] Cf. Parker, Ref. 3, p. 65.

ing being narrower than the bottom (partly visible in Fig. 30).
It is woven of strong ash splints in the checker-work technique
and is supported by two moose-skin strips, one going over
each shoulder. A less commonly used pack basket, but one
more serviceable, as it is water-tight, is the birch-bark article.
The dimensions of this large bark receptacle are the same
as those of the bark pails or baskets described in another
place (page 118). A strip of stout cedar bark forms the
supporting strap, though this is only a temporary attach-
ment. Some of these articles have covers and are, like the
one figured, elaborately decorated with etchings. In the pack
baskets all the camp equipment is carried while on a journey.

FIG. 23

ELABORATELY ORNAMENTED CRADLEBOARD

Back and Side Views

Cradle-boards

The cradle-board, *t'kina'gan* (Fig. 23), is characterized by the curved bracket, attached to the backboard by thongs, forming the bottom and sides. In other respects the board and protecting bar are typical of the Algonquin and Ojibwa of Ontario. The decorations in carving and cutout in Penobscot cradle-boards excel anything else of the kind met with in the east, an extraordinary example being the one figured. A story is recalled of this cradle-board relating how the maker's wife gave birth to a snake (see Penobscot Tales, *op. cit.*, in Bibliography). The father of a prospective child customarily made the cradle-board, and the care exercised in its construction is said to have been the indication of his regard for the offspring. The child was bound in the enclosure, and thus carried on the back of the mother, or leaned in safety against a convenient support. By a Malecite who lives with the Penobscot it is attested that the Indians derived the idea of the cradle-board from the 'Jack-in-the-Pulpit, *Pu'kdjinskwe's·wi awa'sis*, "Pukdjinskwessu's Baby." The baby hammock, to be mentioned later, may be only mentioned here.

Other Aids to Travel

People traveling in the woods, as protection against prolonged rain, strip off a large piece of birch bark, cut a hole in the center for the head to pass through, and let the ends hang down before and behind or over the shoulders. In this way ample protection from the rain is obtained. The improvised raincoat is supplemented by a conical birch-bark hat made by sewing or pinning together the edges of a flat cone to fit the head.

Though much needed in walking over lakes and up and down the river on smooth windswept ice, creepers never seem to have been invented by the Penobscot. A partial help in such emergencies is gained, however, by passing and tying a thong around the feet a number of times. Snow goggles are also wanting, although a fir twig is stuck beneath the hat-brim to protect the eyes from glare, and a piece of buckskin or a handkerchief with eye-slits may shield the face from driving wind and snow in the coldest weather.

An ingenious device for making camp paraphernalia into a bundle which can be comfortably transported upon the back is known as *me'gwayagwɑgan*, "Mohawk bundle," so called because tradition states that it was learned from Mohawk captives. The idea is simply to lay one's blanket out flat on the ground, place the goods in the center, then fold the right and left hand edges inward over the pack line which has been laid across. By drawing the lines together, one has a strong seamless bundle quickly made from an ordinary blanket.

Travel through the extensive forests in the old days did not present the difficulties that one might imagine, at least as far as getting lost is concerned. This was because the whole inhabited area was divided off into hunting territories owned by the different bands of consanguineous families. Each band was well acquainted with its own district, no matter how extensive it might be. Furthermore, there were trails, *a'udi·*, "path," winding through the districts used by the hunters and trappers of the band. Ordinarily there were two main "paths" running perpendicular to each other, north and south and east and west, quartering each tract. Moreover, all the trails were blazed either with the owners' family "emblems" (the animal outlines), or with trail signs not only warning transpassers but leading strangers to the main headquarters or to the temporary camps along the main routes. We shall come to treatment of the bands and their territories later, under treatment of Social Organization. The signs of the trail will be dealt with shortly.

A straight direction is maintained when traveling through the woods by observing the direction in which the snow is blowing, or the rain, or by observing the more numerous branches on the south side of the spruces or the moss on the bark, or the stars, particularly the north star. When these means fail, the hunter can hold a straight course by resorting to the native device of keeping three trees in a line at once all the time he is going. By glimpsing on alternate sides whenever he substitutes a new tree on his line, he avoids throwing himself out of the straight line by the several feet, the width of the trunk. In this way, added to the experience gained by much traveling, he is able to traverse the wilds with astounding expedition and accuracy.

While traveling in winter, the crossing of rivers or lakes on the ice is extremely dangerous and there are many tales of accidents from falling through air-holes or soft places in the ice.   In crossing ice, snowshoes are never worn, even though there be a covering of slush and soft ice, for they could not be loosed in case of falling through.   A long pole is, however, cut and carried.   This prevents a man's sinking beneath should he fall through ice where there is a current.   This device has saved a number of lives during the years I knew the tribe.

Sometimes, in crossing the lakes over treacherous ice, the hunters tie together several of their ice-poles, separating them by cross-pieces a few feet apart like a ladder.   Then by lying flat on the improvised slider and using the axe and hunting knife in each hand to prod his way along, the hunter can get over the soft places and shove the slider back for his companions to use.

Travel indeed forms so much a part of northern Indian life that it is a constant matter of concern.   From the time when the ice breaks up in the Penobscot River, early or in the middle of April, parties are continually coming and going on trips up the river.   The period just before and after the ice break-up is dangerous to those traveling by canoe.   When the ice jam passes Indian Island, generally sometime in April, the Indians congregate on the shore and the cry goes up, "The ice is coming!"   This is one of the events in nature's calendar!

At fairly regular intervals in ascending the Penobscot or other large rivers, are signs and sites of over-night camping stations where parties have been accustomed for generations to halt.   These are usually awesome, scenic spots, high and dry, overlooking considerable stretches of water.   They may be discerned by the much-used fireplaces, camp débris, and grassy plots indicating the well-worn landing places.   Signs and signals are occasionally seen at these stations, left by previous occupants.

In this connection there is, however, another custom fully as much fraught with imagination as anything that could be

expected from uncivilized man's viewpoint. A familiar ancient measure of distance on water, in the forest or along the
shore, and from the mountain top alike, was a "look," called
tegagaʹbimuk, "as far as one can see"; the "plastic mile."
When given a trial in the wilderness its value as a measure is
convincing when following directions given by a guide.

Signs and Signals of the Trail

The merest details of life in the woods are matters of importance to the Penobscot. In the days when forest life was
their continual lot they possessed many devices for mute communication. When the French vessels of La Saussaye hove
in sight of the Indians in Penobscot Bay in 1613, near Mt.
Desert Island, a smoke was noted rising from the shore as a
sign of welcome.[17]

FIG. 24

TRAIL SIGNALS

A slanting stick placed in the ground in a path indicates
direction taken by the one who left it. Sometimes one sees
an arrow marked in the dirt for the
same purpose. Two sticks on a
parallel slant (Fig. 24) indicate direction, and in addition that the camp
is near. A shorter stick points out
the return direction. With the same
idea in view a slice of bark is cut
off a tree along the trail, head high
(Fig. 25). A still more definite
index, where the path is obscure, is
to notch the bark and set in the

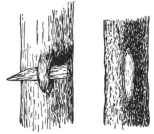

FIG. 25

Trail Blazes

cleft a cross piece, which points out the line to be followed
(Fig. 25).

[17] Cf. Maurault, p. 95; quoting P. Biard.

Natural landmarks, too, are employed as markers of location. To recognize certain peculiarities in the alignment of trees, rocks, or river shores provides means by which particular localities are known and referred to. For instance, the landing place to reach a camp up river for which we were searching, hidden some distance from the main river in the interior of an island, was indicated by a huge elm at the bank with a deep cavity burned out on one side. Without this sign the closest search would have failed to discover the beginning of the faint trail leading from the river.

The story is told of how, when the tribe used to leave the island for hunting or visiting, they left a stick with a partridge's head impaled on it pointing in the direction of departure at the northern end of the island.

Pictographs marked on birch bark served like purposes. As an example of picture-sign writing we have Fig. 26. This

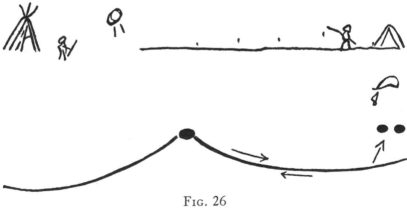

FIG. 26

PICTOGRAPHIC SIGNS

Upper, Charcoal Sketch by Hunter Indicating, "I am Leaving Camp for Two Days to go Beaver Trapping at My Temporary Camp"
Lower, Message Left at Fork of River Indicating that Traveler has Gone by Way of Opposite Branch and Will Return in Two Days

is a drawing of a wigwam on the left, then a man facing to the right, meaning that the writer is about to leave home, then the sun with two marks beneath it, meaning that he will be gone two nights, then a long line, the sign of his journey, or the path, then himself again, facing to the left, that is the hunter returning and the little temporary camp he is leaving. Underneath at the right is the beaver house where he is going to trap, and the small mark beneath this is the trap. The whole thing interprets: "I am going to leave here to go to my small beaver camp (in the direction indicated by the blaze on the tree), where I shall remain two nights trapping; then I shall return."

Newell Lion recalled in his youth being sent a distance from the hunting camp by an old man (Piel Nicola) to get some beavers. While he was gone Nicola had departed, leaving a message on folded birch bark in a forked stick, informing him that he had gone by way of the opposite stream and would return in two days (Fig. 26).

Figure 27 is the representation of a beaver on the trunk of a tree near a beaver pond. It denotes that the colony has been discovered and appropriated by the sign-maker.

Fig. 27

Representation of Beaver Blazed on Tree to Denote Appropriation of Nearby Beaver Colony by Discoverer

In this connection also should be mentioned the birch-bark figures of animals, by which the hunting territories of different family bands were designated. The matter, however, will be dealt with farther on where it properly belongs in the account of the family bands. Thus writes an old author, Nicolar,

Whenever a person enters into some new country and wishes others to know that he has been off. Here the emblem of the band is prominently pictured out. The picture of the wigwam represents the home of the family, a person facing away from it means from home, facing toward it means going homeward. The picture of the sun means day, the moon means month. When a person writes the number of days of his absence, he marks out the sun and under it puts as many notches as there are days of his absence, and if it be months uses the moon in the same manner.[18]

A few miscellaneous body-gesture signals remain to be added:

[18] Nicolar, 147.

To stiffen the forearm with a slight forward motion and upturn of the clenched fist while the arm appears to be hanging innocently at the side, is a signal used by a man to attract a woman's attention to his sexual desires. A variation of the same is to grasp the biceps of the signaling arm with the other hand.

Similarly a man may toss a chip, a pebble, or something within reach, so that it will fall near the girl or woman to whom he means to make a request. Should the woman pick up the object it is a sign of consent.

To thrust the hand toward a person palm downward, with the index-finger and second-finger knuckles spread apart, is a sign of insult, called "*tcɔstci'*." A downward and outward sweep of the hand serves the same purpose.

Like Indians of the north, the Penobscot are clever in making gestures with the lips. By protruding the lips forward or to the right or left while talking they indicate direction. The lip motions also serve admirably under circumstances where silence is required and the hands are engaged, as for instance, in a canoe when approaching game. The movements seem, however, to be involuntary, accompanied by a toss of the head.

FISHING

The Penobscot at all times depended to a large extent upon the many fish of their lakes, river, and bay for a food supply. Some of the old capturing devices are at times still employed.

Customs and beliefs connected with the killing and disposal of fish have been dealt with in my paper on religion. I might allude to the tale in which the different races of fish are traced from transformed people who, driven by thirst, rushed into the water when the Penobscot River was created by Gluskabe,[19] the culture-hero.

To these Indians, practically all of whom lived near the Penobscot River, the spearing of salmon in their annual run up-stream in June, July, or August, was one of the great seasonal events. When the lightning bugs begin to appear

[19] See Bibliography, F. G. Speck, 19.

late in June, they say it is the sign for salmon spearing. The
Penobscot salmon sometimes attain a weight of forty pounds.
During the run, just above falls
or rapids, the men would occupy
some ledge and spear the fish as
they came by. Camps were established in such vicinities. At other
times they went in canoes, the bow
man with a spear watching for fish.
At night a torch consisting of a
green stave, split at the end to
hold a bundle of
folded birch-bark
strips wound with
splints and frayed
at the ends (Fig.
28), was fastened in
the bow of the canoe.
These methods of
catching salmon
were practised until
about 1912, when
spearing was pro-
hibited by the mak-
ers of the game laws.
The fish spear or
leister is neverthe-
less a characteristic
and common imple-

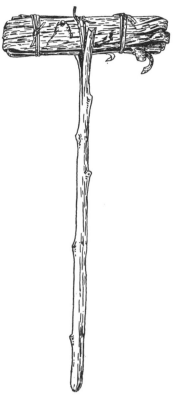

FIG. 28
Torch of Birch Bark for
Night Fishing

ment in the Penobscot villages (Figs. 29, 30).
It resembles those of northern tribes from the
Atlantic to the Pacific and beyond. The shaft,
from twelve to eighteen feet long, is of smoothed
spruce. The outside prongs are not sharp but
serve to grasp the fish so that the central prong
will pierce its back. The outside prongs or
grips are of hardwood, the middle point of iron
nowadays, formerly a piece of sharpened hornbeam. The
central tine is inserted firmly in the end of the shaft, and the

FIG. 29
Fish Spear or
Leister

FIG. 30

Upper left, Man Demonstrating Use of Fish Spear
Upper right, Men in Historic Native Costume, Showing Headgear
   and Kilts (Malecite, St. John River, N. B.)
Lower left, Mask of Deer Scalp Worn in Clown Dance (Man is
   Wearing Moose-skin Coat, 1912)
Lower right, Hunter with Travel Equipment, Snowshoes, Basswood
   Hunting Bag, and Son with Splint Pack Basket

two grips are lashed to the same by splints, strips, or cording. In spears from northern tribes, the method of lashing is observed to be about the same throughout. The spear is called *e'niga'hkᵂ*. Torching for fish is *noda'sɔn·i*.

In the use of this implement, skill develops when one learns to estimate the refraction of the light in the water. But it is difficult to strike the fish squarely. When the spear is thrown from the hand it goes straight down, and after a moment's interval comes shooting up backwards from the same spot, and at the same angle as that at which it went in, permitting it to be cast again.

Just below Indian Island, above the falls, there is in the middle of the river a rocky ledge where the men used to get their stock of salmon. Unheard-of quantities were taken here by the tribe each year until the dam was built. In those days they feasted on the fresh fish and smoked a large amount of it for winter upon pole racks over a fire.

Another kind of "dart headed with like bone" was used "very cunningly to kill fish." [20]

The fish spear (leister) was, and is yet, in general use also for getting pollock and eels. The usual method of spearing from a canoe is followed.

In the winter time, when hibernating eels have buried themselves in the mud of a cove, some families will repair thither and make camp. The men will go out on the ice, make holes through it and prod in the mud with their spears, drawing out eels in quantities. During times of scarcity of other game in the past, whole communities have had to subsist for months upon eels obtained in this manner.

When they are down the bay or river and want flounders, the Indians find some cove where they can see the fish. Then they go ashore, cut and trim a few long spruce poles. The ends are next sharpened and a notch cut in. From the canoes they stick these crude spears into the flounders and pull them up. Turtles are obtained in the same way.

The old way of taking fish, like mackerel, pollock, and others swimming in schools, was to jig them with a fairly

[20] Rosier, p. 372.

large-sized hook, *məgi'kan*, weighted with a stone, without
bait and attached to a long line of braided basswood fibre.
The hook was made from a crotch of willow about four or
five inches long, its point hardened by charring. To the
back of this, a long thin stone was lashed. The line of the
model specimen figured is of a four-ply braid of basswood
inner bark. Armed with this jigging outfit, they went among
the fish and snagged them in the stomach by jerking the
hook up and down in the water.

The pear-shaped stone, the so-called plummet, occurring
archaeologically in Penobscot territory, is said by older men
to have been used both as a slingstone and as a lure for
salmon. In the latter instance it is believed to have been
coated with white deer tallow as bait.[21]

The primitive hook (*məgi'kan*) and line are remembered
by some, and best described by Nicolar.[22] Gluskabe instructed man to take a bird's breast bone (wishbone), rub
one end upon a stone to sharpen it, and attach it to a line of
wi'kəbi, basswood, and this to a pole of hardwood. Fragments of meat were then to be put upon the sharp point for
bait. Gullet hooks; a sharpened bone set obliquely in a split
wooden shank baited with minnow; a toggle of bone splinter.
Casting hooks had tufts of deer hair or duck down for a lure
for bass and pickerel. An alder sapling was the pole.

A scap-net (*kwa'phigan*, "dip-device") used for scooping
fish in shallow places consists of a hoop netted with basswood
cord on a handle about ten feet long. A fisherman standing
on a rock over the water may net many fish as they swim by.
Salmon and shad were regularly caught in this way.

For a long time the net (*ala'pi*) has been used for fishing.
The shuttle used in making the nets is the same as that
found throughout the Montagnais and Cree area. It is
called *lapiki'gan*, "net tool," the specimen shown being made
of hardwood, nine inches long and two wide. Nets are no
longer home-made among the Penobscot, yet we learn that
the almost world-wide "netting knot" was employed. Netting needles varied much in size, the example figured being
rather a large one. Stone net-sinkers, so called by Indians

[21] See bibliography, S. W. Pennypacker II.
[22] Nicolar, p. 33.

and others, are found on Indian Island and other Penobscot
sites as testimony of the early knowledge of netting.

The following quotation from Rosier speaks for itself:
"Towards night our Captaine went on shore to have a draft
with the Seine or net. And we carried two of
them (natives) with us who marvelled to see us
catch fish with a net." [23]   It might appear from
this that the band encountered then (1605) in
Penobscot Bay were unacquainted with the
use of seines. The Penobscot, however, have
another word for nets, *wada'p*, which has reference to basswood.

They used to go down to salt water for
porpoises occasionally in large canoes manned
by two and carrying a sail. Approaching the
porpoises, the bow man shot one while the stern
man paddled up so that the other could stick
a lance into the animal and pass it back to him
to lift into the canoe by inserting his fingers
into its nostrils. This was a dangerous sport
carried on for securing oil and fat. The Passamaquoddy still maintain their reputation as
experts in this line.

For not only large bay fish, but also river
fish—salmon, shad, and others—the harpoon
(Fig. 31), *si'gawan*, with a toggle-head was
used. This interesting implement consisted
of a ten-foot pole with a rectangular cavity
in the end wrapped with an eelskin thong.
Into this aperture was mortised the spearhead,
fastened loosely to the main shaft by a
double strip of rawhide. This was a shank
with single lateral barb, detachable from the
main shaft under a little resistance. The shank or fore-
shaft and head are all in one, about a foot long, made of
hardwood charred in a fire to make it harder, with a barb
an inch long on one side. The tying is ingenious, a doubled
rawhide passed through a hole in the shaft and one in the

Fig. 31
Model of
Wooden Har-
poon for Sal-
m o n   a n d
Beaver

[23] Rosier, p. 371.

shank of the spearhead, and tied with a double wrapped knot. The advantage of this harpoon, they claim, is that a fish or seal when struck cannot break the head off, because it becomes detached and holds firmly by the rawhide until the animal can be lifted out of the water. The same idea, occurring widely among maritime tribes, was used until recently by Penobscot. Although it is said that fire-hardened wood is sufficient for the harpoon head, no doubt bone and stone were used in its construction in the days beyond the bounds of present tradition.

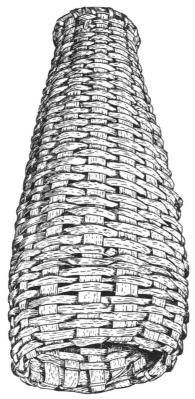

FIG. 32

Splint Basket Trap Set in Streams for Fish

That the distribution of the fish trap, so common among the southern tribes, extended as far as central Maine is shown by the following data.[24] The Penobscot make their fish traps of rough splints in a simple twilled weave from approximately three to five feet in length with the usual indented bottom allowing the fish to enter, but not to pass out. The trap is used mostly for eels. A specimen of the smaller size, about three feet long and one wide, used for eels or for taking bait in ponds is shown in Fig. 32, *nahumu'hkagan*, "eel device."

Several stones are put in to sink it, and dead fish or heads are used for bait. The open end, through which the contents are removed, is closed by a piece of burlap tied over it. A line is passed through a loop in the side so that the trap can be hauled out of the water. This type of eel trap or "pot"

[24] The Malecite also used them.

is widely distributed among the eastern tribes and varies in only a few particulars.

A similar distribution in the north is accorded to another practice apparently at home among the southern tribes; namely, that of poisoning fish with plants. The following account, by an eye witness, of a fishing party in the autumn of 1900 is quite complete. The band was composed of about five families from Indian Island, and camped for about a week on Sunkhaze meadow, to obtain eels. They began by poisoning the stream with decoctions of pokeberry and Indian turnip root. The Indian's time for securing enough eels to last a year is at low water in August. Then the Indian turnip root, which grows in moist ground along streams, and the berries of the poke plants are richest and contain the most poison which stupefies the fish.

The party carried bags of berries and baskets of salt, depending upon game and fish for their sustenance during the trip. The first two days were spent in digging the roots and crushing them with the purple pokeberries upon the surface of flat stones. When a sufficient quantity of the mixture had been prepared, they stripped to the skin and, distributing themselves along the stream for a distance of a mile, plunged into the water, strewing the poisoned pulp thickly upon the surface and diving to the bottom, where they stirred up the muddy sediment with sticks and poles.

When the water was so strongly impregnated with the juices that the workers were driven ashore with inflamed and smarting skins, half an hour was spent in dressing and rubbing the inflamed spots with fresh plantain leaves. By this time the agitated water had settled. Torpid eels began to appear upon the surface, and before an hour had passed the top of the water was spotted with the bodies of dead or dying fish, which floated belly up, unable to escape. The children of the party, having recovered from their hurts, were then forced to enter the water and bring the fish ashore, where they were skinned and salted by the women. After this the eels were placed upon dead limbs and laid in the sun to dry for two days. Then they were hung up in a tent and smoked until there was no drip from the suspended bodies.

Weirs (*sikmohka'gan* (sing.) and *k*ʷ*se'nɑgan*) were of several sorts. The one most commonly seen on the banks of the Penobscot is a fence of brush or sticks projecting obliquely down stream, or a corral with an entrance on one side. Smaller rivers were fenced across leaving a narrow opening near the middle, where fishermen armed with spears, harpoons, and nets gathered in canoes, if necessary, to capture the fish as they passed through. Another contrivance consisted of a lattice of parallel sticks placed horizontally just on or below the surface of the water at the gate of a dam of stones or brush built across the stream. All the water would have to pour over this griddle, and the fish, in trying to get by down stream, would be left floundering upon it where they could be seized by those watching for them. Eels were obtained in this way.

The description of an eel weir on Passadumkeag stream ought to illustrate matters better. In the fall, about a dozen Penobscot families assembled at a point some miles up stream, where an island and abundance of good birch bark for shelters furnished an inviting camp site. The Indians began by constructing fences of willow rods filled in with brush, one running obliquely down stream from each shore. At the apex of these fences were arranged three shallow open-work trays (*sɘnu'djis*), of willow rods placed horizontally. Each was about ten feet long, seven wide, and a foot deep. They were set one above the other, the ends overlapping a little, that at the top having the largest mesh spaces, that at the bottom the smallest. It can be seen from this that the only point of egress for the eels going down stream was through the opening, and that the largest fish would be left floundering in the upper tray, the smaller ones in the lowermost, while the water passed through freely. People stood guard at the trays with large receptacles, baskets or barrels, near at hand, into which they transferred the fish with dip-nets or spears as soon as they were seen. They were then conveyed to the shore where the women were busy splitting, drying, and smoking them. The habits of the creatures were well known to the gatherers, who took advantage of the fall exodus of eels down to salt water. They say the eels began to go down stream early at night, passing by hundreds, then at a certain hour they stopped and did not start to run again till the next night. In the interval, the people took their sleep and enjoyment.

In places where weirs are set for eels pits are dug along the shore some three or four feet wide and about three deep, the number of the pits depending upon the quantity of eels caught. These pits are made for the freshly caught eels to be thrown into, so that they will free themselves of slime, for otherwise they could not be handled conveniently. In several places up the river are to be seen, adjoining old villages or camp sites, a series of such pits overgrown with trees or shrubs, where long ago eeling parties have camped. They form one of the archaeological features of the region. One prominent locality of this sort is to be seen opposite the Teguk rapids halfway up the west side of Indian Island.

CULTIVATION AND GATHERING

The Penobscot were near the northeastern limits of the area of extensive native agriculture. Even at this day, with substantial financial encouragement from the State,[25] the Indians find it hard to reconcile themselves to husbandry, with the passion for the chase so strong in them. At the permanent settlements along the river, chiefly upon the larger islands, the desultory cultivation of a few native vegetables was carried on for immediate use and for preservation against the winter. Different families had their truck patches near their wigwams or in nearby clearings, which were termed ki'hkan, "garden," or nəbi'zunki'hkan, "medicine garden" (ki'hke to plant).

An old-fashioned way of growing climbing beans, still followed by some, is to plant them at the foot of a circle of poles about ten feet long, leaned together at the top like the framework of a wigwam. Three or four of these racks are all that one family cultivates. They say that in ancient times the ground was turned over with sharpened sticks, and when

[25] A bounty on every bushel is annually paid the Indians for corn and other vegetables raised. Cultivation is at present the work of men.

the seeds had been planted dead fish and refuse were put on top as fertilizer.[26]   Other maize complex devices are lacking.

The occasional burning off of berry fields, to clean out and replenish, is one step carried out toward preparation of the soil.   The many islands in the river, still the sole property of Indians, produce abundantly blueberries, blackberries, and huckleberries for the labor of gathering.

A list of native cultivated vegetables includes *skamu'nu*, corn; *adaba'kwal*, beans; *wamptəgwe'wiminal*, cranberry beans (lit. "wild gooseberries"); *we'notcwimi'nal*, peas (lit. "white man's berries"); *wasa'we*,[27] pumpkin, squash ("yellow"); *abədelmuimi'nal*, wild rice ("laughing berries").

In regard to the plants mentioned, the following ideas are held.   Corn was the chief original vegetable, and beans were next in importance.   The wild goose (*wa'mptəgwe*) is believed to have brought beans to the Indians from some region to the south.[28]   The elucidating name "white man's berries" tells the story of peas as far as the Penobscot are concerned.

Wild rice, while not cultivated, was gathered where it grew and was treated much like corn for consumption.[29] Potatoes, brought by the white man, are called *aptcedeza'l*, presumably after the English.   Several indigenous tubers, the artichoke and another called *pena'psk*, as will be seen later, are the Indian potatoes.

Plants employed in the curing of disease have been treated separately with their special functions in an article on Medicine Practices (Speck, ref. 8, p. 316).   The economic uses to which the different varieties are put will now be treated.

FOOD AND ITS PREPARATION

In the fare of the natives meat (*wi·u''s*) was and still is largely the staple all the year round, fish taking a prominent

[26] A comic story is told of an Indian who was planting seeds and putting the fish carcasses on them.   A white man came along for the first time and told him to plant the fish to see if he could raise a crop of them.   The Indian tried it, thinking he had a valuable secret until he told his friends.   This is a sample of native humor.

[27] Oranges are called *wasawesi'zal*, "little squashes."

[28] The Narragansett similarly thought the crow brought them their first corn and beans from the southwest, cf. Willoughby, p. 130, quoting Roger Williams, cf. Williams, p. 114.

[29] Dr. Chas. E. Chambliss also records mention of this fact, Sept. 1932, from a Penobscot informant.

place, while corn foods supplied the pot through late summer and fall until the winter hunt. A standard food is *skamu'nu*, boiled hulled corn. The process begins with scraping the dried corn from the cob by rubbing it over with another dry hard cob. A deer's lower mandible was also employed as a scraper. Then the corn is boiled for a while in a vessel containing a quantity of wood ashes and water. This separates the hulls from the kernels. The cook then empties it into a rinsing basket, *tawigəspata'sudi*, "washing receptacle," and, carrying it to the river bank, jounces it up and down in the water to rinse it clear of lye. The basket referred to is coarsely woven of ash splints, and is oblong in shape. Next the mess is boiled with fat in a pot, and eaten. As soon as the boiled corn left from the first meal gets cold and grows stale it ferments, but it is liked just as well sour. Other things are often put in the corn soup to add a flavor: an eel's backbone, moose leg, deer or moose backbone, and cracked joints for their marrow. Hunters always save the shanks of moose for this purpose. One of these may last quite a season, being boiled over and over again in soup. Neighbors will even send around to borrow one to boil in their soup. With the plain corn, beans are often combined, making corn-and-bean soup. Peas are treated in the same way.[30]

In preparing corn flour, the mill, *tagwɑ'gan*, consists of two rounded pebbles with flat sides which are used as pounders. They rest upon a square sheet of birch bark (Fig. 33). The larger of the two stones is the nether stone resting in the middle

FIG. 33

Stone Corn Pounders and Birch-Bark Table for Crushing Corn

of the bark. With the second stone held in one hand the corn is pounded, being fed with the other hand, while the powder tumbles off the stone on to the bark. Some of the millstones are quite small for the work, not being more than

[30] It is interesting to compare this and the following Penobscot recipes with those of the Iroquois. Cf. Parker (2) and Harrington (1), p. 583.

four inches in diameter, and some of the nether stones were eight inches in diameter. At the upper Penobscot village near Lincoln, a woman formerly had three of these millstones which she operated, holding a pounder in each hand and striking the nether stones alternately with each, while a helper dropped the corn on the nether stone for her. When enough flour had been pounded, it was poured from the bark into another receptacle, or on to a large slab of spruce bark upon which it was exposed to the sun to dry. The crushing stones for the mill were obtained from the river bank or bay shore, and had been worn round and smooth by the water.

Corn meal mixed with maple sugar is a food used in various ways. They call this *pəsida'mən*. Corn flour dough and salt (with an admixture nowadays of cream of tartar) is fried in grease, making flapjacks called *tekle'pɑk*. Bread, *aba'n*, was formerly made of corn flour baked on a flat stone tilted before the fire. *Abanka'gan*, "bread made," or *sawa'bənɑk*, is corn dough baked and dried to be used on a journey or to be stored. Wild potatoes, *pəna'k*, and artichokes are baked in the ashes and eaten with maple sugar poured over them. Fiddle beans, *maso'sial*, are boiled up into a mess of vegetables and are eaten in quantities in spring. The young people of both sexes like to make up parties and go gathering them in canoes. Sand plums, *abədiu'mkiminal*, found growing on low bushes on the sandy places of the northern end of Indian Island, are gathered in quantities in the fall and stewed.

A common method of preparing beans is first to parboil them in water, then to start a big fire in a hole and allow it to die down. This is the widely known "bean-hole." Such an operation is generally performed in the evening, so that, before retiring, the pot of beans can be buried in the hot bed of embers, covered up, and left to bake over night.

Various fruits and berries, blueberries, strawberries, blackberries and grapes, were spread out and dried, then put away in baskets or bark vessels and kept till wanted. Thus in all seasons a fine dish of stewed fruit was possible, either to be eaten alone or mixed with meat and vegetables. Or dried fruit could be soaked in water until soft again and eaten raw.

Originally salt, *sa'lawe* (from the French *sel*), was never used,[31] and the hunters of today tell with wonder of the old-time hunters who used to go into the woods for years never having salt with them to season their victuals. Entrails of game supplied their vitamins, but none of them would care to try them nowadays.

Seaweed, *aska'lzial* (called Irish moss along the New England coast), is said to have been eaten raw or cooked in the ordinary way.

Muskrats, when skinned and cleaned, are stuck on a forked stick, *psaphi'gan*, the forks being pushed into the legs, so that the carcass hangs down, while the end is stuck into the ground near the fire. The carcass is turned until it is nicely roasted. The entrails of muskrats and other animals eaten in camp are thrown on the smoldering ashes and raked off when roasted brown. They are then washed and eaten. Muskrat cut up and stewed, like a fricassee, with other ingredients mixed in, is called *sikpe's·u*. This is a staple of diet in spring when the ice has gone out of the rivers and quantities of muskrat are brought in by the hunters. When eating, they say, whoever takes the muskrat head from the dish has to tell a story.

Cut portions of meat of any kind are boiled in water with fat, or pork, making a kind of stew called *kwa'k^wzu*.[32] Vegetables, beans or squashes, may be added; then it is called *nsa'ban*, soup. Before the Indians had pork they used to get raccoon fat for frying. Stew in general is called *kǝsǎ'bu*.

To prepare a porcupine for eating, the cleaned carcass is singed until the quills are burnt off, but it is not skinned. The process of roasting is followed as for the muskrat.

Moose, caribou, and deer meat are either made into stew, as described above, or roasted on a forked stick, *kulbihi'gan*, "turning device," over the fire, or fried in a pan like steak. Formerly, however, most of it was smoked and made into pemmican, a process to be described later.

A favorite titbit is muskrat tails fried between layers of fat. The tails become soft and juicy and are very sweet.

[31] Cf. Nicolar, p. 144.
[32] This is explained as meaning literally "red buttock."

They are drawn between the teeth and the bones sucked clean. The eyes, tongue, and brain of the muskrat are greedily eaten from the skull when it has been boiled. A similar tasty was made from beaver tails and moose noses, but since beaver killing has been prohibited in Maine, most can now only imagine its delicious taste.

Raccoon and bear grease was kept cold in bark vessels to be eaten at any time. It was mixed with maple sap.

Eggs, *wa'wunal*, of crows, gulls, and other large birds were much relished raw or boiled. To eat them the Indians break the top from the shells and suck out the contents.

Small shad and salmon were greedily eaten raw by children in the spring. They tell how children used to suck the raw fish for the spawn.

Turtles are boiled until tender, although it is rarely that they get so, and eaten. Frogs and snakes, however, were never considered fit to eat.

Fresh fish are planked on a flat piece of wood by a peg through the head, leaned before a hot fire and roasted until done.

Eels are split open, the backbones being taken out and saved to put into corn soup, and the carcasses hung up on a frame like the smoking rack to dry or to be smoked. In winter they are frozen. Boiled over again they make excellent soup. The same applies to all kinds of fish. They are cleaned and split from tail to head and hung on a horizontal pole over a fire.

Oysters and clams are gathered and dried either in the sun or in smoke and put away in bark vessels. To be used they are simply soaked or boiled and eaten in the shape of the usual stew or soup. The shell heaps in Penobscot Bay are universally said by the older Indians to be the accumulations where oyster- and clam-drying operations were carried on in former days.

Porpoise meat cut into steaks is cooked by some by simply throwing it on the embers of a fire. When partly roasted it is ready to be eaten. Many Indians, especially the Penobscot, profess not to like porpoise on account of its rank greasy smell. The Passamaquoddy, however, are extremely fond of it.

A festival known throughout New England settlements as a "clam bake" is a native procedure. The Penobscot prepare it after the following manner. When a sufficient quantity of clams, crabs, lobsters, corn, and cuts of fish is accumulated, a spot is chosen near the water where seaweed is abundant. First a pile of logs is built up, with stones alternating between the layers of logs, the whole being some four feet high and wide. The pyre, as it were, rests upon a hearth of stones. This is fired and allowed to burn down, resolving itself after an hour or so into a glowing bed of embers and red-hot stones. Upon this glowing heap are thrown the victuals, some of them wrapped in wet leaves, while a mass of seaweed is pulled from the rocks nearby and piled over all. After an hour or so (they judge the condition by the smell) the bake is considered done, the seaweed is raked off, and the mess is divided among the participants. No process of baking that I know of produces more savory or wholesome results than this.

Dogs, mink, otter, black cat (fisher), and skunk were not ordinarily eaten by the Penobscot unless they were out of supplies. In starvation time everything was eaten. Hard times in the winter are remembered by some old hunters, when they had to consume the skins and furs they had accumulated, or perish, boiling them for what little nourishment they contained, or chewing them. Even moccasins and skin garments, we are told, sometimes went likewise into the pot.

Anything sweet they call *mehkwani'pugahk*, "sweet taste," and sour things *sawa'pugahk*. Their meat they like well done when boiled, and somewhat rare when roasted. "And this I noted, they would eat nothing raw, either fish or flesh," wrote Rosier in the seventeenth century.[33] At meals the men are always first, the women cooking the food and leaving it for the men to begin on. As soon as the men are through, the women and children enter and help themselves to what is left, which generally is ample. Said Rosier of those encountered

[33] Rosier, p. 369.

in the Bay, "[They] behave themselves civilly, neither would they eat or drink more than seemed to content nature." [34]

Maple sugar mixed with water is an old-fashioned favorite beverage. It is also much used as a sauce for fruits and bread. And when they wanted to induce a thirst they ate acorns. A tea beverage is made out of ground hemlock (Taxus canadensis) or wintergreen steeped in water. Black-birch bark was also steeped for a beverage. Spruce gum is chewed for a pastime. They say that it keeps the teeth in good condition. Drinking water is taken directly from the rivers or from springs. Some families have a hole sunk to the depth of a few feet excavated a yard from the water's edge along the river, which always stays full of clear water that soaks through as in a spring. This combination of spring and well at the river edge is ingenious and satisfactory; it always gives clean water, is never dry, and can be easily and safely dipped up by the children. In the winter, when the river has frozen over, the different families chop holes through the ice for their water supply. It is a pretty sight of a crisp winter morning to see the blanketed women dragging their sleds loaded with vessels for the day's supply of water down on the ice and chopping the hole open while singing and gossiping. It is commonly considered bad for the throat to eat snow when thirsty.

The various utensils, wooden and birch-bark spoons, dishes, bowls, and pot stirrers used in preparing and eating food, are to be subsequently described and figured.

Making and Preserving Fire

I can do no better than to quote Nicolar's description of the Penobscot fire drills in his own quaint style.[35] The apparatus consists of

. . . a speed wheel made from the inner bark of the yellow birch in three or four thicknesses, fastened together so that it will have some weight, and a small soft wood spindle two or three hands long put through this wheel so that when the wheel turns it would turn the spindle. The spindle must be longer from the wheel up than

[34] *Ibid.*, p. 372.
[35] Cf. Nicolar, p. 143.

below it. To the top end of this spindle some fine strips of the
skin of the eel are fastened allowing the strips to be sufficient
lengths so that when the wheel turns it carries the spindle with it
and the string winds around the spindle, the other end of the string
being tied to another stick which is placed in a horizontal position
with one of these strings on each end, and the spindle being in an
upright position so when the wheel is in motion it winds up the
strings and the horizontal stick. When the operator finds the
stick is well up the top of the spindle, presses the stick down, it
stops the whirl of the wheel and soon begins to revolve the other
way, this repeated lively, a blaze is brought at the foot of the
spindle, spunk is applied and a fire is lighted. This horizontal
stick does not only act to turn the wheel but it also helps to hold
up the whole machine. The foot part of the spindle is where the
fire is expected to come must be dry, and the thing that turns on
must be equally so.

A most interesting account of the primitive way of pre-
serving fire, also of transporting it, is furnished by the same
author.[36]

Something must be done by man especially in the matter of keeping
the fire going so that he could have it by him and set up a blaze
when he wished, because there were many instances where people
were obliged to go without it for a long time . . . scouring the
country to find a small speck of fire from which they could gather
their supply. . . . Being patient in a continuous hunt would find
a tree that had been struck by lightning that still retained the fire
that had been brought upon it. But the difficulty was how to
keep it burning while it was being transported from one place to
another. . . . The outer bark of the cedar tree after having been
rubbed fine would take fire easily and keep burning until it was all
consumed, but on account of it having heavy smoke it would have
to be carried in the hand uncovered . . . [later] it was discovered
that some parts of the green hard wood tree produced a dry rotten
wood now called spunk which would burn very slowly and never
go out. . . . It burnt so slow that a very small piece lasted half a
day and emitted scarcely any smoke, so that it could be carried in
a pouch made for this purpose. (To be carried so that it would
not burn the pouch, clam shells were . . . needed after having
been lined with the blue clay and a small aperture having been
left open between the two shells through which what smoke there

[36] Cf. Nicolar, p. 141.

was might escape, these shells were put together and tied tightly and put in a pouch made of whole skin of a woodchuck which can be carried on one's belt outside of all the garments. No part of the skin was sewed, having been skinned whole, only one hole cut lengthwise from the base of the skull down the back long enough to admit the hand. In preparing the skin the skull after having the flesh well scraped off and the bone dried, turned back into its place, it then ready to be hung on the belt where it will not slip out. The tree that produces the best spunk is the yellow birch and the shells used were . . . of the thick and round species commonly known as *quahog*. [By this means] the hunter and others were able to carry fire with them all the time.

In addition to the above, I have heard some old men say that fire could be obtained by rubbing together two pieces of dry cedar wood held in the hands, though no further details were remembered. After the introduction of firearms they often obtained a blaze by discharging a gun into a mass of tinder.

The indoor fireplace in the wigwam was slightly dug out below the surface of the ground, the cooking vessels hanging over it suspended by a withe hook from a cross-pole from one side of the wigwam to the other and resting on the hoop inside the pole framework. Out of doors a few convenient stones are ranged together to enclose the fire, if a small one, and the vessels are set on the edge or suspended by withe and hook from a cross-pole supported on crotched sticks. Another method employed in temporary camps is to hang the vessel from the end of a pole thrust obliquely into the ground near the fire (Fig. 34). One pole is thus needed for each vessel.

Fig. 34

Boiling in Birch-Bark Container Suspended from Pole

The Penobscot in camp generally build their fire of three logs, two side by side on the ground with the fire between them and the third lying lengthwise between and above them. The cooking vessels are suspended from a horizontal pole resting on crotches. This provides an economical and satisfactory cooking fire. It can be banked over night or renewed by adding a few sticks. In starting a fire the blaze is first communicated to a few folds of dry birch bark which are then covered with small twigs. In camp life, if women are present, the lot of tending the fire falls to them; when the party consists only of men, the younger ones have the tasks of making and replenishing the fire. Birch bark is largely used for firewood, although for lasting long the hardwood is chosen. The villagers obtain their wood supply from the thickets preserved for this purpose at the upper end of Indian Island, whence it is hauled on sleds when the snow has come. Some do their hauling in the spring for the next winter. The grand old river is itself a never-ceasing agent of fuel transportation. Hardly any good driftwood gets by the village. There is always some one to spy it and sally out in a canoe to tow it ashore.

Boiling in Birch-Bark Vessels

Before the advent of Europeans, from whom the Penobscot soon obtained cooking vessels, birch-bark vessels were, according to tradition, used entirely. There seems to be nothing in the memory of informants to suggest that vessels of clay were made in this immediate region, although in the shell heaps of the Penobscot Bay area potsherds are found in abundance. I refer to well-known archaeological sources for such evidence. The historic natives were makers of these shell deposits in the bay region.

The widespread process of boiling water by means of heated stones is well remembered here. Folded birch-bark receptacles, to be described soon, were employed, being filled with water and having hot stones dropped into them one after another. The process of putting in hot stones and taking out the cooled ones was repeated as long as the water was intended to boil. The stones were handled with sticks. The food was put in with the stones. However, among Indians north of the St. Lawrence much is said about meat and other victuals being boiled directly over the fire coals in vessels made of birch bark. Instances of it have been recorded by ethnolo-

gists, but few appear to have seen the thing done. While
this subject was under discussion with the Penobscot, I took
occasion, through a wager with doubters of its possibility,
to have it demonstrated. Old Dominick, a penniless patriarch
with a family to support, undertook successfully to bring
two quarts of water to the boiling point, and maintained it
successfully in a vessel of folded birch bark (Fig. 36) resting
directly on a glowing bed of embers. He put a stitch of
spruce root across inside the rims to keep the sides from
collapsing. The water was first allowed to soak the bark on
the inside thoroughly, and the fire was reduced to a bed of
embers with practically no blaze, lest it burn the fastenings of

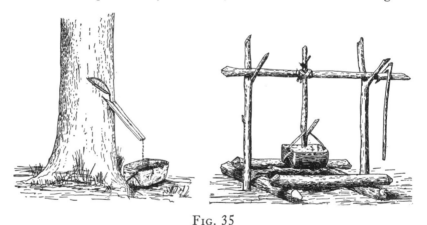

FIG. 35

Left, Use of Birch-Bark Containers as Maple-Sap Bucket
Right, as Boiler Suspended from Crossed Sticks

the boiler. In about twenty minutes a mess of vegetables
could have been boiled with no damage to the vessel. The
outer bark on the bottom was afterward found to be cracked
and charred a little in places. The Indians say that such
vessels did not last long, possibly for but one occasion, but
they are easily made when required. The same can be done,
we are told, by suspending the bark boiler by a withe and
pothook over a blazing fire, provided that the flames did not
burn off the fastenings (Fig. 35).

It was stated in a previous paragraph that although potsherds are archaeologically abundant near the coast there was

no tradition of pottery making in the memory of the people and that birch-bark vessels only were used. We may, however, infer something from analysis of the term *se'ski·dju*

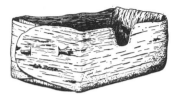

FIG. 36

Birch-Bark Seamless Containers for Liquids, and for Boiling

which denotes the bark vessel and dish. This term may be literally rendered "earthen container." Its application in this instance has provided a puzzle for the Indians with whom I discussed it as well as for ethnologists. Is it a falsity or an anachronism?

Smoking Meat

Moose and deer meat were the meat staples for a large part of the year. Whatever was not consumed fresh in camp was cut into strips several inches thick and hung over a horizontal pole supported by two upright crotches under which a fire was built lengthwise, and smudged. The meat is smoked until it is dried like leather. Sometimes an extemporized roofing of birch bark is built over the rack to keep off rain and to confine the heat and smoke. This smoked meat or pemmican can be kept indefinitely. It was eaten just as it was, or boiled up like a stew. It is called *gespa'te*, "dried."

The description of a meat-smoking camp on one of the islands up the river will convey a more definite impression of this practice; one indeed of no little importance in the economy of hunting tribes. Several moose and deer had been killed near by, and occasion was taken to preserve the surplus flesh on the spot. Some yards in front of the tent, which had a banking of logs heaped with earth several feet high around the sides, two rows of boulders had been placed about five

feet apart. In this enclosure a continuous fire of birch bark
had been kept going for several days. At each end a support,
either a tripod or crotched stick, had been erected for a stout
green sapling extending over the fire bed for not less than
ten feet. Over this the slices of meat were suspended, hanging
close together. The location of this camp was in several
respects well chosen since it was only a few steps from the
river, where the meat could be loaded into canoes, and water
was convenient for regulating the smudge and satisfying the
thirst of the laborers in a task desiccating to man as well as
moose. The sylvan picture is framed by the dense foliage
of surrounding pines affording protection overhead from too
much wind.

Maple Sugar Making

The sugar maple is one of the most valuable trees to the
northeastern Indians, holding a high place in their esteem as
a blessing from the Great Being. It is called *sna'wis.* In
aboriginal times the groves of sugar maples (*ma'kwa'nka'dik*)
were definitely known and regarded as family-inherited property after the manner of the hunting territories. Never were
they worked by others than the hereditary proprietors except
when permission had been granted. It was, however, de-
cidedly a case of usufruct, for the restricted right remained
only as long as the groves were used. When for a season or
two the grove was not tapped, another family group had the
privilege of entering the vicinity and assuming its care. It
should be noted that the sugar groves usually lay within the
family territories, though in the case of the Sockalexis family
the right to a sugar district not within the family terrain was
claimed, the locality being about ten miles up the Penobscot
River near Hemlock Stream, called *kaziu'skuk*, "hemlock
place." Similarly Nicolar Orson had a sugar bush on Sunkhaze Stream and the Raccoon family one on Mud Brook, on
the East Branch of the Penobscot. These restrictions, however, have fallen out of use and largely out of memory with
the last generation.

The women and children repair any time from late in
March through April to localities in which maples abound,

where they camp and prepare to make sugar. Quantities of
birch-bark vessels, boilers and receptacles for the process are
required to be manufactured in advance. The trees are
tapped with a sap runner entirely different from that of the
white man, which is a cylindrical wooden tube. The Indian
sap runner, *alama'nəsak*, is a flat piece of wood about ten
inches long, beveled at one end to fit into a notch cut in the
bark of the tree (Fig. 35). An oblique gash is cut in the trunk
a foot or so from the ground, while the sap runner is made
fast in another notch a trifle below the first, and a bark vessel
is set where the sap drips from the runner into it. A tapping
is shown in figure 35. From these buckets the sap is regularly collected and carried to camp to be boiled down to sugar,
ma'kwa'ni. When the boiling process is done, the hardening
sugar is poured into birch-bark cones about nine inches long,
tied about with a splint or bark cord. In such moulds,
topetci'gan, the sweet substance is kept for transportation
and storage. Incidentally, I have never heard of wooden
sugar moulds or troughs like those of the Ojibwa or Menomini
here. The birch-bark cones, filled with maple sugar, often
serve as presents among friends. A common use for the
sugar is to melt it down with water to make "sugar water,"
or *ma'ʿkwanə'bi*. The bark vessels and stirrers used in the
sugar making are the ordinary home articles to be described
later.

IMPLEMENTS AND UTENSILS

Tools for special purposes are figured and described in
sections dealing with various crafts. The following are implements of general use.

Of prime importance is the crooked knife, *pəka'kani'gan*,
"crooked, or double, tool," and *pəkala'gənigan*, "slicing, shaving tool." A series is shown in Fig. 6. The handles average
about six inches in length, though there is among Penobscot
specimens very little uniformity in either shape or size. The
material, too, differs, some being of antler, apple wood, blue-
berry, and rock maple; the last considered very fine for the
purpose. The general feature of all the knives, however, is
the grip and the bent thumb-rest. The knife is held and used

with the blade toward the body, the curve being uppermost and the thumb pressed against the angular extension. The dimensional proportions are varied to suit the particular grip of the maker.

The blades are curved differently, some being almost straight. The best of them are made of files, ground down and beveled on the upper side. As may be seen, the handle of the crooked knife is one of the most artistically ornamented articles made by the Penobscot. Such treatment is in strong contrast to the habit of central Algonkian and the Montagnais-Naskapi, whose knife handles are uniformly plain. So characteristic is this taste that of the two to half a dozen knives owned by nearly every Penobscot man, more than one half are ornamented. The specimen representing a closed hand (Fig. 6) is probably among the finest wood carvings made by natives in eastern America. Its material is rock maple. Another remarkably carved specimen has small mirrors set in an extension of the handle. Hardly one so poor as not to have a few ornamented crooked knives. Practically all the work for which a complete set of tools would be required the Indian does with this knife, drawing the edge toward the body in shaping material down or whittling corners, making notches to break a stick through, hollowing out cavities with the crook, or planing with the straight part of the blade. It is the same tool, with a few differences in proportions, in shape of handle and insertion of tang, found in native industry through northern North America and part of Asia. Although the history of the form suggests European origin, certain latent problems underlie the constructional concept. Tradition speaks of an aboriginal prototype with a blade of beaver incisors set in the handle, a form widely alluded to in the north, but not as yet collected from living peoples, though known archaeologically.

The Penobscot scheme of inserting the tang of the blade is quite simple. A groove in the handle accommodates the shank deeply enough to allow it to be bound smoothly with a wrapping of rawhide, tanned skin, or ash splint. Sometimes a strip of wood is laid over the imbedded metal in the groove before the wrapping is put on.

The awl, *mago's*, is equally indispensable to the workman. Tradition states that besides bone awls, the tail of a horseshoe crab was commonly employed. Nowadays, however, the universal awl consists of a piece of hard metal, preferably a file, set in a handle of wood or antler. These handles likewise are often modestly ornamented (Fig. 37). Along with them is a horseshoe crab's tail to illustrate the traditional form. A sharpened splinter of a bear's leg bone is said to have been employed as an awl. Probably the most primitive type of bone awl is found in the larger bones coming from the foreleg of the moose (metacarpal), and smaller ones from the deer. These are in their natural form, to be ready for use only requiring to be scraped free of gristle when removed from the leg. The specimens with grooves encircling the wooden handle are interesting because the grooves serve to measure distances from the edge of a bark surface when perforating a series of holes. They are measuring awls.

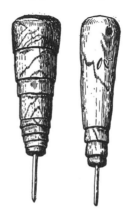

FIG. 37

Wooden Awls with Iron Points

With the awl, the needle, *sɑ'nkɑdi*, was used in sewing, the holes in the leather having first been made with the former. Needles had small eyes. Penis bones of bear, mink, sable, raccoon, and otter, having a natural perforation, were commonly employed. They required only scraping and sharpening. A copper needle obtained from a hunter in the upper village is also figured.

In sharpening edged tools a gritty pebble from the edge of the water is used. One of these was obtained from an abandoned camp, others were slaty whetstones taken from Indian tool boxes.

Native thread consisted of the rind of wormseed plant growing near the water. This was shredded, soaked in water, and then twisted on the thigh with the palm of the hand, making threads from about a foot to three feet long.

The maul, *pugə'magwɑ'di*, is still commonly used in conjunction with the ax for chopping and splitting wood. The ax blade being laid to the grain of the wood, its top is struck heavily with the maul and the material is split out. Such a method is regarded by the old people as the survival of the native process with wooden maul and stone wedge. Flat-topped stone axes, frequently found in the ground around old village or camp sites, are spoken of in this way. The stone wedge of this type is termed *dala'ganis*, "little wedge." I have seen a workman here split out a cedar log a foot in diameter with maul and wooden wedges, and for several hours trim down the ribs and lining of different sizes for a canoe, using only the crooked knife for the shaping and smoothing process. A larger and smaller wedge are used in splitting up logs, the two being driven in alternately and pushed along as the cleavage widens.

Though it may seem incautious to speak definitely of prehistoric stone objects found in this territory, especially since we are not sure in many cases that the forerunners of the present Penobscot were their makers, it would, I think, be a mistake to pass by the opinions of Indians themselves in their bearing upon the probable uses of some of these implements. The stone tools shown are between five and eight inches long, with finely polished, hard, sharp cutting edges and unfinished tops. These are classed in general as knives to be held in the hand for cutting meat or skinning game, and are called *hwi'lsawa'gan*, "slitter" (?).

Modern knives for the same purpose (Fig. 6) have straight metal blades with straight wooden or antler handles. It can be seen, and pondered by the thoughtful, without, however, stressing a conclusion, that the dimensions and manner of use of these and their supposed stone prototypes are similar.

The stone gouges and adze are extremely common in archaeological sites throughout this part of Maine, for evidence of which reference may again be made to the results of long experience in this field.[37] The testimony of the natives concerning these objects is not very detailed, beyond stating that some were mounted, and that others were grasped directly

[37] See Moorehead, in Bibliography.

in the hand for all kinds of wood working.[38]   An old Penobscot at Oldtown told Mr. Orchard that tradition claimed they used to temper the edge of their stone implements by dipping them in hot tallow, and I heard the same thing at the Lincoln village.   The Penobscot call the gouge, chisel, or adze *wala's-knigan*, the name being more strictly applied to the gouge itself.

Several types of one-piece wooden hammers or mallets are used in different capacities.   These are of heavy hardwood, the more generally useful form having an angular head cut out at a right angle to the handle.   The other, specifically a canoe mallet, used in putting slats and ribs in the canoe, is kidney shaped, flat on one side and convex on the other, with the handle at an obtuse angle to the head. Both forms average under twelve inches in length.

The device described in canoe making for spreading or packing against pressure (Fig. 17) might be mentioned again while considering native implements.   It shows considerable mechanical ingenuity, and is often used with the mallet.

In regard to woodwork of the Penobscot in general, a comparatively high grade of advancement seems to have been reached in late historic times.   The diversity of implements, the elaboration of their decorations and carvings support this judgment.

Comparing the Penobscot with the Algonkian north of the St. Lawrence, for want of complete collections from tribes nearer by, wooden implements exceed among the former, the latter exceed in the use of bone material.   Bone, when employed for manufactures such as snowshoes, needles, dice, and minor articles, is worked mostly by filing and shaving.   In the process of dice-making, flat blade of moose leg bone was shaped and polished, and the outline of the dice incised, only remaining to be cut free, trimmed down and rounded by filing.   Animal ribs are tough and durable for tool making.

In the manufacture of articles ivory seems to have been not uncommonly known in olden times.   It is called *wambi'gan*, "white bone," and was possibly obtained by trade

[38] An interesting paper on the subject of New England adzes has been presented by C. C. Willoughby, ref. 2 and 4.

from the Micmac, in whose territory the walrus survived until 1761.[39] I have not attempted to ascertain whether remains of the walrus have been found in Penobscot Bay or not. There is, however, a creature known by name *ao'lwa'kik*ᵂ, "overgrown seal," said to have been common formerly on the rocky islands off the coast (Matinicus Island). Could this possibly refer to the walrus? Ivory articles are mentioned in the myth of the culture-hero (Gluska'be), such as magic ivory dice, and bowls for the bowl game, an ivory ball, a magic ivory pipe, and an ivory bow made of pieces lashed together. The latter is a spring-backed or reinforced bow separately described as a war-bow. In working ivory the same method was said to have been used as for bone.

As to the stonework of former days little can be said, because outside of such implements as corn pounders, basswood shredders, and a few minor articles, none have been regularly used in historic times.

Mention, however, may be made of the sacred character of the flint used in making implements as a factor in the final obliteration of mechanical uses of flint from the memory of the natives. Supernatural associations have attached themselves to flint, whence the name *kɑtɑksu'pəs*, "spirit stone." The great mountain at Kineo contains quantities of this stone which the Indians of former times quarried extensively. Nicolar records a legend concerning the origin of stone implements. Referring to a supernatural woman who for the benefit of the people in mythical times broke up a covering which had spread over the sea, she promised this would fly in pieces to the shore, forming itself in heaps to be made into useful implements. Whereupon, a great quake of the earth shattered the covering. The people, going to the shore, found fragments of stone all about. They gathered these in heaps along the coast, and made small implements. They shaped them, hacking and chipping off the edges to make spears and

---

[39] Gamaliel Smethurst, *A Narrative of an Extraordinary Escape out of the Hands of the Indians in the Gulph of St. Lawrence*, London, 1764. Reprinted and Edited by W. F. Ganong. Collections of New Brunswick Historical Society, vol. 2, 1905, p. 377. An interesting resumé of evidence for the early distribution of walrus on the southern New England coast appears by G. M. Allen, "The Walrus in New England," *Journal of Mammalogy*, vol. II, 1930, p. 139.

arrowheads. The heaps of stones remained on the shores many years, and the people were able to gather and save a large amount for future use. So much was saved that it lasted until after the white man introduced among them tools of metal.[40]

As to work in metal, the Penobscot of early times may have known something of native copper, *suma'lkin*, since copper beads and fragmentary pieces have been found in the region by Willoughby.[41]

Other metals are known by native terms which do not submit readily to etymological analysis in some cases, to wit, iron, *a'lnak;* lead, *pi't·ak;* brass, *wiza'wa'k*; silver, *waba'kek*. The two latter are respectively "yellow metal" and "white metal." These materials are known only through the medium of trade.

Eating Utensils

Food was eaten from birch-bark and wooden bowls, *wala'de*, some of them eighteen inches in diameter for family service, and others smaller in varying sizes for individuals. Birch-bark dishes are figured and described on page 117.

The wooden dishes or bowls were of the same sizes. The one shown in Fig. 38 has a depth of several inches, walls less

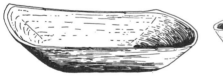

FIG. 38

WOODEN FOOD TRAYS

than half an inch thick, was made of birch knurl and was used in eating vegetables or meats, or as a corn-bread mixer (*to'banka'gan*). Smaller and flatter dishes of the same material had a diameter of about twelve inches and were used optionally as individual dishes or as platters for the dice and bowl game.

[40] Nicolar, p. 105–6.
[41] Cf. Willoughby, ref. 4, p. 13.

Besides the round wooden bowls there were oblong dishes with squared ends about fifteen inches long, resembling the food bowls of the Iroquois and the southern tribes.

For transferring victuals from cooking vessels to individual dishes or bowls as well as for eating with, two kinds of ladles and spoons were used (Fig. 39). The wooden or the bark

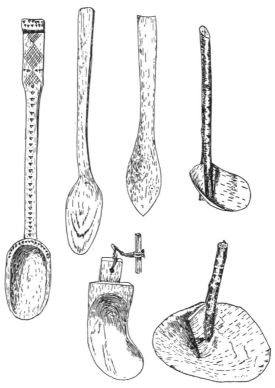

Fig. 39

WOODEN AND BIRCH–BARK SPOONS

spoon, *e'mkwan*, "spoon," usually ranges from ten to fifteen inches in length. When made of bark, a piece cut according to the pattern and folded along the dotted lines is fastened in a cleft stick. These are not only used for eating, but are to be found conveniently at springs for the thirsty traveler, sometimes the handle having a crook to hang it up by. Little punctures in the bark may be noticed plugged tight with a bit of stick. At feasts or similar occasions when the people gathered together to eat, each person came provided with his own dish and spoon.

The wooden spoon has a shallow narrow bowl and a long flat handle sometimes ornamented with carvings. A strip of ash wood, part of the material used in basket making, is often improvised into a spoon, a crinkle in the strip forming the bowl.

An ingenious device for convenience in traveling is the portable wooden drinking cup attached to a toggle by a thong. The toggle is pushed under the belt that the cup may be carried. It is made of a maple knot or root. This style of cup or ladle was common among the eastern Indians.

The pot stirrer, *amspla′kwahi′gan*, is a flat-ended paddle of wood, generally less than two feet in length.

When eating stewed or roasted meat an improvised fork was often used, consisting of a trimmed, forked green stick, *kulbihi′gan*, with which the hot viands were lifted from the pot.

The pothook, *spla′kwahi′gan*, was of yellow birch cut at the place where a twig branches off, and the limber end was twisted to as to form the suspending line (Fig. 5). Some are formed of a cut branching twig suspended from a thong or rope. These are used both in outdoor and indoor fireplaces.

Bow and Arrows

That another type of bow may have been known is vouchsafed by evidence produced some forty years ago by a notorious old Indian character, Frank Loring or Big Thunder.[42] He was an unscrupulous showman, mendacious, but given to practical joking. One of his productions was an "antique" war-bow which he represented as handed down to him by tradition of his foreparents. He made a specimen, and lectured about it, from which I know at least a dozen reproductions have since been made. It was a composite three-piece spring bow, wrapped and braced with raw moosehide (Fig. 62). The bow was about four feet long and made of rock maple in two sections meeting at the center. The pieces were doubly curved. The middle third of the bow, covering the center

---

[42] For historical data and character analysis, see Delabarre, 1935.

joint, had a straight springy stave as a back-spring lashed to the other pieces with a rawhide wrapping. Another strip of stretched rawhide ran from end to end, passing over the back spring, so that the more the bow was drawn the greater the tension on the spring and the moosehide stretched over it. The principle of the backing and the three-piece composition, while thoroughly unlike any other American projector, is nevertheless vaguely suggestive of the sinew-backed forms and the Eskimo composite bow. Such a bow was, by the testimony of Big Thunder's dubious tradition, used in war. An ivory bow presumably of this type is also mentioned in the culture-hero myth. Notwithstanding the censure which acceptance of Big Thunder's fabrication will bring upon one who mentions it seriously, I shall not pass it by unnoticed. If it is to be pronounced an ethnological fraud, so it will stand. And yet Loring was a Penobscot, and as such he could have been guilty of reproducing in his own fashion something actually described to him in youth by Indians then old.

The hunting bow, *tɑ'bi* (Fig. 40), was a simple one-curve rock maple stave, tapering and notched for the string, which was of two-ply twisted sinew. The length was fifty-seven inches. It was quite stiff and had a range of about one hundred yards. In section it resembled other eastern bows of southern New England, presumably influenced by European forms, with a nearly flat face on the outer side and convex on the inner.

A makeshift bow told of by hunters was made in a hurry from a spruce sapling, trimmed but unpeeled, with a rawhide string. Arrows were made of light ash wood twenty-five inches in length. Only the blunt-headed unfeathered bolts, common among all northeastern tribes, are still made. The nocks are only slightly flattened. Arrows are shaped down with the crooked knife from the heart of dried wood. The blunt heads are flat or conical (Fig. 40). The method of feathering was two or three sections of feathers several inches long wrapped at their lower end to the shaft, the upper end free. Crow and hawk feathers were used. The blunt-headed bolts are called *pa'hkwal*, (pl.), the barbed flint or metal arrows used formerly being called *sawo'nal* (pl.).

An arrow-carrier, *pa'hhkwainu'di*, "arrow receptacle," known through individual tradition, consisted of a strip of

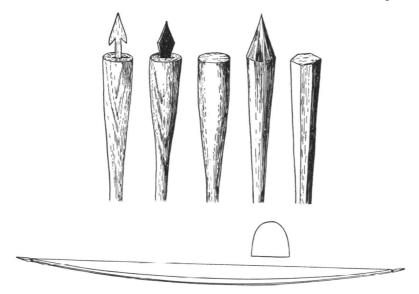

FIG. 40

Upper, Series of Arrow Ends
Lower, Bow, Showing Half-Round Cross Section

leather several inches wide worn like a bandolier over the shoulder, with about twenty double slits in it to accommodate the arrows. The arrows hang vertically before and behind; those behind can be grasped over the shoulder as the bandolier is pulled about. Basket quivers are remembered only by name.

An interesting account is given by Rosier (1605).

In one of their canoes I saw their bowes and arrowes, which I took up and drew an arrow in one of them which I found to be of strength able to carry an arrow five or six score stronglie, and one of them took it and drew as we draw our bowes, not like the [East] Indians. Their bow is made of Witch Hazel and some of Beech in fashion much, like our bowes, but they want nocks, only a string of leather put through a hole at one end, and made fast with a knot at the other. Their arrowes are made of the same wood, some of

Ash, big and long, with three featheres tied on and nocked very artificiallie; headed with the long shank bone of a Deer, one side very sharp with two fangs in manner of a harping iron.[43]

That curious conservatism of the Indian stands out in the fact that toy bows are made now in practically the same style as that described above, except that the string is run through a hole in both ends instead of in one.

Birch-Bark Vessels

The tough, pliable, and easily obtained bark of the canoe birch (Betula papyrifera) was an indispensable article in the economy of the northern Indians. It furnished material for house coverings, canoes, culinary utensils, in the historic period taking the place of pottery and antedating splint basketry. Besides special articles, into the construction of which birch bark enters, as described and figured elsewhere in this study, there are products of general utility. Birch-bark cooking vessels, dishes, and receptacles, storage vessels and carrying receptacles, large and small, are of three fundamental types.

Cooking vessels, we have observed, were formerly made of birch bark. Since they had to hold water, they were made of one sheet of material, folded without seams and fastened at the sides. Varieties of boiling pots, kettles, and water vessels, called *seski'djo*, are shown in Fig. 36. The vessels sometimes had hoop rims, and often bales by which they were suspended from the fire-hook. A maple hoop or a tough ash split is used.

To boil in one of these vessels, a hot but smouldering fire had to be maintained lest the flames burn off the fastenings. Another way was to set the vessel on two green logs over the embers. I have witnessed this. On one occasion it required less than twenty minutes to bring cold water to boiling. The vessel is shown in Fig. 36, having suffered no damage, although the older Indians say that such kettles did not last long. When they cracked they could be repaired with pitch, but were then good only as receptacles for dry contents. Vessels of this type used as common receptacles about the camp are called *ku'n·adjo*.

[43] Rosier, p. 372.

The next type of bark vessel is more properly a dish or bowl used as a receptacle for food, an eating dish, or for general purposes. The pattern differs from the preceding. The seams in the bottoms of the dishes, however, are fairly tight, and all are well finished with rim hoops. Typical forms are shown in Fig. 41. The outer surface of the bark

FIG. 41

BIRCH–BARK DISHES AND PANS

is turned in, rarely out. The bark dish is called *wa'ladc*. Some have two rim hoops of maple, one on the outside and one on the inside, some have only one, which is either inside or outside, and others of later make have a rimming of sweet grass bound with the hoop.

Still another way of folding the same pattern produces a seamless, water-tight soup dish or food receptacle. In this the four corners are bent double and folded, the four folds running in the same direction, and the hoop is bound down on the rim. This type of dish differs in shape from the preceding in having constricted instead of flaring walls.

These three types of receptacles were formerly common possessions of each Indian family. But now they are made and used only on hunting trips where the bush economy causes this and other native properties to persist.

The last and perhaps most characteristic type of vessel, *migɔna'gwe* or *migɔna'dju*, is one which has a rectangular base and seamed sides sloping inward, used for storing meat, vegetables, grease, clothes, and trinkets. It ranges from a tiny, toy-like box to a receptacle capable of holding about a bushel. Some are provided with lids, some with bales, and some with straps for carrying or hanging. Some are provided with two leather loops by which they are attached to the belt and used as a berry pail, *sagi'bi*. Two maple hoops stitched on with spruce root or basket splint form the rims

FIG. 42

BIRCH–BARK VESSEL WITH ETCHED CURVE AND LINEAR DESIGNS

(Figs. 42, 43, 44). Since these receptacles were of more permanent value, elaborated etched decorations are often seen on them. They have passed out of use. I need hardly mention the wide distribution, and similar characteristics in technique and decoration, of objects like those described among the northern Algonkian tribes. Round birch-bark boxes, *seski'dju*, of plainer form, are those shown in Figs. 43, 44, 45. They are made by sewing a ring of bark to form a cylinder, with a hoop rim, fitting in a round bottom of wood or bark and supplying a similarly made cover to fit inside or outside. The sewing is done with ash basket-splints or spruce root. These boxes were used for storing small objects about the house, beads, trinkets, and for berries. In size they ranged from three inches in height and five in diameter upwards to a foot or more. Some are decorated with etchings. Cylindrical boxes were also made of bent wood. An old example of the wooden-hoop box from the Penobscot is in the Heye collection (Fig. 46). It is a little over a foot in length and one half as wide, the shape being oval. The sides of the box and cover have been steamed, bent, and secured fast by pegs around an oval bottom of wood.

Rhythmic lines and zigzags are incised on the walls. This article is stated to have been a man's tool box.

In considering distribution of techniques and ornamentation [44] of birch-bark containers in the northern hemisphere, the methods of sewing will come in for some attention. An

FIG. 43

BIRCH–BARK BASKETS
Round and Rectangular

examination of Penobscot specimens yields the following classification of stitches and joinings:

A plain in-and-out stitch of variable distance for common articles is used longitudinally (Fig. 47, a), or transversely (b). The latter is generally reinforced underneath with a strip of splint or spruce root to prevent it from tearing through. As shown in Fig. b, this is a common method of joining, known as the regular "canoe stitch," and used

[44] See W. C. Orchard.

FIG. 44

Upper, Birch-Bark Decorated Baskets, Rectangular and Round
Lower, Ash-Splint Clothes Basket

FIG. 45

DECORATED BIRCH–BARK BASKETS
Rectangular and Round

for canoe bottoms and gunwales, wigwam covers and bark vessels. Where the stitch has to run on the edge of the bark, spaced groups of stitches are made at different intervals (c and d). The advantage here is that there are not too many holes to weaken the edge of the bark. The edge may also be doubled by the addition of an extra flap of bark for strengthening. A compact, solid wrapping and

FIG. 46

Wooden Oval Box with Incised Carving

stitching (d) is nevertheless sometimes seen, every third or fourth stitch going through deeper down from the edge of the bark (e), or sometimes only a third or fourth or eighth wrapping will pass through the bark, the others merely winding around the hoop. Several varieties of a similar

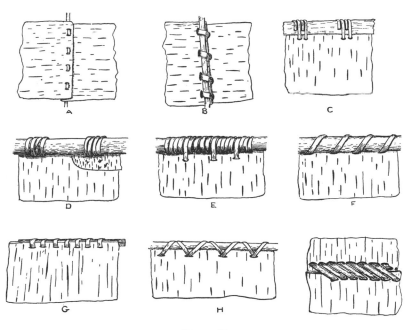

FIG. 47

Stitches for Fastening and Rimming Birch-Bark Containers Sewed with Spruce Root or Splints

binding are shown in f and g. These latter forms of
rimming were often formerly fancifully ornamented by inter-
weaving lengthwise a different colored strip of stuff, or porcupine quills. A criss-cross rim stitch (h) is also common. It
serves at the stern and stem of the canoe, or where two
surfaces of bark come together to an edge. Here the fluted
reinforcement is also employed.

Bark Getting

The birch bark, *ma'skwe*, in the manufacture of native
utensils is of two kinds, summer bark and winter bark. In
the summer time the bark is not as good as that peeled in
winter, since it does not separate so readily into layers.

The winter bark, required for important construction like
canoes and wigwams, is obtained as follows. The tree is
felled so that it will fall upon two logs for a bed, about six
inches or so from the ground. Then a slow fire is made
under one side, and a lengthwise cut is made along the top
of the log. The edges of the cut are loosened and, with a
wooden chisel about six inches long, the bark is forced from
the log little by little. Warm water poured on helps the
operation. When the one side is thus peeled off, the other
side is rolled above the fire and similarly treated. The
process corresponds to removing the skin from an animal's
body. Some say that the bark chisel of wood was formerly
a stone implement similarly shaped. The edge of the wooden
chisel is fire-hardened. No hammer is used with it, the pressure of the hand being sufficient. When freed from the log
the sheet of bark is rolled up and made ready for transportation. When it is desired to scrape the rough shreds from the
outside, a knife is used, though in earlier times a sturgeon
scale served the purpose of a scraper. A good piece of prepared bark, however, has the outside layer, which is white
and rougher, entirely removed. It is called *wəlasα'gwal*,
"good bark," (i.e., with short scar-marks). The remainder
is used for less important articles. The terms applied to
different qualities of bark are: *ka'ka·sα'gwe*, "brittle (with
eyelets or scars)"; *maso'sigwe*, "big bark"; *ma'skwe*, the
general term for birch bark. The Penosbcot used to think,

when they were about to go and peel bark, that by eating no breakfast their bark would come off better and be freer from knotholes.

Basketry

The making of plain baskets for domestic use is a well-established feature in the later native life of the region. An extension of the northern frontier of the splint-basketry industry has, it seems, been gradually effacing the southern boundaries of the more primitive birch-bark technique. Among the Wabanaki tribes the latter has completely succumbed to the former within the short space of approximately sixty years; somewhat less than this among the Micmac. Certain peoples like the Algonquin of Quebec and Ontario have conserved both crafts side by side, though generally in the conflict of types the simpler birch-bark technique ultimately gives way before splint basketry. My views of the northward diffusion of the latter have been outlined in another report.[45] While the shape and functions vary somewhat, here, only two or three types of basket weave occur even now. The ordinary weave is the checkerwork or over-one-under-one, while a hexagonal twill, like the snowshoe mesh and the weave formed in the melon basket, comprise the other two forms. The materials used in basketry are mainly black or brown ash for the splints, and maple for the hoops and bales.

The process of Penobscot basket making has been made the object of study by Mr. W. C. Orchard, whose manuscript contains an illustrated account of the preparation of material and the process of construction.[46] My own remarks will therefore be much condensed, covering more the general economic aspects of the art. Women's work baskets, in which they keep basket-gauges, knives, and material in general (Fig. 44), are about twelve inches wide. Another type, square in form, was used as a receptacle for dried berries. Having no angles, roundish baskets are said to have been designed for use in canoes which might be damaged by sharp-cornered

[45] *Decorative Art and Basketry of the Cherokee*, Bulletin Public Museum of Milwaukee.

[46] MS of W. C. Orchard, Museum of the American Indian (Heye Foundation), N. Y.

baskets heavily laden. The statement applies chiefly to the moosehide canoes. Types called melon baskets are used much in the fields for carrying vegetables. Baskets in general are called *abaznu'de*, "woodwork receptacle." [47]

The process of construction is briefly as follows. An ash log, cut about ten feet long, is laid upon blocks and pounded with the back of an ax for about an hour or so to loosen the layers of fibre. Next, the layers are stripped off and planed smooth with a knife, or more commonly, nowadays, by a metal blade set in a clamp. These layers may be kept in rolls or coils until needed. They are generally from an inch to two inches wide. The important step of cutting these lengths into splints of the thinness required for basket making comes next. For this purpose a modern instrument of native invention called a "gauge," *ali'kpesa'wagan*, "stripping tool," is brought into use. The gauge is a tool of wood, varying according to the owner's fancy, from four inches to six in length. There is a handle section and a block part. Into the latter, little blades cut out of watch springs are set and held fast by a transverse bar of wood or metal, so that the sharp edges of these teeth face inward. By holding this in the hand, and starting the strip of splint over these teeth, the splint is drawn against these, being slithered into as many pieces as there are teeth, plus one.

Basket gauges are most important tools in the native woman's outfit. As a rule ten or more are kept in a basket, forming a set for cutting different widths (Figs. 48 and 49). In each, the teeth are at different distances apart, so that splint strips of any standard can be uniformly cut. The finest are about 1/16 of an inch, and the coarsest about 1/3 of an inch wide. It is impossible to write a description of the forms taken by the gauges, hardly any two being alike. A wide play of fancy in carved decoration is lavished upon them, as may be observed from the figures. Some of the specimens shown seem old; their invention may date back to the middle of the last century. Much of the splint stripping is said, however, to have been done formerly with the

[47] The noun ending -(*n*)*ude* indicates "receptacle, container, carrier."

FIG. 48

CARVED GAUGES FOR SPLITTING ASH SPLINTS
USED IN BASKET MAKING

teeth.   Similar gauges are encountered among all the Algonkian who make baskets, north of the St. Lawrence, as well as
the Iroquois and Huron, though group differences in construc-

FIG. 49

Basket Splint-Cutting Gauge Elaborately Carved

tion and shape enable them to be distinguished.   None of
them, however, have such profusely ornamented gauges as
the Penobscot.   The range of carved ornamentation here
includes varied and original realistic representation of animal
heads, human hands, in three dimensions or in relief, carved
finger grips, openwork combinations of incised triangles, cross
hatchings, tree figures, double curves, beveled edges covered
with series of notched triangles, and numerous motives to be
found treated in more detail under the heading of Decorative
Art.   A darkening, either in black or red, is in some rubbed
into portions of the incised surface to add to the contrast
effect, and sometimes the wood is dyed dark red or brown
with alder bark.   Several remarkable examples of native
carving may be seen among the gauges, the conventionalized
eagle's head carved out of beech wood for instance, and the
openwork curved handle.

When the splints have been cut and treated as above and
dyed the desired colors, the weaving is begun upon a flat
board resting on the lap.   The checkerwork bottom is made,
then the ends of these splints are turned upward to form
standards, in and out of which the fine splints are woven as

filling. Much variation is possible in shape and dimensions, some of the workers lately preferring to construct their baskets over a mould. The rim is secured with a hoop wrapped with a thin splint, and sometimes covers are fitted to the whole. The plain blades, or braided lengths of sweet grass, *mski·'kwal*, "grasses" (Savastana odorata), are now abundantly used in the weaving and rimming of baskets.

The ornamentation of baskets in color was of old produced by introducing different colored splints. Besides this technical effect, painting was sometimes executed on broad splints, or extra dyed splints were inserted over the foundation splints to form a "false embroidery."

Besides ash, cedar was occasionally used in basket making, though not so much among the Penobscot as among the Malecite. Cedar does not require beating like the ash, the layers of the wood coming off easily when green. Cedar baskets are, however, not so strong as those made of ash.

The basketry of the Penobscot, like that of all the eastern tribes, has been tremendously stimulated by trade in the last generation or so. Many innovations both in form, function, and in the implements for basket manufacture, have crept in, though the art is fundamentally native. Sweet grass is much more used nowadays than formerly, some informants even stating that it was not used at all in basket making before the latter quarter of the last century.

The verification of splint baskets as being native New England of the colonial period is to be found in the collection of old Penobscot figured and described by Mrs. Eckstorm in her monograph on Penobscot industries.[48]

Bags and Pouches

Pouches and bags of skin with or without the hair, some formed of the whole skin, some of a trimmed, two-seam pattern, and others of woven cedar and basswood bark, of all sizes, were common. Bags in general are called *manu'de*, "receptacle."

The most complex of these were the woven bags of basswood for carrying provisions, or for containing personal prop-

[48] Eckstorm, pp. 27–30, pls. III–IX.

erty. They range from six inches in diameter to several feet (Fig. 50), with proportionate handles or shoulder straps. The weaving process employed in making these articles is given on page 136.

A common form of bag for pipe and tobacco, fire-making implements, and other necessities of the men, was

. . . the pouch made of a whole skin of the woodchuck which can be carried on one's belt outside of all garments. No part of the skin was sewed, having been skinned whole, only one hole cut lengthwise from the base of the skull down on the back long enough to admit the hand. Sometimes the incision is made in the breast. In preparing the skin, the skull, after having the flesh well scraped off the bone, dried, and turned back into its place, is then ready to be hung under the belt, where it will not slip out.[49]

FIG. 50

Woven Basswood Carrying Bag

This is the widespread Algonkian man's belt-pouch, and is called *bitsənɑ'gan* in Penobscot. Some little pebbles were often put in the skull to make it rattle.

An old specimen showing how this type of pouch came to survive in cloth is one for percussion caps, fourteen inches long with an opening down the under side four inches long with little flaps on the ends, the whole symbolizing an animal's entire skin with the flaps as legs. A worsted flower ornamentation is on the outside. This is also worn folded over the belt like the cased-skin pouch of which it is a copy.

An example of moose-hair embroidery which, although made by a Malecite woman on St. John River, represents the kind of work formerly done by the Penobscot, is the bag in Fig. 51. This pouch, twelve inches long, is for pipe and tobacco, made of tanned deerskin with a draw or wrapping thong and fringe. It is attached to the belt or carried inside of a larger pouch. A small moleskin pouch used for trinkets or for tobacco, measuring six inches long, is shown in Fig. 52.

Sealskin (harbor seal) was formerly used. We hear of large game bags several feet across, gun cases, and smaller

[49] Nicolar, p. 142.

pouches and bags made of this skin. A specimen was obtained from an old Penobscot woman, though probably made by the Passamaquoddy who did much of this work. It was used to carry small pocket articles, or tobacco. Another was made of a seal's paw.

Knife sheaths, *pidala'gwɑdi*, were commonly made of buckskin or moose skin sewed with a thong. A loop enables the

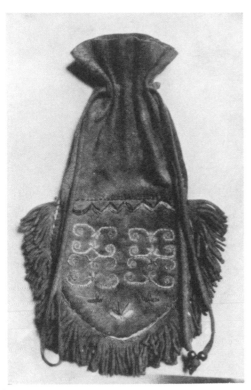

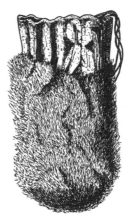

FIG. 51

Pipe and Tobacco Pouch of Deerskin
Decorated with Moose-Hair Embroidery

FIG. 52

Small Mole Skin
Pouch

sheath to be attached to the belt. Penobscot knife sheaths were plain. The foreleg of a deer, skinned so that the white spot is shown, is made into a knife sheath which was exceedingly attractive to native eyes.

A wall pocket for the reception of odds and ends was made of a squirrel's skin half turned inside and suspended by a string. Seal bladders were commonly used as receptacles or bags for seal oil, which was used in cooking. They are called *wa'bɔskwe*, "white" (?).

Skin Dressing

Moose, deer, and the larger animals whose pelts are to be used, are skinned as soon as killed and the hide rolled up green to be taken home for dressing.[50]   A convenient night is customarily chosen for the job of tanning.

FIG. 53

SCRAPER OF WOOD AND IRON

For Removing Hair from Deer and Moose Skins

Beforehand, however, the skin has been scraped free of hair with a tool, *djekhau'sude* or *tcekhi'gan,* "scraper," made of wood like a spokeshave with a piece of metal for a blade (Fig. 53).   It is used by a man who spreads the wet skin over a log supported obliquely on the ground (Fig. 54) and shaves the hair off by a motion away from the body.   In the cold

FIG. 54

BEAM UPON WHICH HIDE IS CLEANED OF HAIR

winter time another process for removing hair is employed for large hides.   The hide is stretched by selvage cords run through slits in the edge of the skin, inside a rectangular framework of poles, *alhe'psan,* which is leaned upright against some support.   The operator, with a different type of scraper, *mənela'gan,* made of a tough piece of wood ten to twelve inches

[50] Consult also Eckstorm, I, pp. 51–52.

long, having a metal blade set in perpendicularly near the end (Fig. 55), stands in front and with a downward motion scrapes the hide clean. Next the grease and fat are scraped off and the texture is softened with a toothed scraper or

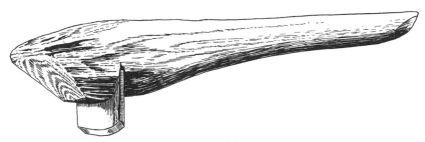

FIG. 55

SKIN FLESHING TOOL WITH METAL BLADE

grainer (Fig. 56) made of hard wood. This is also done on the frame.

When the skin has been soaked in oil or grease and washed, it is ready for the all-night tanning process. The several men who are to do the job strip off most of their clothes and heat up the house with a good fire. Then they bring the hide or

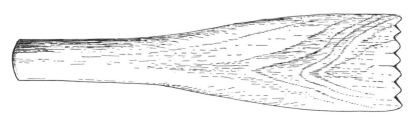

FIG. 56

SKIN FLESHING TOOL OF WOOD

hides inside and pull and stretch them with their hands in the heated room, working all night sometimes before the skins have dried soft. Two men seize a skin and pull and wring it between them, with the perspiration running down them. They laugh and tell stories to make the work less irksome. If they have kept well at it, the hide, when it is at last dry, will be soft yet extremely tough and pliable.

The labor is hard, hence well-dressed pelts are highly priced. The next thing they do is to sew up the skin like a bag and hang it with the mouth opening downward over a funnel, nowadays a barrel, under which a smudge is lighted. Here it is left until well smoked. By varying the quality of the smudge different shades of tan are given to the skin, a smudge of cedar bark, for instance, giving a fine dark brown, sometimes a pinkish tinge. Birch bark produces a darker color. In this way formerly the Penobscot dressed skins for their clothing.

To make waterproof moosehide for moccasins or skincanoes, they left the hide raw but kept it for a long time well greased with moose or deer tallow. The more it absorbed the more waterproof it became. They are only occasionally so prepared nowadays.

The skins of smaller mammals are commonly kept and used in the green state. The skin is first removed by cutting it across the lower abdomen and down the hind legs lengthwise, then pulling it off entire towards the head; the pelt is stretched on a proper sized frame, *dugbulhawa'gan*, made by bending a stick to form an oval, one end being notched into the other, for muskrat skins.

The commonest thong material for sewing, snowshoe netting, wood sewing, lines, and wrapping stuff, except for splint basket-stuff, is rawhide or "babiche," as it is known throughout the French-speaking north. To make this, the skin is cleaned of hair, as described above, then spread out on a board and cut with a knife around the edge, the cut following the border of the skin all around. Or the cuts are made zigzagging in from the side of the skin, a number, often seven, parallel to one another, so that when they are cut apart at the ends the whole hide is separated into one long strip or thong of the thickness, usually somewhat less than a quarter of an inch. The thong is then rolled up into a ball or skein and kept green in a receptacle (formerly bark) until needed. Before being used, however, it is left in a vessel of water and soaked until soft. To stretch the thongs, two deer tibia are used as grips for the twisting (Fig. 57). Working on skins is attended to by the men, as it is considered too heavy for

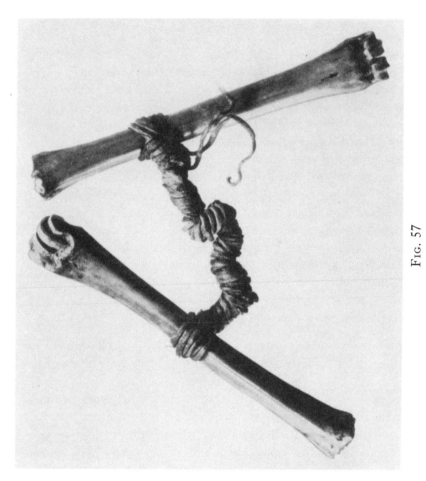

FIG. 57

DEER TIBIA AND "BABICHE" THONGS IN PROCESS
OF STRETCHING

women, except perhaps during the stages in which it is being smoked and finished.

Sewing

The sewing of buckskin and birch bark is done with several different kinds of stitches, which are determined by materials as well as by the purposes of the joining. The thread stuffs are: rawhide thongs, *wlo'ges*, sinew thread; rolled basswood bark thread, *wuskwɑ'bi;* the tough threads of the skins of worm-root, *pske'taguk;* thin ash splints, *wi'kəbi;* stripped spruce root, *wa'dəbi;* and latterly rattan. In sewing together the edges of skins the two are laid edge to edge and sewed with the ordinary whip stitch. Thongs of thin rawhide or tanned hide, and twisted sinew, are employed. The tough vegetable threads, basswood and worm-root fiber, were twisted with the palm on the thigh and used for leather sewing. In bark sewing, however, more diversity and specialized ingenuity are shown, a condition which may possess evolutionary significance in the history of the technique. The stitches with ash splints and spruce root have been previously discussed (page 121). The functions of the animal penis-bone needles have already been mentioned.

Weaving

In addition to the basketry techniques, the Penobscot practised several other forms of weaving which, though still remembered by some of the older people, have long been out of use.

The gray wool which grows thickly near the roots of the hair in the mane of the moose was used as material for thread. The wool was combed from the hair, then rolled on the thigh with the palm of the hand into a kind of yarn. Of these materials, it is said, mittens were made. It is also possible that blankets, socks, and other articles for warmth were woven of moose wool.

Like the far northern Algonkian, the Penobscot remember that various articles of clothing were made of woven strips of rabbit skin. I was told that one of the methods of construction was to braid together broad strips and then join these together by sewing to the width desired.

The inner bark of the basswood tree was, it seems, the material most extensively used in native Penobscot weaving. A few remarks from my own observation relevant to the process of obtaining the bark may be of interest. On several occasions among the islands up river, I attended the gathering of this material. Basswood trees which are free of branches some distance from the ground are sought to be stripped, so that the withes, as they are peeled off, may be as long as possible. The tree bark is cut through with an ax, and the outer bark is loosened at the cut and pulled off upwards in long streamers. The white knotless inner bark is thus exposed and next separated with a knife, so that it may be grasped in the fingers and stripped off in strong strips. As the lengths are obtained they are rolled up into coils and carried to the canoe to be brought home. One old man with whom I traveled had the beguiling habit of singing songs to the pulling of the bark because he thought the bark came off stronger and freer on account of it. Some of the strips not more than two fingers in width and almost as thin as paper held our combined weight when we tried to swing from them. "See what my song do, boy!" said he. "You nebber seen *wuskwa'bi* (basswood bark) come off like dat before." The raw bark is kept in coils until needed. Before the bark is to be used it is boiled for about half a day in a vessel of water containing wood ashes. The lye softens the fibers and extracts the slimy juice which would otherwise make them stiff and brittle when they dry. The stuff may be dyed at this stage. The strips, after being shaved down with a knife to the desired width, are ready to be used as a coarser or finer weaving material.

At this juncture another operation is generally required for the finer work. While drying, the strips are drawn between the thumb and a round smooth bone or stone about six inches long, called *djikta'khigan*, to soften them. Actual fiber thread can be made of it by shaving off thin shreds and twisting them while wet on the thigh with the palm of the hand. Although such articles have long been out of use, nevertheless blankets and mats are recalled to have been formerly manufactured of basswood-bark twine by means of a crude loom.   From a suspended horizontal bar the warps were hung, and with the fingers the finer woof filling was woven or twined in.   Further details were lacking.

Perhaps the commonest method of basswood-bark weaving, one which has survived until recently, is braiding.   The woman who practises this ties a number of lengths to some firm upright; a tree if working out of doors, or a post in the house.   Then she braids them together, moving away from the fastening as her work advances.   The only articles I observed in the making were sled or burden drag-lines and head pack-straps.   For these, six or eight strips somewhat less than half an inch wide, when well braided make a head band about two and a half inches across.   New lengths are inserted when the ends of the strands are reached, the additions not weakening the substance perceptibly.   Figures 22, 30, and 50 show some examples of basswood braiding.   A finer article was made by Alice Swassion at the village near Lincoln.   In it the strands number a dozen or more and are about an eighth of an inch thick.   A zigzag design in blue covers the broad part, which presents a woven surface three inches across.

The weaving of showshoe nettings with rawhide thongs is a matter of vital interest.   As has been described, this technique is the hexagonal twill.

One should remember, however, in estimating the relative importance of weaving in the life of this zone, that the presence of an ever ready supply of birch bark, serviceable for so many purposes, operated unfavorably upon the development of the art of weaving.

One of the few specimens of weaving available for description is the small basswood pouch (Fig. 50) from the upper Penobscot village near Lincoln.   It is five and a half inches square, and is made of basswood fiber of natural color boiled in wood ashes and shredded as usual on a smooth stone held in the hand.   Its construction is as follows.   Across a strong triple-ply strand, twenty-five double-ended woofs were started by the braiding process, resulting in a diagonal checkerwork fabric.   A broad strip of the required length was produced; the sides were folded together and sewed up to form the pouch, and then rounded and turned down for the flap.   The

narrow suspension piece is similarly braided. Weaving and
the making of receptacles is woman's labor. Besides lines of
braided rawhide and of basswood fiber, ropes of braided eelskin are known (*naha'muabi*, "eel rope"). To make them,
large eel skins in the raw state are selected and cut in strips
about an inch wide, then braided in three ply. Such lines
were more serviceable indoors where they were not subject
to wetting.

Dyeing

Dye materials for coloring basket splints, porcupine quills,
and moose hair, bark-cords or strips, and articles of wooden
ware were extracted from vegetable substances. They gather
the materials, put them in a vessel over the fire, cover them
with water, and boil the mixture until the water is highly
colored, after which it can be either diluted or boiled down to
a still darker shade. The stuff to be colored is then soaked
and steeped in the coloring. The native colors are all rather
deep and somber except when used on quills and moose hair.
To supplement those I obtained, Mrs. Eckstorm [51] gives
original notes on dye materials which I quote in parentheses.
Cedar leaves and cedar bark give a rich olive green (Cedar
twigs and elmbark, set with copperas). Alder bark gives a
dark red (Solomon's seal, various berries, blueberries and
bloodroot, set with alum). Rotten wood gives a dark blue
(Indigo). White maple gives a light blue. Ash bark and
ash bark ashes give yellow (Root of gold-thread). By adding
more and more cedar dye to the dark olive stain, a black dye
will be produced. Hemlock or pine bark gives a dark reddish-
brown (Alder bark set with copperas).

Veins of clay found here and there in the country gave red,
yellow, and other colors, so they say. From these a powder
was made, which, mixed with water, formed coloring matter.
Red was abundantly obtained at different places on Olemon
Island. Here are the primary native color terms: *me'kwi'guk*,
red; *me'kaze'wik'*, black, brown; *wabi'guk*, white; *wiza'wiguk*,
yellow; *wasasa'tstik*, yellow, ("pumpkin color"); *e'nigewa'tstik*, blue color; *e'skibagwa'tstik-*, green, "leaf color."

[51] Eckstorm, 1, p. 24.

The general term for color is *a'tstik*, a lighter shade is designated by *mamala'tstik*, "shaded or spotted color," a darker by *me'kaze'wiguk*, "dark," also "brown."

Wabanaki tradition describes for a former period complete body clothing made of the skins of animals. From the time of early contact with the French and English, however, cloth obtained in trade came to be substituted for skins, though, as we are told, in the transitional garments native patterns of tailoring were preserved. The indications of Iroquoian influence may also be remarked. On the other hand, it cannot yet be stated just how far the Iroquois themselves adopted Algonkian ideas of garb during the period of their acclimatization in the north. Native styles of ornamentation also survived in the new clothing materials, bead-work and ribbon appliqué taking the place of moose hair, possibly some porcupine-quill embroidery and painting. The account of the elements of native costume is derived from tradition, from old pieces preserved among the Indians and in museums, and from models made by old people who remembered seeing or using them before they became obsolete by about 1850.[52]

The men ordinarily wore moccasins, leggings, a breech-cloth, a short skirt or kilt, and a characteristically northeastern long-sleeved coat. The women, for as far back as can be remembered, were clothed likewise in moccasins, leggings, a breech-cloth, a skirt reaching about halfway down the calf of the leg, and an upper garment reaching below the waist. Upon their heads they wore a conical high-pointed cap.

Long, square-cut, sleeved coats, *baskwana'si*, "back cover," were characteristic of the men's full dress costumes of a wide area, including the Penobscot, from Southern New England to the Micmac and northward through the Labrador peninsula. No particular differences have been noticed between Penobscot, Passamaquoddy, Malecite, or Micmac long cloth coats, though the descriptions given here are based primarily

---

[52] In connection with these notes Mrs. Eckstorm's valuable section on Penobscot dress should be consulted (see Eckstorm, pp. 68–70.)

FIG. 58

CHIEF'S LONG COAT OF BROADCLOTH AND WHITE BEADWORK

upon Penobscot articles. Since essentially similar garments
are found among the Naskapi and Montagnais of Labrador,
the evidence for their being a native type stands as a plausible
assumption until the contrary be proved. The pattern of the
long coat, which seems in historic times to have been a garment intended for dress occasions, is quite simple. It reaches
halfway to the knee, has a square-cut bottom, is open down
the front, and includes sleeves, *pitənα'gan*, and across the
back a broad flap-like collar with lapels (Fig. 58). The
field of ornamentation is upon the collar, the shoulder seams,
which were sometimes covered with decorated epaulets,
around the cuffs, up
the front opening, and
around the lower border
of the skirt part. The
whole field of art in
clothing characteristic
of the region consists of
series of designs bearing
a prophylactic plant
and flower symbolism,
with certain interpre-
tations of a civil char-
acter in a later period
of confederation (1750?)
acquired through the
stimulation of Iroquois
alliance. In all extant
specimens, beadwork
and ribbon-work take
the place of the early
painting and the sup-
posed moose-hair work.

FIG. 59

Early Type of Moose-Skin Sleeved
Coat with Painted Designs

A supposedly au-
thentic specimen of the
Penobscot man's coat
of the earlier period is
shown in Fig. 59. It is made of tanned moose skin with
fringe down the sleeves, across the collar, down the front

and around the skirt.   It is open down the front and has one fastening of thong.   Around the cuffs, down the front opening and around the skirt runs a diamond and zigzag linear design in dark blue dye.   Around the skirt is a diamond design of the type found similarly employed among Algonkian tribes east of the seventieth degree of longitude south of the St. Lawrence [33] and northward throughout the Hudson Bay region.   Similar long coats of deer and caribou skin, and open down the front, were worn by the men in summer and winter.

In a period within memory the men's leggings, *kwene'zonal*, also mostly of red and blue cloth, reached from above the knee to the ankle where they were tucked, in winter time, into the top of the moccasin.   Such cloth leggings have a flap several inches wide decorated with beadwork and ribbon appliqué, while leather ones had fringe along the seam.   The breeching cloth, *wule'ge*, "diaper," of tanned skin was tucked under the belt before and behind.   Nothing is stated of decorations on the breech cloth.   The hips and thighs were in later times covered also with a pair of short pants called *pɔ'ldjisɑk*, "breeches" (derived from English).   Leggings, as remembered by some of the old people, were also made of muskrat skins sewed together, fringeless and plain.   Wealthy hunters also wore, pulled over the leg, leggings made of the entire tanned skin of a large otter.   Both of the latter fashions were for winter use, no imagination on our part being required to conceive their warmth and barbaric splendor.

The man's kilt, however, is an article of local occurrence, reported in the east only among the northeastern Algonkian and Iroquois.   No Penobscot specimens, unfortunately, are now available for description.   Originally a deer-skin wrapped about the loins, this garment came to be an elaborately ornamented element of attire.   Cloth and beadwork with whatever ornamentation they carried, a memory no longer preserved, later replaced the buckskin (Fig. 30).

[53] Distribution based upon Mahikan evidence in literature (A. B. Skinner, *Notes on Mahikan Ethnology*, Bulletin Public Museum of Milwaukee, vol. II, No. 3, 1952), and especially F. W. Hodge and W. C. Orchard, *John W. Quinney's Coat*, Indian Notes, Museum American Indian, N. Y., vol. VI, 1929, pp. 343–351.

FIG. 60

MEN'S CEREMONIAL CAPE–COLLARS

Bead Work on Broadcloth
Upper, Ancient Style of Decoration in Double-Curves
Lower, Later Style in Floral Patterns

The men—who often went naked above the waist upon occasions when the coats were not worn—had separate decorated wrist-bands or cuffs for dress occasions, and a broad decorated cape or collar, *pa'tɑn* (Figs. 60, 65).   A relationship is perceivable between the long coat with its ornamented collar, cuffs, and skirt, and the separate collar, cuffs, and kilt, detached from the body of the coat and worn as ornaments, as though the ornamented areas of the long-coat had become detached to be worn over the bare skin.   Sometimes a shirt (*ɑtu'thɑ'wi*) of skin was worn.

The men's headdresses are of special significance.   There are the hunting caps with two ears, *wazə'muwi'sik*) (Fig. 9), intended for decoys, besides others of a more decorative nature.   The decorated headband with gull, great blue heron, eagle, or hawk feathers fastened stiffly upright all around was a common article of fancy dress —the coronet with rigid feathers.   In this connection the pose of the heron with beak pointed skyward was given as the reason for its "holiness."   The beaded headband also sometimes had partridge wings, one on each side, or a partridge tail in front or behind.   The most typical ornamental headdress was, however, the decorated headband with a circlet of feathers or a single large feather upright at the rear (Figs. 59 and 61).   Weymouth [54] (1605) described a "kind of coronet . . . made very cunningly of a substance like stiff hair colored red, broad and

FIG. 61

NEWELL GABRIEL

In Full Ceremonial Dress

[54] Quoted by Willoughby (ref. 3), p. 506.

FIG. 62

CLARA PAUL

In Native Full Dress of Period about 1840
Note the Traditional "War Bow" and Silver Brooches

more than a handful in depth." By this curt description we recognize that remarkable warrior's insignia, the deer-bristle "roach," the history and distribution of which commencing, it may be, in eastern North America remains an important topic for interpretative research. Head coverings in general are termed *agwu'skwe'zun*.

We now come to the special articles of woman's attire. Of major importance is the skirt, *ala'bizun*, "lower covering strip" (Fig. 62), a simple doubled length of skin, in historic times of cloth, reaching from the waist to the middle of the lower leg. Upon the seam, which is prolonged into a flap, beadwork and ribbon-work furnish ornamentation. The specimen figured is of red strouding with bands of blue ribbon. The ribbon-work at the sides is of blue and yellow. Such skirts, as will be seen, were more or less profusely decorated with silver brooches, evidently another emanation from Iroquoian culture. The skirt is forty inches wide and thirty-eight long. It is pulled up at the waist and made secure by a string. Underneath the skirt the women wore leggings (Figs. 62 and 63) reaching from the knee to cover the ankle. Like the men's leggings these had decorated outer flaps.

The woman's upper garment or waist is said to have originally been made of weasel or hare skins sewed together after the legs had been trimmed off, so that the edges would meet. The later historic overwaist is of some bright colored calico stuff (Fig. 62) with a frilled edge reaching well below the waist. Large silver brooches, in the more prosperous early colonial days, ornamented the breast of this garment and served as clasps down the front opening. The overwaist is called *ma'tlet*.

Even as late as the last generation, the women wore the long peaked, hood-like caps, *gwənuskwa'kʷsəs·ak*, "long pointed," so characteristic of the northeastern peoples (Fig. 63). As with Indian garments where cloth was substituted at an early period for buckskin, so it happened with the "squaw-cap." Then, too, the moose-hair embroidery was transferred to beadwork. The average Penobscot cap is fourteen inches long, with a rounded lower edge, the squared lower edge being

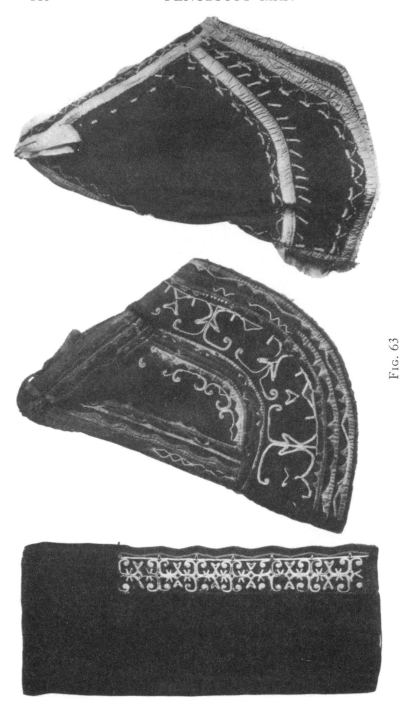

F_{IG.} 63

WOMAN'S BROADCLOTH LEGGING AND CAPS

With Designs in White Beadwork

a Micmac and Malecite distinction. One specimen was of
dark blue cloth with beadwork and ribbon-work, having
several rows of cylindrical beads in imitation of the original
wampum. It showed the manner in which the latter was
originally used as a means of decoration. Another is of red
cloth with white beads and ribbon appliqué. These hats
are understood to have been proper only for married women.
There are, nevertheless, instances in which they have been
used by men, especially in winter. They are evidently derived from the protective hood worn when traveling in snowy
forests. Some of the women wear the head-covering continuously, some seldom removing it even at night. Hand-
kerchiefs nowadays have replaced the peaked caps.

Birch bark seems also to have played some part in clothing.
It is a matter of tradition among old people that conical hats
of birch bark were worn in rainy weather, and that similarly
made birch-bark capes went with them. In dances, and as
a form of ornament, it is also stated, a kind of skirt or kilt
of the same material, and leggings or greaves for the lower leg
were used. This approaches a costume of birch bark, which,
I was informed, also served anciently as a suit of armor if
made thick enough. Plain conical bark hats for protection
in the woods against inclement weather and snow are still
occasionally made by hunters.

The Penobscot still make moccasins of deer and moose
skin. Several types of footwear prevail: the loose slipper
worn indoors and when the wet moccasins are drying after
a day's journeying, the low heavy shoe-pack or oiled moose-
hide moccasin worn in the woods, and the entire moose hock
serving as a boot for winter wear. A characteristic of the
Penobscot man's and woman's moccasin, ma'ksən, is a wide
vamp to which the sole is puckered and sewed. The creases
in the puckering of fifteen pairs of moccasins from the tribe
range between twenty-eight and thirty. The pattern is cut
so as to draw up the front just a little, the upturn being
considered convenient in walking through grass. Decorations of recent Penobscot-Malecite specimens consist of three
characteristic flowers in beadwork, connected by stems with
a few conventional leaves. An old pair of Penobscot mocca-

sins in the Peabody Museum, Cambridge, shows the same
general figures in moose-hair work, from which design the
beaded patterns seem to have been derived.   In later work,
from the hands of adopted Malecite, the beadwork is sewed
on velvet attached to the vamp.   An attractive creamy
white tan is seen on the house moccasin.   The heavy dark-
colored moosehide moccasins for outdoor use are sewed
with a stout thong.   A thong lacing goes around the top and
is fastened with an invariable knot.   The young have a
saying that when this works loose it is a sign that the wearer
is being thought of by a lover.   In summer time it was worn
over the bare foot, in winter time over several layers of warm
stockings formerly made of hare skin, and nowadays of
knitted wool.   Ordinarily the foot wrappings, *asi'ganal*, consisted of quantities of old skins or rags.   Leather taps are
sewed over the heel or toe or both when they wear through.

The moose-hock boots, *abu'nkaznak*, are exceptionally
serviceable in this country during the snows of winter
and the thaws of spring.   To make them, the skin is
peeled from each whole hind leg of the moose.   The hair is
left on and the entire hock may be tanned in recent days,
though formerly they say it was left raw.   The middle of the
lower joint is cut through and bound closed with a tight seam.
Except perhaps for a little taking in at the rear top, the boot
is now complete.   Some have a lacing across the front, though
this is an innovation.   As foot coverings, they are warm,
waterproof, do not chafe while snowshoeing, and do not slip
as badly on the ice as moccasins.   Kept in the wet state,
untanned, they were left at the back of the wigwam away
from the fire, rolled up tight when not in use (also Eckstorm,
I, p. 50).

In Rosier's time (1605) the dress of the natives of Penobscot Bay was described as follows:

Their clothing is Beaver skins, or Deers skins, cast over them
like a mantle, and hanging down to their knees, made fast together
upon the shoulders with leather; some of them had sleeves, most
had buskins of such leather *tewed:* they have besides a piece of
Beavers skin between their legs, made fast about their waist, to
cover their privities.[55]

[55] Rosier, p. 368.

An article on the dress of the New England Indians by Willoughby [56] gives information from early sources on the dress of the tribes south of the Penobscot. No evidence has been met so far to show that the feather mantles made by the southern New England tribes were known as far north as the Penobscot.

Both sexes wore mittens, *maldje'sak*, in winter, made of fur or woven and knitted from moose wool. They were attached over the shoulder by a thong to prevent their being lost. None of native make, however, have been obtainable. Socks, *kəne'zonal*, were also knitted from moose wool twisted into threads between the thigh and palm, and then knitted with two sticks.

Hairdressing and Face Painting

The men formerly wore their hair long, reaching to the shoulders or the waist, generally confined by a headband. Boys had theirs sometimes cropped like a bang across the forehead. This is still observed by a few. Though the men have now, as they did formerly, combs and brushes to manage their hair with, yet the greatest laxity prevails in its arrangement. One of the marks of old-fashioned conservative Wabanaki hunters is a tousled head.

The women parted their hair in the middle and gathered it behind the head where it was tied into a cylindrical knot or "club," over which was wrapped and tied the end of an ornamented strip of skin or cloth. The skin of a water snake was frequently so used. This hair ornament, of cloth two by twelve inches long, is said to have been more in vogue among married women, who wore their hair up. One still finds old-fashioned women wearing their hair tied up in a roll or coil at the back of the neck with a rag or kerchief tied about the head. Sometimes they wear a single braid. The hair-pad is called *pahkwa'bəlɑgaŋ*. Another style, still occasionally followed, was to tie it with a string at the back of the neck and allow the rest to flow free down the shoulders. The ornamented strip was formerly fastened to the place

[56] Willoughby (ref. 3).

where the locks were bound.   The women think that braiding the hair, particularly that of children, augments its growth.

Says Rosier of the men (1605), "They suffer no haire to grow on their faces, but on their head very long and very black, which those that have wives binde up behind with a leather string in a long round knot." [57]

The little that could be gathered regarding face painting is as follows: The men regarded painting as a formality intended for war, dances, and festivities.   The paint, *wəla'·man*, obtained from varicolored clay streaks on the islands, was kept in a bowl which was covered to preserve its magic potency and color.   Because the veins of the "earth whence the clay comes lie in darkness, so the paint must be kept in darkness."   Before ceremonies, the men, one by one and alone, went into the wigwam where the paint was kept, and decorated themselves.   Some of the individual patterns, purely aesthetic in purpose as remembered, are: a blue and a white stripe on each cheek from the nose to the angle of the jaw; three vertical blue or white lines above bridge of the nose; one blue between two white bars, or the reverse, on the cheeks; and three white and two blue vertical bars on the forehead.   Black, red, yellow, and blue stripes were also put on the cheeks extending from the eye to the corner of the jaw. The usual areas of painting seem to have been between the eyebrows and above the nose, from the corner of the mouth to the chin and the cheeks.   Warriors also painted their naked backs to indicate exploits.   "They paint their bodies with blacks, their faces with red, some with blacks, some with blew." [58]

Special paintings were still used in 1914 in some of the dances and ceremonies.   When the mourning is removed from a widow, a dance is given in which the participants wear across the forehead a bar of red put on by an old woman. This denotes renewal of joy.   A black bar about three inches wide was put obliquely across the face of men during the election ceremony, as a sign of mourning until the new chief was installed, when it was cleaned off.

[57] Rosier, p. 368.
[58] Rosier, p. 368.

Quantities of red paint were probably obtained from disintegrated iron ore in certain portions of the soil of Maine, much of the supply having come, as Moorehead shows, from the present vicinity of Katahdin Iron Works. The extensive use of it in this region is shown by its abundance in prehistoric graves explored by Willoughby in the neighborhood of Penobscot Bay.[59] Olemon (wəla'·man, "red paint") Island was a favorite resort for parties desiring supplies of paint.

People up to a few years ago commonly dyed their finger nails a bright yellow for beauty's sake. The dye was obtained from the ripened blossom of the snapdragon, adjəs·ika'siawan, "stain finger nail." To apply it the blossom was tied to the finger nail for a few minutes. The stain would remain for weeks and was fancied by young men and girls.

Personal Toilet

In caring for their persons several articles were made use of. Combs, na'skun, are made of wood, two and a half to three inches across with deeply notched teeth (Fig. 64). The men used the same articles to curry their favorite dogs with. For a hair brush or comb cleaner, an article possessed by nearly every Indian family, the dried skin of a porcupine's tail is brought into use, ma'-dawes·walo'sis, "porcupine's little tail" (Fig. 64). Frank Jo, from whom I obtained one of

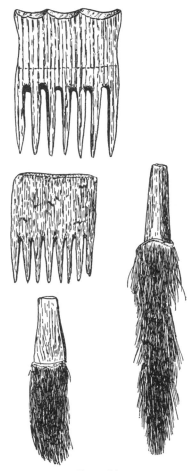

Fig. 64

Wooden Combs and Porcupine-Tail Comb Cleaners

[59] Willoughby, ref. 4, p. 49.

the tails, declared: "I lost my little boy some years ago and went hunting. I came across an old porcupine and killed him; cut off his tail for a brush. But he looked at me so sadly that I was sorry I killed him. He looked just like the little boy. I am sorry to part with that brush, but you may take it."

A wooden back scratcher literally *gitcigibskuna'lzodi'*, is used among the older women. Evenings they sit around and scratch themselves under their clothes in private, with puffings and snorts, it feels so good. The usual scratcher is a piece of thin ash, fourteen to twenty-four inches long, with a bend an inch or so wide, sometimes notched and carved. With the long handle one can reach far down the limbs and back without removing the clothes. To display one or to refer to it invariably produces laughter, though they are sometimes given mischievously as presents. Inferentially the back scratcher appears to be a relic of vermin times, when the people dressed solely in skins and were infested with lice. No one could for a moment, however, now accuse the Penobscot of harboring filth.

A toothpick is made from the raccoon's penis bone, which is white and strong. By chewing the end of a piece of soft juicy wood they keep the tooth surfaces white. About the camps, a chip, or a piece of splint serves the purpose of toilet paper, but off in the woods the men cut and shave the sides of a twig down to an edge resembling a rustic knife. They used to trim the hair by means of a clam or mussel shell, sawing this against a flat pebble. Toothpicks, *ska'nis*, "little bone," are still used, made from the penis bone of mink, sable or otter, and from the pointed bone (metacarpal) found in the foreleg of the deer.

So far as could be learned, there was no custom of pulling out the face hair, although Rosier mentions it.[60] Straggly, stiff mustaches and occasional short thin beards are common among the darker men. The practice of shaving, which many now follow, is said to augment the growth.

In the old days lice were removed from garments by holding them directly over a fire, the heat of which would

[60] Cf. Rosier, p. 368, see quotation on preceding page, note 57.

cause the vermin to drop into the flames. Skin clothes were washed by beating them between stones in the river.

Ornaments

It is difficult to draw the line between unconventional personal ornament, and amulets, yet here the idea of adornment seems to exceed.

Necklaces of red beads, several rows wide, were formerly worn by the women, partly for ornament, partly to protect themselves from excessive bleeding and blood affections. One or two aged women still follow the custom. Woven necklaces (Fig. 78) of beadwork, the weave being that of wampum strips and similar neckbands, direct imitations of the wampum, were made. One specimen is thirty-two inches long and seven-eighths of an inch wide, with alternating green and red triangles, bordered in white. Another small one for a child is one-fourth of an inch wide, having a green background with red, black, and blue spool-like figures, and a pendant hammered out of a dime. Girls' necklaces of loose-strung glass beads were fastened to ribbons tied about the neck.

A necklace, *wusku'-zəwan*, common among the men, especially hunters who regarded it as a sign or boast of success,

FIG. 65

SOL NEPTUNE

Penobscot Chief in Full Ceremonial
Dress, About 1875

consisted of deer antler prongs and deer hoofs bored and strung on leather. Necklaces of bear's claws, when worn by men, indicated high rank, and were considered as a protective charm if the wearer had killed the bear himself. A specimen strung on red beads is shown, the bear, a so-called "ranger bear," having been killed in 1876, and the necklace kept as a trophy.

Armbands, brooches (*niskama'nɔl*), headbands, and medals of cold-beaten silver were worn by the men (Fig. 65). Within memory, no one in the tribe has practised silversmithing, so I have nothing further to say of the process than that it included beating, hammering, and punching. The brooches range from one-half to six inches in diameter and were etched. The larger ones were chiefs' insignia, to be worn on the breast. There seems to be little doubt of the derivation of silver ornaments, if not the industry itself, from tribes west and south of them, who, in turn, had them from Europeans.

Wampum was also extensively used by both sexes in the construction of necklaces, collars, and neckbands. The importance of wampum as a means of recording will be dealt with under a separate heading. Several collars and necklaces are illustrated there.

III

DECORATIVE DESIGNS AND TECHNIQUES

DECORATIVE designing throughout the northeast was fairly alike in technique, in interpretative symbolism, and in motive. The native populations on both sides of the St. Lawrence seem to have had, during the historic period to be sure, the same relative categories in their art. The Penobscot and other Wabanaki divisions shared common properties. The problem of original design content in this region is, however, by no means a simple one, for the occurrence of realistic floral motives here as the basis of decoration raises inevitably a question as to its extent of influence exerted upon local art forms by Europeans. It is well known, of course, that from the twelfth century onward, floral motives came into great prominence in the development of design throughout western Europe. That northeastern Algonkian art has responded generously to the stimulus provided by early association with white people there can be little doubt. The whole question which is coming in for full, but rather delayed attention in discussion of recent art history is how to account for the beginnings of floral realism among the northeastern Indians without being prejudiced in the direction of accepting a European origin for them when indications on the surface seem to point to this as the simple answer. Nevertheless, until the matter of the original design properties of the northeastern Indians is cleared up, it will continue to remain open for discussion from both angles. It requires the accumulation of some dependable information on the art of the region in the period prior to European contact, as well as more complete distributional studies of historic techniques and concepts of decoration. Interest in the possibilities of this engrossing theme induced me to present, in 1914, a short survey of the character and distribution of the design motive—the double curve—most distinctive of the whole northeastern territory.[1] Penobscot designs figured prominently in this

[1] *The Double-Curve Motive in Northeastern Algonkian Art.* Anthropological Series, No. 1, Memoir 42, Geological Survey of Canada, 1914.

essay. Then, after a final visit to the village at Oldtown to test out and elaborate the knowledge of Penobscot motives already acquired, I prepared a monograph giving illustrations of practically all the specimens of decoration from the tribe existing in the collections of the country, and offering evidence of an early symbolism, with interpretations traced through several periods in the art of the tribe until its final recent disappearance.[2] The study in question is destined to be one of a series dealing specifically with decorative processes of northern Algonkian tribes until material representing developments over a wide area becomes available for consideration.[3] This having been done for the Penobscot, it remains to incorporate only a shortened summary of ornamentation and technique drawn from the paper referred to.

In its flourishing era, as it is known from specimens and the evidence of tradition, Penobscot, like other Wabanaki art, found its chief expression in white beadwork on a foundation of red and black broadcloth. The lines of the white designs were open and fine, and took the form of curves turning inward, facing each other. This has come to be termed the "double-curve" motive. Preceding the late historic period, it has been assumed that the same designs existed, originally painted upon the leather garments for which cloth material was substituted after the coming of the traders. We next trace a period in the advance of art in the region when the double-curve figures began to give way to pure floral patterns worked out in lines tending toward actual realism after the style of European decoration. There is evidence to show the transition of Wabanaki art through all three phases. A survey of the designs most typical of the tribe will bring out the predominance of the double curve, followed in later times by realistic floral art. The aspect of the problem, however, changes when one considers the bearing that the painted designs of the still uncivilized Naskapi of the Labrador peninsula have upon it. For unless European derivation be proved

[2] *Symbolism in Penobscot Art.* Anthropological Papers, American Museum of Natural History, N. Y., vol. XXIX, Part II, 1927.
[3] *Montagnais Art in Birch-Bark, A Circumpolar Trait,* Indian Notes and Monographs, Museum of the American Indian, vol. XI, no. 2, 1937.

for the latter, they will stand as existing prototypes of the painted designs of adjacent culturally related areas where floral motives are mentioned in early documents as properties of tribes from the Labrador coast through the lower St. Lawrence and the Maritime provinces as far south as southern New England.[4] What effect the Penobscot contribution may have upon the accumulation of positive evidence touching the question of aboriginality of the flower-like curve figures here still remains to be seen (Figs. 66, 67). Whatever ultimate decision on ancestry may be accorded the design content of the northeastern Indians, the fact emerges uncertainly in view of the conflict of theories, that from the era shortly after European contact the Wabanaki peoples were garbed in skin clothing bearing designs answering to the description of scrolls if not leaves and flowers. From this we may infer that the typical double curves so predominant in the older manufactures of the Penobscot, as we meet them in the illustrations appearing in the studies already published, had become characteristic culture properties of the natives, and had acquired culture value in their aesthetic, social, and magic-religious reactions.

A few remarks borrowed from the memoir referred to will serve as a summary for the present purpose. As regards function, a significant and at the same time an unusual feature characterizes Penobscot designs, which so far as I am yet aware, is unrecorded of other tribes outside of the northeastern area, and has recently been commented upon by Boas for America in general. The plant representations were, before the decadence of native views, associated with the protective and

[4] Among the older authorities who invite us to consider the history of the technique is one from New England. Daniel Gookin (1647), the first Indian Commissioner of Massachusetts, in *Historical Collections of the Indians of New England*, is the author of clear testimony in regard to the material and decoration of the pails and baskets of the natives of his time. "Their pails to fetch water in are made of birch bark. . . . Some of their baskets [are made] of barks of trees, many of them very neat and artificial with the portraitures of birds, beasts, fishes and flowers upon them in colours." This appears to be the earliest reference giving definite description of the bark receptacle in terms that we can recognize as applying to the birch-bark constructions and their ornamentation. Gookin's remarks allude to observations made among the tribes of New England and could have been strictly applicable to the Penobscot as we know their art and industry from contemporary sources. As such his description applies to the related groups whose techniques and forms of decoration we find preserved for our consideration to the present day. It is accordingly no longer upon dubious or feeble bibliographical support that our knowledge of the early floral designs rests.

FIG. 66

DOUBLE-CURVE DESIGNS IN BEADWORK AND CARV-
ING SHOWING MODIFICATIONS FROM SIMPLEST
TO THE MOST COMPLEX FIGURES

FIG. 67

POWDER HORNS INCISED WITH DOUBLE-CURVE
DESIGNS

Also Used as Dance Rattles

curative properties of medicinal herbs which are so important
to these Indians. While it may be going too far to assert,
from present-day sources, that the designs were placed upon
objects for the definite purposes of invoking magic protection,
it seems probable, nevertheless, that originally among women
this purpose prevailed. Discussing matters among the older
people, I gradually became aware of a therapeutic function
subconsciously underlying their floral art. I infer that what
exists now, merely as a vestige, was formerly a marked trait.

In a few instances, however, we encounter a different
spirit of symbolism in the floral and double-curve designs.

It was among the men that the double curve seems often to have been employed as a symbol of peace, *gizagwo'dawak*, or *gizau'ditpitak* (Fig. 68). The opposed half-curves represented social and civil bonds holding the people of the tribe together as a common body. Such an interpretation cannot, however,

a

b

Fig. 68

Double-Curve Designs with "Political" Symbolism

be ascribed to every occurrence of the double curve. This applies more when used upon dance ornaments, beaded coats, capes, collars, cuffs, pipes, and wampum, objects employed as symbolic regalia in political celebrations and ceremonies.

Decorative techniques follow lines determined by the object to be decorated and the materials employed. The typical double-curve designs, for instance, occur upon garments and allied articles, formerly of moose or deer skin, but characteristically on broadcloth ornamented with beadwork. The realistic flower figures also predominate upon articles of the same materials which comprise head dresses, women's pointed caps, chief's collar-capes, cuffs, lacings and collars of coats, leggings, wristbands, belts, pouches, women's skirts, and dress moccasins. Illustrations throughout the volume show their varied form and use.

An interesting substitution for embroidered designs on border areas of these articles is to be found in the ribbon appliqué sweeping curves and angular ornamentations which are so common in Iroquois, Delaware, and central Algonkian ornamentation. The colors and outlines of the lines, dentations, scallops, of the ribbon appliqué patterns find an analogy as well in the painted border designs of the distant Naskapi—a significant occurrence indeed.

In carvings on wood, stone, or etchings on birch bark, the double curve is also found. And the geometrical figures, triangles, diamond, and composites occur abundantly in addition to realistic animal likenesses. The flower designs are usually lacking upon birch-bark vessels, birch-bark baskets and dishes. These objects are ornamented mostly with etched double curves and life forms, which, like the techniques themselves, are of an older genus. Again in wooden implements such as basket splint cutters or gauges, knife handles, cradle boards, boxes, spoons, and wooden objects in general, powder horns, horn dance rattles, and articles of soft stone such as pipes, both the double curves and simple curved and geometrical ornaments occur in profusion.

PORCUPINE QUILL AND MOOSE HAIR DECORATION

Embroidery with porcupine quills was, I believe, not extensively practised by the Penobscot, from what can now be learned. Pipe stems were at one time, however, commonly decorated with quill wrappings in varied colors. An example

FIG. 69

STONE TOBACCO PIPES WITH MOOSE-HAIR
EMBROIDERY AND PORCUPINE-QUILL STEMS

is shown in Fig. 69, the details of which are described by Mr. Orchard. Each quill encircles the stem once, the turned-up ends abutting on one another in the center of the under side (Fig. 70). The quills, before being used, have their barbed points trimmed off, and are kept in bundles. When

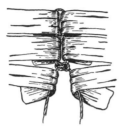

FIG. 70

Detail of Fastening Ends of Porcupine Quills in Decorative Wrapping on Pipe Stem

needed for work they are wet in the mouth and flattened by being drawn between thumb and a flat, round-edged piece of moose bone. A variety of false embroidery is produced on the upper side by interlaying quills perpendicularly to the wrapping—a device common in America, especially in the northern regions. While birch-bark vessels were thought by some informants to have been ornamented with quill-mosaic like that still done by the Micmac and northern central Algonkian, no Penobscot specimens of unquestioned identity have been preserved to prove its occurrence here.

Mrs. Eckstorm, with sufficient caution, regards several examples in the Abbe Museum to be of Penobscot origin.[5] I should, however, prefer to consider them, like the examples of moose-hair work, as intrusions; in this case indirectly from the Micmac.

The technique of moose-hair embroidery on leather is represented by only two old specimens from Penobscot in the Heye collection, identical with that of the Huron and Malecite, where it was until recently alive.[6] Bunches of from three to five hairs were sewed to the buckskin with the whip stitch, to form floral designs. As in Huron symbolism, the figures (Fig. 69) represent vines, balsam fir, trees, and stumps, with zigzag borders. The occurrence of the moose-hair technique which I listed in 1914 for the Penobscot is now seriously open to question. Mrs. Eckstorm has convincingly shown that the articles obtained from them were probably em-

[5] Eckstorm, I, p. 38–43, pl. XV–XVI.

[6] From the Malecite on the St. John River in New Brunswick I have collected similar articles. Cf. Speck, "Huron Moose Hair Embroidery," *American Anthropologist*, (N. S.) Vol. XIII, No. 1 (1911).

broidered by Huron with whom, over sixty years ago, they communicated.[7]

BARK ETCHING

The birch-bark etchings are made by heating bark that has been peeled in winter time and wetting it until quite soft, when it can be readily etched down to the lighter under-layer with a knife-point. A rich dark color is given to the bark by applying a hot rag saturated with a dye made by boiling alder bark. The designs incised appear in the lighter color of the under bark, while the dark outer bark serves as the background. In the bark etchings of the Montagnais, the process is the opposite, where all the dark part is scraped away, leaving the design. Greasing, when all is done, greatly improves the appearance of this work. The double curves appear to great advantage on such a surface, and representations of moon crescents, trees, and game animals are numerous.[8]

SINGING AND MUSICAL INSTRUMENTS

The Penobscot had comparatively few musical instruments, only the hand rattle, the drum by tradition, and a kind of end flute, the form of which has been forgotten. The hand rattle for dancing is the only instrument of which we have definite knowledge, it being quite extensively used yet in social dances. This instrument, *aha'lnan* (from English "horn"), or *aha'lnosis*, "little horn," was formerly a small hollow gourd containing dried pumpkin seeds, pierced by a stick for a handle. In later times this became entirely replaced by a cow's horn scraped thin, containing buckshot, and plugged at the end with a disc of wood, in fact an ordinary powder horn of flint-and-cap-lock rifle days. These instruments were often highly decorated with etchings in characteristic double-curve designs and realistic representations of animals (Fig. 67). An earlier form variation was made of a cone of birch bark closed at the top with bark and fastened

[7] Eckstorm, I. p. 38.

[8] For detailed discussion and analysis of birch-bark techniques and decoration in the northeast, see Montagnais Art in Birch-Bark (Bibliography, Speck, no. 4), and for Penobscot treatment and illustrations, Speck, The Double Curve Motive, 1914. Mrs. Eckstorm devotes some space to the topic in her monograph, I, pp. 46-8.

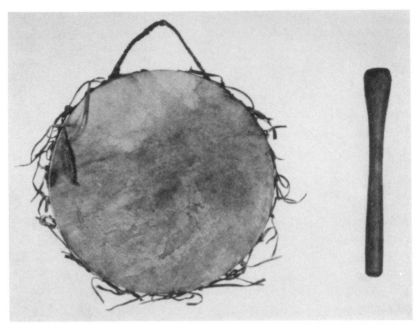

FIG. 71

DOUBLE–HEADED DRUM AND WOODEN BEATER

on a wooden handle. The rattle is held in the right hand by
the dance leader, its broad end up, and is struck against the
open palm of the other hand, or, to vary the sound, vibrated
sidewise sometimes on a level with the head, sometimes down
near the floor. The leaders are very wiry and nimble, adopting various grotesque attitudes while their arms and legs are
going. One peculiarity about the rattling is that the beats
do not correspond to foot beats throughout the dancing, nor
to the rhythm of the music.

The details of the drum, *pekhola'gan*, "instrument beaten,"
are as follows (From a specimen made in 1912 by the dance
leader [Fig. 71]): On a hoop three and a half inches wide and
eleven inches in diameter, a head of green deerskin is stretched
on each side, laced all around with babiche somewhat irregularly. A wrapped handle of rawhide is fastened on one side.
Across one face two strings of babiche are strung to act as
snares, while around the opposite face a row of babiche strings

represents fringe. The drumstick is of cedar, ten and a half inches long and one and a half wide at the head. The presence of the snare here is interesting, since the same is also encountered through the Algonkian area north of the St. Lawrence in Labrador.[9] The Penobscot regard the buzzing noise made by the snares as "singing."

To furnish a primitive tympanic accompaniment for dancing, we have beating without a drum. In one dance, the *Nawa'dawe*, or Micmac Dance, the single singer furnishing the song strikes a rattle or short stick on the floor, or on the bottom of an unturned bark vessel, to beat time.

A flute, *bi·bi·'gwadi·*, "blowing (onomatopœic) tube," was known, but particulars as to construction are not forthcoming. It was used by shamans on account of the magic influence of its tones. It was also said to have been used to furnish music for dancing. As among the southern and western tribes, the Penobscot played love tunes on their flutes and called them "lonesome songs." A story told by an old man at Lincoln illustrates the idea.

There was an elderly woman who never got married, but who kept company very much with a young man. Her name was *ɑmi'knak*ʷ (a species of bug with a hard shell). The young man played very beautifully on the Indian flute. At last a quarrel arose between the lovers, and they separated. Some years after, *ɑmi'-knak*ʷ was one of a party of berry pickers in the country north. The young man followed her, and one day while the women were among the berry bushes picking, he climbed a tree and began playing one of the old favorite songs. *ɑmi'knak*ʷ heard it, and when the women went back to camp she told her friends what had happened and began to cry. "Oh! It makes me feel so sad, that lonesome song. Boo-hoo!" It did not take long for her to join forces with her lover after that.

The songs are of half a dozen or more different kinds. There are the dance songs chanted in unison by leader and dancers, sung alternately in syllables by the leader and chorus of dancers like antiphonies, and those sung only by a one- or two-man orchestra in which the dancers do not join. Details

[9] Specimens collected by the writer from the Montagnais and Naskapi, cf. Turner, pp. 324–5. See Speck, *Naskapi*, Univ. of Okla. Press, 1935.

of these procedures will be given with examples later. Besides compositions of this type there are songs for special occasions, such as burial, marriage, canoeing, gaming, and others, as well as simple humorous or obscene songs for pastime occasions, and lullabies. There was also an important class of myth-songs to which whole stories were formerly sung. Those intended for special occasions will be given under their appropriate headings, while a few examples not falling under other headings appear below. In all cases they were recorded on the phonograph and transcribed by Mr. J. D. Sapir. In native terminology an ordinary song is *ali'ntowa'gan;* a "dance song" is called *pəməge'wintowa'gan.*

Here, as elsewhere, dance songs consist chiefly of meaningless syllables, one group or bar of which is uttered by the leader, while the alternating group serves as a response rising from the chorus of dancers. Alternating or "round" songs of this type have been recorded from the entire eastern and southern area. The dance leader, who shakes a hand rattle, sings a burden of from three to five syllables, upon the last note of which the body of dancers unites in another dependent burden of shorter duration. Then the leader repeats his burden, perhaps varying the tones a little. So the dance concert continues, with the rhythmic alternating syllables accompanied by rattling and the stamping of the dancers' feet. Occasionally the leader or some dancer utters an outburst of expressions such as "*Wi·dju'ke'mine,*" "Come and help us out!" "*Na'kskwesi'zak,*" "Girls!" "*Ski'nosi·stak,*" "Boys!"

The remarks above apply more strictly to the characteristic Penobscot dance songs. There are some other dances and songs differing considerably from these, which bear evidence of having been introduced from the Micmac and Malecite. The effect of Penobscot dance songs to the European ear is plaintive and sad in theme. But in action quite the contrary is true. The effect of the united action of the participants, the drolleries of the leader, the rhythmic outbursts of the chorus, and the unrestrained hilarity of all present are highly enlivening. In fact, the very dance song which is to my own ear the most plaintive when sung alone,

forms the most hilarious performance of all.   This is the
Maˤtagiˈposi· or Snake Dance.   (See page 283.)

I offer here a few examples of the leader's part and the
chorus responses separated from contexts which appear in full
later on.[10]

Wedding or Round Dance
(P. R. 16) [1]

yau nĭ   ho yau'nĭ ho

(do.) (P. R. 11)

ka'yu wa'nĭ   ya'hya he

(do.) (P. R. 108)

kwe' hai wa'   nĭ ho'

kwe'hai wa'   nĭ ho'

(do.) (P. R. 66)

kwe ya'   wa he no'

kwe ya'   wa he no'

Canoe Song

The magic power of song syllables was thought to have a
quieting influence upon the forces causing rough water, and
also to strengthen the canoe men.   A number of years ago
an informant (Charlie Daylight Mitchell) was crossing from
Deer Island to Eagle Island in Penobscot Bay during a
heavy sea.   He was in a small canoe in the company of an
old man who chanted the following song all the way across.
The singer tempered his voice to follow the pitching of the

---

[10] The numbers in parenthesis are the catalog numbers of phonograph records in
the University Museum, University of Pennsylvania.

canoe as it mounted wave after wave. He said that the boat rode the waves much more easily while the old man was singing.

The meaningless syllables are, repeated over and over again,

kwe ha' yu we, ha' yu we hi'
kwe ho' yu we, ho' yu we.

Myth Song

The following is an example of music to which myths were sung. Some of the old women are said to have had many of these song myths, but I am not sure whether all myths could be so sung, or whether certain ones only were set to music. In this song the musical theme is repeated over and over until the story comes to an end. The tale, as will be seen, is the popular one of the deserted woman.

The words to this are:

metcigak nlɑ'bin <small>I can just about see them</small>	elɑbɑ'zim'uk <small>going away</small>
da'li· nɑga'lɑnɑ' <small>There she was left</small>	mɔna'anizuk <small>on a little islet</small>
mɑdjega'dunke <small>she began to pick</small>	gadezi'minɑl <small>gooseberries.</small>

The explanation is, "A woman was left all alone on a lonely island (by her family); all she could get to eat was gooseberries." It would seem from this that the song myths were not straightforward narratives, but consisted of disconnected ideas and expressions relevant to the subject, intelligible enough to those who knew the story, but incoherent to others.

Woman's Song

The following song is current among the women. While there attaches an obscene side to it now, they claim that formerly it was a "perfectly proper song," a sort of ballad. Several versions are to be heard at Indian Island, though it is rare to hear one in public.

(P. R. 29)

The words are:

ta'nia' gilwe'djosin, e'dudla'dɑk e'dudla'dɑk.} repeat twice
<small>Where you come from, so hot, so hot!</small>

—— —— [11] ta'pnimɑ'k, si'ptugla'dɑk -la'dɑk
—— —— <small>testicles, stretching hot, hot!</small>

[11] A man's personal name of two long syllables is sounded here. I prefer to omit the one originally supplied in the rendition given. The song is evidently of Malecite origin.

All of which means, freely rendered, "Where you come
from it must be quite hot, because so-and-so's testicles are
hanging so low!" The dashes represent a personal name.
Comic songs improvised as occasion arises make mention of
the names of men and women in various humorous associations.

Comic Songs and Lullabies

The following is a typical Penobscot song which may be
heard about the village or in camps. It serves as a pastime
song, with the nonsense syllables as given below. Set with
some comic words, it becomes a ballad. Again one is likely
to hear it used as a dance song at some festivity.

The burden is: he' hai gwa' ni ho' yu wa ni', repeated over
and over again.

This is similar to the preceding. When first heard it was
used as a lullaby in the Penobscot village at Lincoln. At
other times it is heard as a work or pastime song. Comic
words ridiculing someone are often put to it.

(P. R. 30)

Ends with whoop

The burden is: ho' hyu we' hi· ho a hi· he' ho' hyu hwa' ni· ho a'hi· ho' ho' hyu we' hi· a'hi· ho' (repeated indefinitely).

An old lullaby familiar to the Penobscot, and also used as a "counting out" song by children in games, is:

(P. R. 21)

The syllables of this strain are:

tci' ni po' li na' a wis'
a'ka li's
antɑp
a' a su'wa

The syllables are grouped like words in the above order although they mean nothing. This lullaby was sung by an old Penobscot governor, and seems also to be well known among the Malecite, from whom some think it was borrowed.

The following are drinking songs, emotional attempts, ballads which the Indians like to sing when "feeling good," often when they have been drinking.

(P. R. 29)

widju'kemine'-ga	nid'abesis'-ga
"Come help me-ga	my little friend-ga!"
e'wigwe'doda'm-ga	e'ligadu'smi-ga
She looks guilty-ga!	been drinking-ga!
gi'wɑdjida'si-ga	Mi'kmaskwe'sis
got lonesome-ga!	a little Micmac woman!

Here, as plainly appears, the Micmac woman is supposed to be speaking first, then the singer explains her condition. Notice the -*ga*, imitating drunken talk.

The following is a love song describing a young man's thoughts of his sweetheart. Unfortunately the text was not obtained.

(P. R. 73)

Other song burdens used with familiar dance songs appear as phrases interjected between repetitions of the usual meaningless syllable-bars. Translations of several are:

(*a*) gada'wusmi' ya hye   I'm thirsty, *ya hye*
     sawahtu' ya hye   Tired, *ya hye*
     debənete' tc ya hye   Soon, *ya hye*

madjə'smi ya hye   I'll commence to drink, *ya hye*
beskwa'dasi'mges ya hye   Even in the face of firing, *ya hye*
be'skwut·e' ya hye   Just the same, *ya hye*
eligi'n meskuda'wa ya hye The likes of me will be found,
                                         ya hye

The above sounds like a fight song, possibly a reflection of some ancient war dance through its allusion to bravery in the "face of firing."

(*b*) *a* I come walking,   *a* from afar,
       a I am coming,   *a* from afar I come walking
       a Now here I come.

The Penobscot, like other northern Indians, were extremely fond of whiling away time with games of chance, strength, and skill. Some of the amusements are, however, simple and colorless. Their games show many common Algonkian features, though some may have been overlooked in accounts of other tribes because of their informality.

The most prominent game formerly was the common dice or guessing game, *wa'lade hama'gan*, "dish game." This was played with a flat wooden dish (Figs. 33 right, and 2 upper right), derived from the household eating bowl, and six bone or antler dice, diameter seven-eighth inch, flat on top and convex on the bottom (Fig. 72). Dice were as highly prized as wampum by the Penobscot and were ornamented with incised arcs.

FIG. 72

Bone Dice Used in Bowl Game

The dice is a complex game. I give rules of the game as taught me by a few players at Oldtown and Lincoln who still used it, though it should be noted that some passes arise in the counting which cause them to argue hotly about the proper procedure.

To begin with, there are only two throws that count, the one when all the six dice come either faces or tails up, and the other when five come alike either way. The former, called *wu'likadi'gan*, "good treasure(?)," entitles the player to one of the four flat counters. The latter throw, *nə'gədo'ləmi'gat*, "five -(?)," entitles him to take three small counters; thrown twice in succession gives nine small counters, and three times in succession, one flat stick, the equivalent of a "six alike" throw. Upwards of three alike in succession, or different throws in succession give only the independent values. The counters, consisting of one crooked stick, four flat ones and fifty-six thin round sticks are named and valued as follows:

nodəmi'gewa'dju	"(?)"	⎫
wawa'gədjis	"crooked back"	⎬ crooked stick
wuni'gesu	"old woman"	⎭
wu'likadi'gan	"good treasure"	⎫
sɑ'gəmo	"chief," "governor"	⎬ flat sticks
tca'his	"joice" (Eng.)	⎭
aba'sizɑl	"little sticks," round thin counters.	

The game begins by each of the two players having a turn alternately, until one throws a count, which entitles him to successive throws until he misses. This first part of the game is likened to "traveling," and the counts appear as above. The rule here is that the crooked stick cannot be taken until all the others have been taken, and then it counts only the same as one of the plain small counters (aba'sizɑl), two of which have to be paid to the taker by the other player, unless there are two left in the pile to accompany it.

When the crooked stick has been taken, the game is called *glia'lgwe* "drifting," the procedure being likened to travelers drifting down stream.

As soon as this stage is reached, or when all the small counters and flat sticks have been won, the counting continues differently from before. When a "five alike" is thrown, the player puts in a separate pile one of the small counters from his accumulated pile. This stick is then called a *tegadi'gan*, "treasure (?)" or "debt (?)," and in the final paying up in settlement of the game, it is worth four small sticks from the first pile of the other player. For two successive "five alike" throws, three of these *tegadi'gan* may be put out, or for three successive "five alike" throws, one of the next kind, equal to a "six alike," can be put out.

When a "six alike" throw is made, a small stick, to which is assigned a different value, is put in a separate pile. This stick is called *sɑ'gemo*, "governor," "chief," and is equal to four *tegadi'gan*, or to one flat stick from the first pile, or to sixteen small ones. It will be seen, then, that in this stage of the game, two different piles of the small counters are formed, both having different values. Usually, when playing during the "drifting" stage, the players add to and take from the debt pile, by canceling, according to each winning throw. The game may be prolonged until one of the players has won all the counting sticks of the other player, or it may be brought to the settlement when the winning man thinks his opponent is too far behind him to be able to pay the equivalent of his counters.

The game proceeds according to the above scheme until one player gets a large enough "debt pile" to challenge his opponent to pay up. The paying up process is conducted according to the second rating of values. If the challenged one cannot pay up, he is defeated. There is, however, one saving chance left him if he possesses the crooked stick in his pile. This gives the holder three last throws, which, should they come either "five alike" or "six alike" in succession, win him the game outright.

The following resumé may help to elucidate the system of counts.

COUNTERS

	THROW	FIRST TIME	TWICE IN SUCCESSION	THREE TIMES IN SUCCESSION
FIRST STAGE	Six dice alike (*wulikadi'gan*)	flat stick (*wulikadi'gan*)	two flat sticks nine small sticks	three flat sticks
	Five dice alike (*nə'gədo'ləmigat*)	three small sticks (*aba'sizɑl*)		flat stick

This stage is ended when all the small sticks and flat sticks are taken, which leaves only the crooked stick (*nodəmi'ge-*

wa'dju) requiring two small sticks to accompany it from the opponent's pile.

SECOND STAGE "drifting" *glia'lgwe*	Six dice alike	small stick *sagəmo* "governor"	two "governors"	three "governors"
	Five dice alike	small stick "*tegadi'gan*"	three *tegadi'gan*	one "governor"

These small sticks of different denominations, "governors" and "*tegadi'gan*," are kept in separate piles to distinguish them.

This stage ends when one player wins enough to challenge his opponent to a final count.

THIRD STAGE· "Paying up"	One "governor" = four *tegadi'gan* in pile accumulated during second stage.
	One "governor" = one flat stick, or sixteen small sticks in pile accumulated during first stage.
	When challenged to pay up or settle, the player can draw from both piles at the above values. Possessing the crooked stick gives him a chance to win outright if he makes three counting throws in succession.

The Indian ball game, or lacrosse, *a'lni abaskʷ hama'gan*, "ball stick game," was the most organized outdoor game. It is, however, now remembered only by a few of the older people. The men were divided evenly in sides, there being no limit as to number. Horizontal goal sticks were erected on the chosen ground. Each player, stripped to the skin, was provided with a racket (Fig. 73) resembling the Iroquois

Fig. 73

RACKET FOR LACROSSE GAME

ball stick. The ball, made of stuffed buckskin, was tossed up midway between the goals, after which the players strove by means of their rackets to get it through their opponents' goal. The side gaining the number of goals previously decided upon wins the game and the goods which were usually wagered upon it. Other particulars are not available. This game, however, was a great event in early days, when it was played by teams from the different Wabanaki tribes at their gatherings.[12]

The snowsnake game, *so'he*, *sowehe'k*, "skid," was a favorite winter pastime. We hear that by the arrival of the month of March, the boys were accustomed to throw away their snowsnakes lest they turn into real snakes. Until thirty or forty years ago it was played by both men and boys, but not since. They had a number of sticks carved out of hardwood (rock maple) about three feet in length, tapering from a rather heavy upturned head, an inch and a half wide, to a slender tail with a notch in it for the finger, something like an arrow notch. The sticks were oiled or scorched to make them slippery. The heavier head end was carved variously, the usual form being in imitation of a snake's head with mouth and eyes. Decorations on the body of the stick were made either with paint or by smoking. By winding a splint over the stick, smoking it black with birch bark and then removing the splint, a sharp contrast in the original white wood and black was obtained (Fig. 74).

FIG. 74

WOODEN SNOWSNAKES FOR GAME

The eyes and mouth were colored red. Men and boys owned numbers of sticks which they made themselves or won. The sticks were of different patterns suited to different condi-

[12] A description of this game at Penobscot will be found in an article by W. W. Newell, *Journal American Folk-Lore*, vol. III, No. VIII, 1890, p. 32.

tions of snow, and each had a name. The name given to the favorite stick was generally *wino'sis*, "old woman." The sticks were thought to possess animation and were talked to as though they were pets. Some typical names remembered were: *pdeske'sus*, "rattler"; *keska'wiat*, "fast one"; *to'lbe*, "turtle"; *skuk^w*, "snake"; *pəmu'le*, a supernatural creature; *awe's·us*, "bear"; *ezəba'nəs*, "raccoon"; *wadjoi'min*, beech nut (head); *kiwa'kwa*, cannibal giant.

Any number of people could play. On a day when the snow was judged suitable, a player would go through the village calling for others to come and play with him. The party would then proceed to a level place and mark off a line for a starting point. A path or runway was made by dragging a round log about six inches wide through the snow. By turns each player would throw his stick, sending it bounding over the snow by an underhand release held near the tail with the index finger in the notch. This was the method of throwing on ice or crusted snow. For soft snow, an overhand throw was used, when the stick bounded through and over the snow like a living creature. Often a place was chosen where the stick would dive beneath soft snow and come out on a stretch of ice. At the point where the stick came to rest, the thrower stuck it upright in the snow to mark his throw. When all the players had thrown their sticks, the one who had sent his the farthest won them all. There do not seem to have been any particular rules in this game. Before throwing the sticks, however, the players addressed them and sang songs at the starting, repeating the songs over and over again as the stick sped along.

An example of address and song is: "Now little snake, you must do well, and defeat them all. Now I am going to sing for you, ready go!"

Then putting his strength behind the stick, which had been resting on the snow during the above, he sent it forward with the song

él he we' sin su'he si'z αm na'be dji'ptun wi'no si'z αm

which means "go quickly, my little snowsnake, and catch the old woman." As the different sticks are thrown, their names are substituted for "old woman," which means here the opponent's leading stick. Other invocations to the snowsnakes were: "Frog, rush ahead and kill them." "My snowsnake is not betting, only trying it out!" "My snowsnake, open your mouth, follow on and win the pile of snowsnakes (*ma'mowa'tak*, "pile of wood")." These are spoken of as snowsnake songs.

Culin quotes the following account from Mr. Willoughby:

When a man wanted to play this game, he took a number of his suha (suhe) sticks and went through the village calling "su he! su he!" One or more of the players would take a boy by the feet and drag him down some incline, thus making a track or path in the snow. Down this path each player in turn, calling out "*suhe!*" threw one of his sticks, as a spear is thrown. To mark the distance, this stick was stuck up in the snow beside the path, opposite the place where it stopped. When all the sticks had been thrown, they became the property of the man whose stick had covered the greatest distance. He then gathered them all up and selecting such as he wanted, calling at the same time "*suhe!*" throw the others up in the air, and they became the property of those strong and quick enough to secure them.[13]

Another game was played between men with slings, *ala'kagan*, the idea being to sling stones as far and accurately as possible. The men were provided with carefully made sling sticks about a foot and a half in length, with a thong at one end having a loop for the thumb and a groove at the upper end near where the thong was attached (Fig. 75). A round pebble was placed in the groove and held down by the thong, which was in turn kept taut by the thumb through the loop until released. With such a sling, stones could be

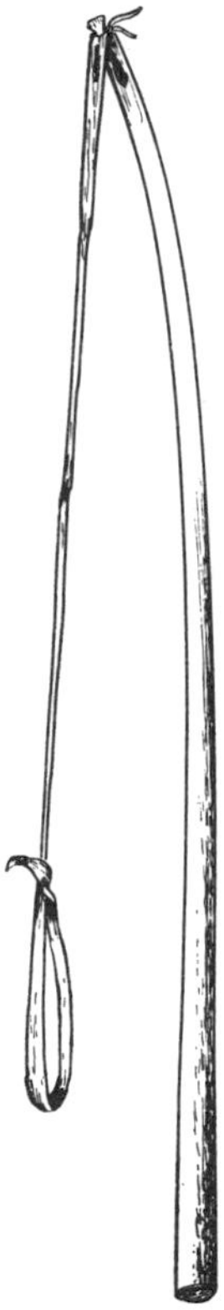

[13] Culin, p. 407.

FIG. 75

Sling Stick for Throwing Stones

thrown a great distance, even across the Penobscot River. It is
told how, after getting paid for spearing salmon, they used to
scale silver dollars across the river just for fun in the early
days. No one seems to know whether the sling was ever
used as a weapon or for hunting. It functions, however,
somewhat as does the primitive spear-thrower in other hunting
cultures.

The game known as *aba'sizɑl*, "little sticks" resembling
"jack-straws," is popular among adults. The set of sticks,
all being about seven inches long, made out of cedar, with
their counts is as follows:

4 gikɑ'mkwɑhan	"canoe pole"	50 counts each
4 temu'kwetahi'gan	"sword"	10 counts each
4 peskwɑ'di	"gun"	10 counts each
4 ca'bɑl (Eng.)	"shovel"	10 counts each
1 wuni'ges·u	"old lady," crooked stick	10 counts each
4 tca'his	joist	10 counts each
4 tamhi'gan	ax	5 counts each
4 tɑhɑ'ngan	paddle	5 counts each
50 aba'sizɑl	little sticks	1 count each

The *pi'nsis*, "little pin," is a piece of bent basket-splint
to be used in lifting the sticks from the heap. Two players
engage. The sticks are held in a bundle in the hand and
allowed to fall on the table or board. The first trial must be
made with the bare hand, or else the player may pay his
opponent one little stick and use the pin. The object is to
remove sticks from the tangled heap without moving any of
the others. As soon as one player fails to secure a stick, the
other takes up the bundle, drops the sticks and takes his
turn. When all have been taken, they match up their win-
nings, pay off and count up the winner's balance. This
game, which is regarded as a modification of an older form,
is supposed to symbolize a log jam.

The ring and pin game, *a'dwis*, has two forms among the
Penobscot. One is merely a lover's pastime, and is played
with a maple pin about ten inches long joined at the middle

with a thong to a cone shaped bundle of moose hairs or, as often happens, of wrapped pin or green arbor vitae (cedar) twigs (Fig. 76). The regulations are simple; each party gets two chances to see who can impale the bunch of twigs the greatest number of times. Sometimes a number of people play at it, sitting around in a ring, each having a throw until he misses, after which it must be passed to the next. The players decide how many points will win. The counts are one for each time the bunch is caught.

In another form this was a gambling game. Six moose phalanx bones, strung on the thong with a little piece of leather on the end to keep them on, take the place of the bunch of pine or arbor vitae leaves. The stakes are put up and each player has

Fig. 76

Toss-Pin and Bundle Game

ten throws, at the end counting up one for every bone that he has caught. When all have played, the man with the highest number wins.

In the springtime, a common daily amusement of the boys is to hunt about the village and over the island with bows and blunt-headed arrows for squirrels, blackbirds, robins, and in fact anything worth shooting at. It is no uncommon sight to see from a dozen to a score of boys together engaged in this sport, searching along the river shores for a muskrat, or running in a crowd up into the woods on the hill after a rabbit or bird, with one arrow fitted to the string and a few more held in the hand with the bow.

A frequent amusement among the young is head rubbing, *tkwa'din*. The contestants clasp their hands behind each other's necks and rub foreheads together until one gives up. A peculiar sidewise gouging on the opponent's temple is the master move. This is played, they say, to harden the head and develop indifference to pain. They think, furthermore, that it prevents headaches.

Boys amuse themselves by blowing chokecherries through a hollow stem of arch angelica bush (*bagwa'luse*) about a foot and a half long. With it they try to knock over small birds. This toy reminds one of a degenerated blowgun.

An old-fashioned toy consisted of a triangular piece of stiff birch bark about a foot high, with a small wooden ball attached by a thong to its apex. A hole was made just a trifle larger than the ball in the middle of the bark. With this toy a person amused himself trying to let the ball drop through the hole when the triangle was held in a vertical position.

In winter, when the river is frozen over, some young men and boys may nearly always be seen playing ice shinny. The goals consist of pairs of sticks set up at a convenient distance apart. With shinny sticks, ordinarily homely affairs of green wood, they strive to knock a block of wood through the opposite goal, with no particular regulations, except that the block cannot be lifted from the ice. The regular modern game of hockey or "ice polo" is well known and is played by the Indians of Maine and New Brunswick with considerable success against white teams, but the essentials of the original game are about as above.

Canoe tilting is called *ta'gwa*. Two men man each canoe, the rear man paddling, the bow man armed with a long pole with padding on the end. The canoes then come together and the bow men try to push each other overboard. Canoe racing affords considerable amusement.

Foot racing over a short course or over a path going around Indian Island is a common occurrence for sport and for muscular and endurance training. Numbers of men frequently race in squads over this path, which is about three miles long and quite rough. Sixteen minutes is said to be the best record.

Various forms of wrestling are carried on, and in this the neck grip seems to be common. Facing in opposite directions lying on the back and trying to overturn each other by locking the inside legs is said to be an old-time method.[14]

[14] The field of modern sports, football, baseball, pugilism, and track has always attracted the young Penobscot men, some of whom, Sockalexis, Neptune, Nicolas, Solomon, Sapiel, and others, have become well known professionally.

A game called "roosters," common among the Micmac, is said to have been played by the Penobscot. Each opponent has his hands tied together with a sharp stick held in them. Then a pole is run under his knees and elbows as a further obstacle. The contestants try to prod each other with their sharp sticks. Their awkward positions, growls, and gurgles while fighting provide an amusing scene.

Another amusement is *do'tuwesi'zɑ'k*, "little pines," a game for women chiefly. Anywhere from six to a dozen tips of white pine sprigs are trimmed squarely across the ends to represent dancers. They are stood pointing upward upon a slab of wood, then by jouncing and shaking this, a lifelike imitation of human dancing is produced. As the player sways and jounces the board, she sings dance songs while the pine tips twirl, topple, slide, or circle around, sometimes in pairs jostling one another. They eventually fall, upsetting each other till all are down. The onlookers are greatly affected by the grotesque pantomine; they encourage the performance with expressions of "*hai! hai!*," "*tâɩ́ tâɩ́*" and "*u'ye!*" When one of the "dancers," after tumbling over, becomes righted again, as frequently happens, they cry "*Ee!* She's glad to wake up again! She's come to life!" The last "dancer" to remain on the board is praised for her skill and endurance, as the pine tips are supposed to be women. The toy is then passed to someone else. It is a common thing to see an old man amusing children with this toy. Formerly the women had an actual dance which was called the Pine Dance (p. 299) which this toy represents.

The children also have *da'thasoldibna*, "we play old ogre." One of them assumes the rôle of the monster who eats children, *kiwa'kwe*. Another is their protector, while the devourer tries to catch them as they take refuge, with screams, behind him or her. When a child is caught, the monster makes believe to devour him by biting his clothes and growling, all of which greatly terrifies the rest.

They make little spheres or marbles of fir balsam pitch and roll them down a sloping board. The players whose marble goes farthest takes all the others' marbles.

The bull roarer is a well-known toy. It is called *Pəmu'le utohɑ'gan*, "Pemule's paddle," from the story of how Pemule travels through the air whirling his stick.[15] The roarer is usually made of cedar about ten inches long and is attached by a thong to a stick about eighteen inches in length.

The buzzer was an amusement among children. It is made of wood, in diameter about four inches, with a doubled deerskin thong twenty inches long. Some buzzers are said to have been a foot in diameter producing a noise resembling the sighing of the wind. Some are nicknamed "white man's saw-mill." It is possible that the buzzer was a native device, considering its wide range through North America from the Eskimo southward in conjunction with the bull roarer. Both are believed to affect the wind.

Top spinning for divination was formerly a children's pastime. The top, *libu'gumuda'gan*, consisted of a circular disk of bone (being of moose jaw) about two inches in diameter with a wooden peg through it, extending about an inch above and below. The upper surface is said to have been ornamentally painted. The game was played by children who formed in a circle, asked some question of the top, spun it, and waited to see toward which one it pointed after coming to rest. Personal questions such as, "Who will be married first? Who will wet himself or smut his clothes?" were put to the top. Wishes also were made by all the children, and whomever the top pointed to would obtain his or her wish.

A game called *wine'sosis*, "little old woman," was played by the children. It was something like tag. One little girl would impersonate an old woman trying to capture children, and the others would plague her and dash away until someone was caught.

Small children have various amusements. They tie a hare's foot by a string and drag it around treating it like some pet animal. Miniature wooden guns, snowshoes, revolvers, and the like furnish the youngsters with practical

---

[15] This creature is believed to travel over the world once each year swinging the "roarer" in each hand. He comes to see what is needed to help when the people burn grease to call him down as they hear him coming through the air. He has no body.

toys. A little strip of birch bark is frequently held between the lips and some tune blown through it as one would do with a stalk of grass. I have also seen them playing with bundles of fallen leaves, counting them out like money, or as forfeits.

In the winter time sliding down hill on toboggans or sleds takes up considerable of the children's time. Unorganized sports of the children are many. Crowds of boys jump, race, wrestle, fight, climb, and throw missiles, in their play contests. Or one boy will shove or punch another who will try to catch and punish the rogue, involving the rest in the mêlée.

But one cat's cradle is known, called "crow's nest." Repeated inquiry has failed to bring any more besides this one to light. It is a form of the figure widely distributed called "Leashing of Lochiel's Dogs." [16]

Male and female dolls, *a'mskwadje'kkan* (Fig. 77), were made of corn husks and dressed up with corn tassel for hair. Braided pieces form the body and limbs, and folded ones the clothing. These are, however, rarely seen among the Indian children.

Fig. 77
Corn-Husk Dolls

In winter time, when the river is frozen smooth, nothing is more common than to see the children amusing themselves on sleds propelling themselves along at a high rate of speed with a pair of iron-shod sticks like their elders, who have a more serious purpose in going up river by this means for wood or meat. Much amusement is given in nice weather during the winter out on the frozen river near the village, by trying to trip or throw each other.

A pastime among children consists in trying to make pretty figures by biting series of indentures into pieces of very thin folded birch bark. They try to rival each other in the variety of patterns produced in this way. By folding the

[16] String Figures, C. F. Jayne, N. Y. 1906, p. 116–120.

thinnest bark two or three times perpendicularly, biting some lines of tooth marks into it, then unfolding it, fancy symmetrical figures are obtained. When native arts were practised these outlines furnished motives for decoration. In the same way the Montagnais women of Labrador use them as patterns in beadwork and birch-bark etching, though the idea seems not to have survived in the decadent art of the Penobscot.

A toy figure appears in the small braided figure of sinew from a deer's leg. It is called a man of skin and bones. The old man who made this in play had a little story. He said, "This is the man of skin and bones. He ran all his flesh off chasing the deer. The deer also ran himself to skin and bones. So when the man killed him there was no meat on him to eat." This ludicrous effigy is a joke on too ardent hunters.

An amusement resorted to by people in the woods, when a porcupine has been killed, is to take a certain bone from its hip, wrap something about one end for a grip, and then see who has a strong enough wrist to break it.

Several other games of undoubted European origin are known. One is essentially the European game of "cat," called in Penobscot *gwino'sgwe'is·uk*. A double pointed "cat," with one, two, three, and four notches on its respective sides is knocked into the air and batted with a stick, the player counting up as much as is indicated by the uppermost notches. Another men's game, of European derivation, though even claimed by some to be native, is checkers, *kwakwa'niga'n*. A bark or wooden board and wooden men of alder were used; the rules being as usual.

A form of base ball was played by men. The field had four posts at the corners. There were a pitcher, batter, and catcher. When the batter hit the ball, which was a large soft one, he ran around outside the posts. If the pitcher stopped the ball short or caught it on the bounce four times, the man was out, until which time he could keep on batting and scoring runs. This game may have been an Indian sport older than modern baseball.

The telling of humorous anecdotes about people is a pastime much in vogue. The Wabanaki are indeed a jolly

people; with most of them any time is play time.   An obscene
toy consisting of a small wooden box with a slide lid, containing a crude man's figure with abnormally exaggerated private
parts was found in possession of some men engaged in snowshoe making.   One of them owned the effigy, causing considerable amusement roundabout.   Indulgence in the pastime
of humorous narrations is incessant.

Since humorous anecdotes play a prominent part in social
life, but seldom appear in the conventional ethnological accounts, a few examples from the camps may prove of interest.

Some Penobscot on their way down the bay encountered some
strangers working over a lot of lobsters which they had just caught.
They were employed by someone.   As the Indians came by, the
strangers, to taunt them, began calling out nonsense syllables trying
to imitate the Penobscot language.   The Indians retorted, "Very
well! We'll be back again soon."   When they had finished their
trip, they came back over the same route and landed where the
strangers were still working.   "So!   Now we'll take those lobsters
you said you wanted to give us."   "What lobsters?" said the men.
"We didn't say we would give you any lobsters."   "Oh, yes you
did," said the Indians.   "As we were going down, you called us in
our language and promised us a lot of lobsters, so now keep your
promise."   There was nothing else to do but comply, and the
Indians turned the joke and received a canoe half full of lobsters.

At the last tribal visit of the Passamaquoddy to the Penobscot,
the former were received with a great dance and celebration
(*Ska'wehe*, cf. section on ceremonies).   The Penobscot women
cooked a feast.   The Passamaquoddy ate it and went to bed.   But
something was wrong with the food, no one knew why.   During
the night, the visitors' bowels were affected, and they soiled their
beds.   By morning when the Penobscot went over to see their
guests and renew the celebration, they found them gone, and
discovered the trouble.

The white man once upon a time asked the Indian if he knew
how to whistle.   The Indian told him he could whistle and said
he would show him.   He happened to be peeling bark at the time,
and had a long strip on the ground one end of which he was holding.
"Stand on that end there, and I'll show you how the Indians
whistle," said he.   When the white man stood on the bark the
Indian jerked it from under him and he fell on his rear.   "That's
how the Indians whistle!" cried he.

TRADITIONS OF WARFARE

Living constantly under the menace of invasion from the Iroquois, the Penobscot developed a combative spirit which, according to tradition, preserved them at times from annihilation. After the appearance of Europeans, with consequent encroachments, hostilities increased on the Penobscot borders only to be ended by a general treaty of peace with northern New England Indians in 1749.

Tradition also speaks vaguely of a short period of warfare with the Malecite and Micmac. Outside of the long-continued struggle against Europeans, during which European arms were quickly adopted, the main sources of information refer to conflicts with the Iroquois. The purpose of warfare on both sides was to subdue, not to gain territory. Nicolar in his treatise also makes this clear.

From the Iroquois viewpoint we know that the expansion of the league required the subjugation of the more simple neighboring Algonkian tribes, and that expeditions were constantly being sent eastward to force them into the league. The exposed position of the Penobscot, just off the edge of the fighting territory of New Hampshire and Vermont, laid them open to the first fresh attacks of their enemies. From the Penobscot viewpoint, however, the Iroquois had a hard time of it, seldom winning a victory, and only succeeding in getting the eastern tribes to join the league when the latter had grown tired of resisting and had become compliant through the influence of judgment rather than fear. The event which closed hostilities between the Iroquois and the eastern Algonkian was the great treaty of peace at Caughnawaga at which the Penobscot, Passamaquoddy, Malecite, and Micmac were represented. Mrs. Eckstorm places the date as 1700. Delegations continued until between 1866–72 (Eckstorm, III, p. 213).

Prior to this, many a long trip through the woods and snow from the Mohawk to the Penobscot River to attack some unwary village resulted in the surprise and destruction of the Iroquois. But the fact that the Penobscot never embarked on punitive expeditions away from home bespeaks for them a less aggressive spirit. As fighters we hear of them only repelling enemies from their own territories.

War in general they call *a'odin;* "to fight" is *mi'ga'hke.* Their implements of war included the war ax, stone- or iron-headed tomahawk, *təmahi'gan,* "cutting instrument," the bow, *ta'bi,* and arrow, *pa'hkwe;* the knife, *tse'kwak^w,* lance or spear, *eniga'k^w,* and a wooden club, *mskwa'djis.* The fact that there is no native name for shield might seem to indicate its absence.

For the stone-headed tomahawk tradition mentions a flat beach pebble, the middle of the long sides pecked or battered away a little to form notches for the handle, which was made of a single piece of ash bent once around the stone and lashed back several inches on itself with rawhide. The later historical tomahawk type, had a triangular blade and a spike, the iron heads of which were supplied by French traders. A specimen was recovered from a well on Indian Island.

The war club was made of a single heavy gnarled birch root, with the stock as a handle. These clubs were used in personal encounters, it is said. Many fancy examples are made today for commercial purposes, with elaborated animal and human carvings. The old ones were plainer.

Bows and arrows have been described before. Concerning spears Rosier mentions their "darts headed with like bone," [17] which were probably used indifferently for hunting and fighting. Guns, after they were obtained from traders, became known as *peskwa'di,* "exploding tube."

The cries and yells uttered by fighting men were believed to have power to stupefy and even kill the enemy by their magic force. Individuals had their own particular yells. A high tremolo call, produced by vibrating the tongue between the alveolars, is one kind still used for signaling purposes. The same yell, made by hitting the open mouth with the palm of the hand, is common.

Scalps were taken from enemies, we are told, a piece about the size of the palm being removed from the crown, dried and preserved by the warriors.

It was more customary in this region, however, for the victors to cut off enemies' heads, retaining them as trophies.

[17] Rosier, page 372.

As will also be learned from the anecdotes, when captives were made one would be spared to have his nose, ears or hands cut off. Captives were otherwise mutilated and then liberated to return home as a warning to their people of what might be expected another time.

As is mentioned in one of the animal tales, the creature who has killed his enemies' family leaves the corpses in lifelike attitudes with little sticks prying open their eyes and mouths to deceive and taunt their friends. So, in the war tradition, we learn that the same was often practised by men—in this instance animal myth and human custom coinciding. One example of the latter will be found a few pages on, the mythical instances occurring in the adventures of Raccoon. Dr. Paul Radin encountered a similar correspondence among the Winnebago.

It was tabooed for women, especially young girls, to cross over the path of warriors or hunters, whom it would weaken and bring general bad luck. The old Indians tell of a test that the warriors used to put themselves to when traveling up and down Penobscot Bay. Near Camden, Maine, there is said to be a steep hill of loose shifting sand visible from the water. Here the warriors would land and try to outdo one another in running to the top. It is said to have been very difficult and was considered a great proof of strength to succeed.

They had the custom of settling intertribal disputes by duel. The story is related of two war parties that met to fight upon the ice of a lake or river. The leaders challenged each other to settle the matter by single combat. A stick was planted upright in the ice, and the two contestants, armed only with wooden clubs, fought it out around the stick.

The Passamaquoddy and the Mohawk have similar legends and I presume many of these have been passed back and forth from tribe to tribe, as stories are, until the actual incidents and parties concerned have become confused.

Warriors painted themselves in various ways, as noted previously. They painted marks on their backs to indicate how many men they had killed.

Some interesting war customs are given by Nicolar.[18]

In time of war, no mercy was shown to the defenseless, old people and women were despatched, even babies were slain, no prisoners were taken, only such ones the enemy knows to be most beloved were taken to be cruelly tortured to irritate the feelings of the prisoners' friends. Burning at the stake was the principal measure; exchange of prisoners was never practised. The only way to rescue a friend from the enemy was to keep fighting to rout the enemy. The war was carried on mostly in the night time, the invaders watch closely and when they found the others to be in sleep the attack was made.

The shamans also played an important part in war. "They had the power in giving the war cry or yell, to cause the enemy who hears it to fall to the ground helpless." They also "carried off captives to torture them, or carry them far from home and leave them either to die or find their way home without food. The woman captives liberated in this manner were allowed to go unbound, but the men were always bound so that they could not feed nor otherwise help themselves." [19]

War Anecdotes

Most of the facts remembered, which I give directly, deal with the Mohawk. The Penobscot shamans always knew when the Mohawk were coming. They could detect them with their power. Upon one occasion while the men were hunting, the shaman (*mədeo'linu*) called the women and old folks of the village together and told them to dress up as men and play at lacrosse with great energy. This they did, and when the Mohawk scouts beheld the active and apparently ever ready young men of the village making such a display they concluded to give up the idea of attacking and went away.[20] Whenever a Mohawk party was defeated and captives were taken, the Penobscot saved some of the men and sent them back to their tribe with their ears cut off, or otherwise mutilated, to carry the news. Generally, it is said, a sentinel was kept continuously on watch at the head of

[18] Nicolar, p. 109.
[19] Nicolar, pp. 111, 115.
[20] Substantially the same story is told among the Passamaquoddy about themselves in a threatened attack by the Micmac. Cf. Leland and Prince, p. 26.

Indian Island, because the Mohawk always drifted down the river when they came, following the old Indian canoe trail from Caughnawaga.

At the rips on Mohawk Stream some miles above Indian Island, a band of Mohawk were once encamped. They were busy raiding the Penobscot families who lived up the Passadumkeag waters. One night eleven Penosbcot boys from Indian Island started out and came upon the Mohawk camp while all were asleep. The boys stole in, captured the Mohawk chief and took him back to Indian Island where the Penobscot burned him at the stake. The rest of the Mohawk fled.

Upon another occasion a party of the enemy was in camp near the same rapids waiting for a chance to descend upon the Island. Once in a while a peculiar thing happens on Mohawk Rips; the water, instead of flowing down stream, is turned when the river is high and flows upstream for a short time. One morning the Mohawk saw this change in the current. Overawed by the manifestation of magic, which they took this to be on the part of some Penobscot shaman, they packed up and went back to their own country.

Whenever the old people saw chips of wood on the river bank or saw them floating by in the current, they used to say that the Mohawk were coming and that the chips were a sign that they were building rafts somewhere up river upon which to come down. Once, after receiving such a warning, a party of warriors started upstream to find the Mohawk and drive them off. When they reached Mohawk Rips, the enemy's camp was found and attacked so suddenly that all the Mohawk of the band were killed. One of the chiefs took refuge on a large boulder in midstream and was the last to fall.

The Mohawk were encamped at Mohawk Rips, whence they were attacking Penobscot families and camps wherever they found them. In one camp they killed all but a young woman and her child, sparing these to carry home as captives. The woman and her child were kept with their captors in the camp at the rips. Now the Penobscot heard of this and planned to rescue their kinswoman. They came in the night and fell upon the Mohawk. It was winter time and the bands fought on the river on the ice. The Mohawk were losing; the Penobscot men began killing them all. But one Mohawk remembered the captives. He left the fight, went back to the camp and struck the woman with his tomahawk where they had bound her. When the child in his cradleboard fell over on his face in the snow, the Mohawk, in order to kill him, threw his tomahawk at him and hit the cradle board, knocking off a piece near the top. Then the Mohawk ran off. When the enemy were all killed, the Penobscot men ran to the camp and found the boy face downwards in the snow. He was not hurt, but smiled when they lifted him up. The rescuers returned with him to the Island and he was named *Adamhi'gan*, "Cut with an ax." When he grew up he became a leader of the men and killed so many Mohawk that he was nicknamed "Mohawk killer."

In one of their fights up river, the men captured a Mohawk and brought him to the Island, where on a square boulder near the spring just outside of the village at the end of the main path through it, they killed and buried him. Not long afterward they found the grave filled with stones. The Mohawk had come secretly, removed his body, and filled up the hole with stones.

When the New England troops in 1724 destroyed the Indian village and mission of Norridgewock, founded by Father Rasles, a woman with her baby boy in a cradleboard upon her back escaped by swimming across the river. The baby's name was *Sankǝde'lak*, "Stream emptying into a river." Later she found her way to Indian Island where the boy grew up and raised a family. The Denis family is descended from him.

There was once a company of old women camped near the large pointed boulder that projects from Passadumkeag Stream five miles or so east of its mouth. Their sons and husbands had gone into the interior to hunt, leaving them until their return. A sad fate befell the poor old women. The Mohawk found them helpless, and killed and scalped them all. Not satisfied with this, they impaled them on sharp upright stakes through the arms, fixing their mouths and eyelids open with cross-sticks, leaving them to appear

as though they were alive.   In this condition the men found
the old women when they returned.   The rock is called
Scalped Rock in memory of this episode.

Ma'ndoa'mek^w, "Spirit fish," "Devil fish," was a great
war chief and at the same time a shaman.   Once during his
life a large band of Mohawk struck the head of Penobscot
River and descended to besiege the village at Oldtown.
Ma'ndoa'mek^w learned of the approach through his magic.
He could trace their advance from day to day.   One day
several canoe loads of Penobscot boys, who had been a few
miles above the village fishing, came down past the island
loudly singing war songs with a number of heads of the black
chub (*a'wuskhowɑk* "spies") fastened on sticks in their canoes.
Some people hearing their noise came out and told them to
stop.   When Ma'ndoa'mek^w saw them he knew that enemies
were near.   He organized a party and ascended the river to
where he knew the Mohawk were camped.   When he got near
he chanted a medicine song which put the Mohawks into a
sleep.   Then the Penobscot men went in and cut off their
heads, bringing them back to the village on sticks in the same
way that the boys had brought the chubs' heads.   When
Ma'ndoa'mek^w died, another chief was elected to his place.
He wanted to be called by the same name, but he persisted
so much that the people instead called him Mi'tcigəna'mek^w,
"Excrement Fish." ·

SMOKING

The Penobscot seem to have known the cultivation and
use of tobacco, *adama'we*, from an epoch antedating the coming of the whites.   One could venture a suggestion of Iroquois
derivation for it.   They entertained Weymouth's crew with
their tobacco, "which was excellent, and so generally commended of all to be as good as any we ever smoked, being the
simple leaf . . . strong and sweet taste." [21]

Tobacco was, according to one story, believed to have
originated from the bones of a mythical female being, the
"first mother," [22] who directed her husband to kill her and

[21] Rosier, p. 373.
[22] Cf. Nicolar, p. 62. This woman, the first mother created by *Gluskɑbe*, left a
family in hunger and discontentment, but by means of her death provided corn from
her body for their nourishment and tobacco from her bones for their contentment.

drag her body over the ground. The body became the corn plant and her bones the tobacco, as is related in the myth.

Said Gluskabe to the people, "This blade will give strength to the mind; burn it and inhale the smoke it will bring freshness to the mind and your heart will be contented while the smoke of it be in you. . . . Remember her (the mythical female) when the smoke of her bones rises before you; yea more, whatever be your work, stop in your labor until the smoke has all gone to the Great Spirit." [23] A more authentic version, however, accredits Gluskabe with stealing the first tobacco from a monster grasshopper who lived upon an island, and bestowing it to people.

Smoking, *wuda'ma*, "to use tobacco with the mouth," is extensively indulged in by both sexes from early age. The old native plant has of course been entirely forgotten long ago and the trader's tobacco has taken its place. Varied mixtures are used as of old. Some mix the dried and crumpled bark of the squaw bush, *nespipa'mk*^{w}, with it, and some admix a little dried sweet fern (Comptonia asplenifolia) leaves called *Me'gwai nespipa'mk*$^{'w}$, "Mohawk tobacco." In the tobacco pouch, the men say, a piece of dried beaver castor adds a delicate sweet flavor to the weed. Oil from the beaver's scent sac was also mixed with squaw bush. When, in the woods, the tobacco has run out, or when they are too poor to afford better, the Indians often fall back on the squaw-bush bark; satisfactory proportions are two-thirds squaw bush to one-third tobacco.

The story tellers always smoked while reciting. At the end of their sentences they drew in a quantity of smoke with a noise, allowing it to float out through mouth and nostrils with the next sentence. In the council, a speaker is invited to speak by the chief's passing him the pipe. As with all Indians, tobacco is a medium of friendship. They treat each other and strangers to it; they smoke together when talking things over, and invariably after a meal, whether at home or in camp, the men sit apart from the rest to enjoy a pipeful. I was rather surprised, though, at perhaps half a dozen of the elder men who do not use tobacco at all. Some of the

[23] *Ibid.*, p. 64.

Indians leave a little tobacco at springs when they take a drink in the woods, as a recompense to the local spirits.

The pipes in general, *dama'gan*, fall into two types, those with keel-based bowl set at right angles to the stem (Fig. 69), and those with the curving flaring bowl. The typical pipe is stone, *pəna'pskwa's·ən*, "stone pipe," made of black slate or what is locally called "air and water" stone. The stone is cut with an ax and the shaping is done with a knife and file. Considerable variety is shown in pipe shapes. The most elaborate (*a*) is ornamented with curved lines joining hearts, said to indicate the bond of friendship between the parties who smoked it. A realistic eagle figure is lightly etched on the front of the bowl. A graceful and well-executed specimen (*c*) is of the curved variety with a realistic salamander clinging to the bowl. The mouth, eyes, and two rows of holes on the back representing spots, are filled with red ochre. This salamander seems to be a favorite motive in eastern Indian art, appearing on spoon-handles, pipes, clubs, and other articles. A single specimen of clay bowl is on record here (*d*). Nothing was known about it by the owner. Examination shows it to be of a fine-grained clay burnt black. I was told that such pipes were made by burning a chunk of clay, then cutting and boring it down with the knife as though it were a lump of stone. The front of the bowl suggests crudely the human face. The wooden pipe (*e*) is complete in one piece, made apparently of chestnut. The older women have a number of these, from one of whom the specimen shown was coaxed. Another pipe (*f*) is interesting as an example of a makeshift constructed rapidly in the woods in camp. The bowl is of cedar, plugged at the bottom with a birch-bark wad; the stem is of squaw-bush split, with the pith cleared out and the stem bound together with a strip of cedar inner bark. The maker of this pipe got me to twist alternately the alder stick which he had cut around deeply, while he held what was to become the bowl until the latter came off in a cylinder of bark and outer wood, a quarter of an inch thick. To make a pipe like this and scrape and dry enough squaw-bush bark for a good smoke requires less than half an hour altogether, and the article is good for some time.

Fig. 69, upper left, was similarly made of alder and used by a hunter who had lost his pipe and tobacco. The bottom hole is here plugged with a bit of wood cut like a handle.

A word as to the pipe stems. The usual material is squaw bush, although an unidentified willow twig is said to be just as good. The stem is sometimes split, hollowed, and bound together again, or else, if possible, the pith is pushed out with a stiff wiry fir twig or a wire.

More common in the old days, when Indians had a fancy for such things, were stem wrappings of strung beads and porcupine quills.

MNEMONIC WAMPUM RECORDS

As my study of Penobscot ethnology progressed I came to realize the extreme importance of civil and ceremonial traits involving the use of wampum among the six extant tribes of the Wabanaki group. My principal informant, Newell Lion, furthermore awakened me to the immediate necessity of recording what could still be learned of former wampum procedures while several aged persons who remembered seeing them in operation were yet living in the tribe. He was one of them himself. The task once commenced was carried to completion as far as conditions permitted during the next two winters, and the results were brought out in several publications: One [24] a paper on the confederacy of the Wabanaki tribes; the other [25] a more extended monograph covering the wampum topic within the same area (terminology, wampum in mythology, its evolution in form, as currency, as ornamentation, in ceremonies, in marriage proposal, and its historical perspective). Much of this was drawn from Penobscot sources. To avoid repetition here of the treatment given in those studies, I have merely cast a brief outline of the salient features of wampum usage as we see it portrayed in one period of Penobscot national life, between 1700 and 1870, when the arms of the Iroquoian alliance, stretched toward

[24] The Eastern Algonkian Wabanaki Confederacy. *American Anthropologist*, n.s., vol. XVII, no. 3, 1915, pp. 492–508.

[25] The Functions of Wampum Among the Eastern Algonkian. Memoirs of the American Anthropological Association, vol. 6, no. 1, 1919. pp. 1–71.

the east, held in their grasp the Wabanaki hunters in the forests of Maine.

Intertribal compacts, negotiations of a civil nature, were, as we know, mnemonically recorded by means of shell wampum beads woven into strips and kept by the council. Even in events of lesser importance, like marriages, the wampum was used. Considering the fact that the material was regarded as a precious article, used mostly, and throughout its history, in personal ornamentation, it would seem that the idea of employing it for political purposes might have been introduced from the Iroquois where this feature of its use was so prominent. Tradition states, and in fact we know it be true, that strips or belts of wampum were distributed by the Iroquois after peace had been established among the eastern Algonkian tribes. In regard to this event Nicolar wrote as follows:

A treaty was made and to make it lasting a large collection [of beads] was made from all parts of the country, which was after woven into a wampum band two hands wide and twenty-one hands long, and along in the middle part many different characters were woven in representing what the band was made for who were concerned in it. This band was the grand council fire which was left in the care of the *Me'gwɑk* (Mohawk) who were very faithful to their duty until recently when they began to show signs of a change in demeanor. When this was discovered the visits to the council fire were after a while stopped. This discontinuance was brought about by the actions of the *Odɑ'wɑ* (Ottawa) which was soon followed by all the other tribes. The spot selected where the grand council fire was to be established was at the head of the first big rapids of the great lake river (Caughnawaga, at Lachine Rapids on the St. Lawrence, the Mohawk center.) And the name given to it was *Ktci Sku'dek*, "Big Fire." As has been stated before, all the tribes visited this council fire every seven years, and during the council days all kinds of sports were enjoyed by the young. At first the Mohawks seemed pleased to have the people come, and took pride in being able to entertain decently all that came. They seemed delighted in serving as the keeper but after a long while wanted to be the commander; boss. This the people could not tolerate and quit going there. The last visit made from the east was only fifty-three years ago (1840), and some of the young men who went with the old men on that last visit are still living. One feature of the federation that can be called pleasant was that the people divided themselves into classes, the father, the eldest son and the youngest son. Ottawa was the father; *Wabana'ki* "Dawn Lander" [Abenaki, i.e., Penosbcot, St. Francis, Passamaquoddy, and Malecite] the eldest son; and Micmac was the youngest son. And after the division was made the oldest Micmac present was undressed and put into a cradle-board and there he was kept tied and fed all day like a little baby. Every time the delegation met at the grand council fire this performance was repeated.[26]

In regard to the political use of wampum in the Wabanaki area it seems clear that the institution, if not rooted directly in the principles of Iroquois organization, was at least greatly stimulated through the influence of its genius. This, however, does not decide the question of the history of disk wampum used as decorative material. It is considered primordial by the Penobscot, whether rightly or not, and is common in archeological sites excavated by Moorehead through the southern part of Maine.

Wampum both white and purple is generically called *wa'babi* (pl. *wa'bɑpig*), meaning "white band." The form and material are identical with the New England wampum made of quahaug (Venus mercenaria) and conch (Busycon).

As to the tradition of its manufacture and use, Nicolar says:

The parts of the shell got fit for use are rubbed on some gritty stone to shape them. Then the awl is used to make the holes. The making of the holes was the slowest part of the work therefore when it was made it was considered valuable. It was never intended to be used as money. True there were many instances where it was exchanged for other things yet the principal object was that it be used as pledge of honor; say for instance when ever a person or persons wished their words to be taken honorably and give wampum with these words. This was sufficient to settle the matter desired. Matches for marriage were made by the old people and here the wampum was used as a pledge.[27]

The ordinary wampum in use among the Penobscot and their neighbors was the smooth finely bored variety, cylin-

[26] Nicolar, pp. 137–139.
[27] Nicolar, p. 145.

drical in shape, averaging about one-quarter of an inch long
and one-eighth of an inch wide, white, purple, or marbled.
It is the same as that found among the Iroquois and Delaware.

Another variety, however, is found in the graves of this
section of Maine, which judging from its roughness and size
is an earlier form of bead, the predecessor of the later wampum. The bead disks have an average diameter of one-fourth
of an inch.

The form of wampum strips is that of a necklace or a
collar (Fig. 78). The beads are strung one at a time, on

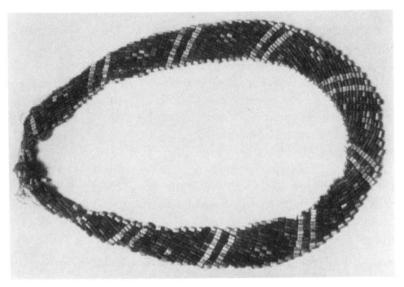

FIG. 78

WAMPUM COLLAR

The Enclosures Between Bars Symbolize Union of Nine Bands or
Tribes Represented by Crosses

doubled threads, suspended from a piece of obliquely cut
leather, the upper outside thread turning in, and passing
between the doubled warps at each course of beads. The
bead-woven fabric is consequently built up by hand, each
warp in turn becoming a diagonal woof between a row of
beads. A curvature results, so that the strip, when hung
over the neck, lies flat upon the chest.

The symbolism of the wampum collars is not very elaborate (Fig. 79). White rectangular Roman crosses or triangles upon a solid purple ground largely comprise the motives. The crosses are said to represent the parties concerned in a compact or in a civil event, as the case may be. Triangles represent wigwams, local or tribal groups, as do also the crosses. Symbolic wampum strips or "belts" were exchanged between negotiating tribes and were kept and rehearsed in council as

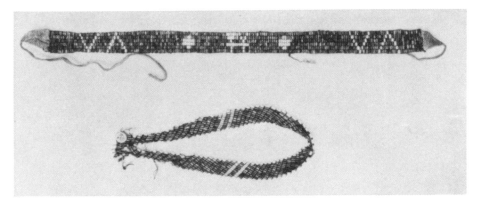

FIG. 79

Upper, Wampum Belt Representing Agreement between Penobscot and Other Peoples
Lower, Collar Representing Friendship

memorials of the event. All those coming from the Penobscot now preserved in museums seem to be the latter. The chief was originally the custodian of such objects. The Penobscot, however, have not continued to preserve oral or written records of the treaties, commemorated in wampum, to give any of the terms of agreement between themselves and the Iroquois, as have the Passamaquoddy.[28] In the memoir on wampum previously referred to, facts are compiled from information given by older Penobscot concerning the specimens in museum collections.

Figure 78 shows a wampum collar twenty-four inches long and one and one-half wide. The background is dark purple with double white oblique cross-bars enclosing crosses, some

[28] Cf. Prince, ref. I.

of them imperfect.   This belt is said to have been made and retained by the Penobscot in commemoration of a treaty of friendship between the tribes represented by the nine crosses. Eight of these tribes were enumerated by the governor of the tribe: the Penobscot, Passamaquoddy, Malecite, Micmac, Iroquois (Mohawk), Chippewa (eastern), Ottawa, and the "Flat Heads" (possibly the Têtes de Boule on the upper St. Maurice River, Canada).   This leaves out of account the Abenaki of St. Francis who, being well known to the Penobscot of that epoch, might have been the ninth tribe represented by the enclosed crosses.

IV

CHARACTERISTICS OF SOCIAL LIFE

FAMILY BANDS

WE NOW approach a most important topic of Penobscot life, a collection of data fraught with hopeful possibilities for gaining an insight into factors underlying the development of Algonkian society, and also with possibilities for serious misjudgment.

The social grouping which dominated Penobscot life in former times (until approximately 1870) was the family group. This corresponded to the secondary family unit of loose structure comprising persons related by blood and marriage, owning hunting and fishing rights in certain lineally transmitted districts marked by traditional bounds known geographically to the groups. The family groups also held associations with particular animals whose figures were adopted nominally as their emblems. Personal names of the groups were commonly derived from the associated animals. The family bands among the Penobscot numbered twenty-two in all, according to my informants in 1910.[1]

The family hunting territories, more or less geographically defined, were generally determined by groups of lakes or by river systems in the interior, and by bays or rivers and estuaries on the coast. The local bands or families were under the leadership of patriarchs. The rights to the district descended by inheritance through the male line to the active hunters of the family, i.e., to sons, to nephews, or to sons-in-law. It constituted what is termed "naked possession" of the land—usufruct tenure without title further than that conveyed by continued occupancy and use of its resources for the support of the family. The bands, moreover, were known by some special animals from which descent was claimed, or which, as in several instances, were associated with a legendary family hero. Certain features among the

[1] A list of twenty-four family bands was obtained by Dr. Frank T. Siebert.

latter were not unlike what is encountered among "totemic" divisions on the northwest coast of America.

Although we may speak of the family group here having had "totemic associations," it should be remembered that no restrictive regulations of marriage (exogamy), diet, or conduct, except in several individual instances, are recorded in connection with the groupings. It is hardly necessary to criticize in detail Morgan's [2] attempt to demonstrate clan organization among the northeastern Algonkian, further than to state that his ideas concerning the so-called clans of the Abenaki arose through approaching the problem with a preconceived impression. His list of Abenaki clans (evidently St. Francis Abenaki, judging from the dialect in which it is recorded) is manifestly a list of family hunting groups like those of the Penobscot.[3]

[2] L. H. Morgan, *Ancient Society*, N. Y., 1878, p. 174.

[3] F. G. Speck, "Abenaki Clans: Never!" *American Anthropologist*, vol. 37, no. 3, 1935, pp. 528–30. See also Bibliography, F. G. Speck, nos. 9 and 10.

Dr. Siebert, who subjected the question of sib organization among the Penobscot to closer examination with aged and competent informants (men of the Gabriel and Stanislaus families) in the early 1930's, is inclined to go somewhat farther in acceptance of a formalized sib status of the family groups. Since I regard the source material he obtained and his understanding of its meaning to be a definite contribution to the points of sib identity discussed above, I shall quote with his approval the comments he made after going over my material. (F. T. Siebert correspondence, June 1, 1939.) "Our only major point of difference (discarding Morgan entirely) is that I believe the Penobscot family groups are really weakly developed gentes. I think both the detail of your data and mine will satisfy all the requirements in the definition of a sib— *a named, formal, totemic, exogamous, unilateral group*. The only weak point is that of exogamy and I have stated my reasons for believing this was the case. You and your informants were probably confused by extratribal unions of the same totemic group, since I know there are both Malecite and Passamaquoddy "Bears" intermarried at Old Town for several generations. . . . My data shows reasonably well that the Penobscot family band functioned as a rather weakly developed sib. These were exogamous for the tribe but not for members of the same "totemic" division in neighboring Wabanaki tribes. Thus a Penobscot "Bear" could marry a Passamaquoddy or Malecite "Bear" (of this there are several examples) but not a member of the same sib in his own tribe. The small number of members in a family band, considering there were at least twenty-four such groups in a tribe numbering between 600 and 1000 people at the time of European settlement, combined with the originally strict Penobscot regulation preventing marriage between first and second cousins, seem in themselves to exclude marriage within the family group. Furthermore each of these patrilineal sibs or gentes possessed a "grandmother," the oldest woman in the gens, who presided over most of the domestic affairs of the group and had the power of rejecting any suitor from outside the gens who was proposing marriage to one of the young women of the gens. In addition each gens seems to have possessed a "welcome" song of its own, and to have had a strong sense of its own individuality and aloofness in social functions; a feeling which tends to persist to this day among several of the more conservative Penobscot families. On the whole the Penobscot seem to have

The Family and Kinship

The terms expressing relationship between members of the family include forms which may be interpreted from several points of view according to the theories of specialists in the field of social organization. The Penobscot relationship terms have been given in an article published in 1918, referred to in the Bibliography under my name, for which reason it is not urgent to reproduce them here. From the article some points may, however, be summarized. No positive indications of relationship between types of cousins or between nieces and nephews or uncles and aunts occur to suggest the operation of exogamic groupings, clans, or sibs. For the same series of terms there are no distinctions between individuals on the mother's or the father's side except for aunts. The term for niece is derived from that for daughter. And cousins of all classes are frequently addressed as brothers and sisters. There is the tendency for a widower to consider his deceased wife's sister as his next spouse (the sororate), and for the widow to marry her husband's brother if circumstances favor it (the levirate). A patrilineal tendency may also be discerned in the relationship of a male to his father's brother, who may adopt him or give him his training in hunting. The intimacy of relationships through marriage, showing in the terms used in reference and address to the "in-laws," may likewise be understood in the light of the "secondary family" framework in Penobscot society. In short, there are pointers to a recognition of the enclosing bonds of the family as the basis of Wabanaki society. It would seem that a loose

stood in a transitional cultural zone between the sibless nomadic Algonkians to the north, and the Iroquois and middle Atlantic Algonkians to the south and west who possessed a more complicated social structure. The position of the Penobscot was in a stage similar to that of the Ojibwa, who possessed sibs without moieties. It is a mistake to believe that Penobscot village life was not as completely developed as the hunting phases of the culture."

I am also moved by Dr. Siebert's material and reasoning to lean now toward his proposed definition of Penobscot sibs. A process of reinforcement of the family as a social integer may have been operating through the known historical relationship with Iroquois. The source material coming from a bygone epoch of native society inevitably lends itself to varied interpretational opinions. Dr. Siebert's views and his additional notes are accordingly included here for the benefit of technical readers who will see in these deliberations the evidence for regarding the problem of Wabanaki social organization as a still open one.

secondary family group, with paternal inheritance and name identity, obtrudes itself as affording an idea of the under-structure of the kinship scheme. No restraint exists between a man and his mother-in-law, no avoidance habit, but rather a filial-maternal feeling so far as custom is concerned. And the observed social customs favor the view.

It is believed by some informants that the family group names were associated with the animals of the chase most abundant in their territories, those furnishing their main supply of flesh and fur. Likenesses of the animal eponyms were painted or carved on landmarks such as trees and rocks, or represented by birch-bark cut-out silhouettes posted here and there on the borders of the hunting ranges. The boundaries thus marked were explicit in purpose. And we are reminded by informants that the same were employed as personal signatures on treaties. Furthermore, the men in general of each particular family band were known, to outsiders especially, by the names of their animal emblems.

The territory of each family group was regarded as inalienable property by the proprietors, to whom the hunting and fishing rights were restricted. It was even customary for cruising parties to secure permission to travel through the districts of another family group, while, in addition, it was emphatically wrong to hunt or trap outside one's own territory. Trespass was prevented by the exercise of magic power on the part of shamans in the family groups to conjure against intruders. Old *Ezəba'nəs*, "Raccoon," (family No. 15), laid a curse on his hunting territory against anyone who might invade it, by declaring that such a person would be found floating there dead. The right of sale may have been exercised at times, but it is not remembered by Penobscot informants. Newell Lion did, however, know of a Micmac's refusing six hundred dollars for his hunting ground on Kegemakugee lake, Nova Scotia.

The family hunting district was designated by the term *nzi·'bum*, meaning "my river." The determination of the country, in the native mind, from the point of view of its waterways becomes evident. And we note that "north" is literally "up river," in reference to the Penobscot River. The term *wagado'nkagan*, "(his) hunting territory" is the embracing designation for the same (F. T. Siebert).

Cross-paths, consisting of blazed trails, were maintained in the hunting districts, running north and south and east and west, along which the owners made their hunting and trapping excursions. The trails radiated from some favorite camp which made a local headquarters, temporary camps or stations being located at a day's journey in different quarters. The direction of these trails was determined more or less by the lay of the land, the lakes, and river courses in each particular territory. Upon these trails blazed signs, already given in a previous section, showed the direction of the camps for the convenience of strangers entering the districts. The animal emblem of the band was employed as the sign of proprietorship on the blazed trails. So it appears that in the old days the whole interior wilderness was covered with a network of trails, allowing little reason for anyone to get lost for very long in the woods. The hunters or trappers of each band operated in one quarter of their territory at a time, thereby allowing the game to increase unmolested in other quarters. Thus the game was "farmed" by each band.

Definite reference to the family hunting territory institution among the Penobscot is forthcoming from the records of a conference held with the Indians at Fort Pownall in 1764. The pertinent passage I quote from Sister Leger's *The Catholic Indian Missions in Maine (1611–1820)*, who cites it from the original in the Massachusetts Archives. "They said it was their custom to divide the hunting grounds and streams among the different Indian families; that they hunted every third year and killed two-thirds of the beaver, leaving the other third to breed; beavers were to them what cattle were to the Englishmen, but the English were killing off the beavers without any regard for the owners of the lands." [4]

When a family territory became overcrowded, or when the game in it became too scarce to support its occupants, a division was made among the members of the band. Some

[4] Leger, p. 115, quoting Joseph Chadwick, "An Account of a Journey from Fort Pownall up the Penobscot River to Quebec, 1764." Printed also in *Bangor Historical Magazine*, vol. IV, 141.

families would separate, packing up their paraphernalia, and emigrate up some river in canoes until they reached an un-occupied, unposted region such as was to be found in the interior to the north. Here, when a suitable region was dis-covered, they settled and founded the nucleus of a new band by assuming an animal emblem and posting their new habitat with the representation to show proprietorship by preëmption. These facts indicate quite graphically the probable north-eastern Algonkian drift, from west to east generally speaking; one group branching off from the other under like circum-stances. Considerations like these, taken in connection with the high development of modes of travel, the temporary character of domestic utensils, and the general cultural sim-plicity of the tribes will, when more is known of the neighbor-ing Wabanaki, afford helpful material for the solution of the problem of Algonkian migrations.

In recent years investigations made among the northern forest tribes, not those of the treeless barrens, from the Ojibwa to the Montagnais disclose an essentially similar social and economic organization as that described here. The division of the country into either large or small family hunting territories was fundamentally similar. In this "prim-itive" type of organization we observe, as I conceive it still, one of the earliest Algonkian social characteristics. If one admits that sociological factors are slow developers in this area, that in the northern deciduous forest area social struc-ture of the hunting peoples was harmoniously adjusted to the habits of game animals, then we may assume the institution described to be at the core of northeastern Algonkian culture.

Some data of a more specific nature may now be reviewed: the legends of family associations.

One of the most interesting features of this unelaborate family organization is the belief in descent from animals, or in the idea of associating the first formation of the group with some animal or creature with which an early family hero had an adventure.[5] As will appear shortly, a group of families

[5] In regard to the possibility of a weak totemic complex existing in former Penob-scot society, I may say that the indications appealed to me at first with mild force, indeed as something more to be suspected than accepted in view of the apparent

claiming their association with aquatic creatures (whale, eel, sculpin, crab, sturgeon, yellow perch, lobster, frog) form a group with a common origin legend, and, besides being mythically related, also coincide territorially, since some of their districts are grouped near the lower part of Penobscot River and Penobscot Bay. These were designated as the "saltwater families." No further political links seem to have developed. One additional fact, however, has some significance, which is that of the two families highest in rank, from which the tribal chief could be chosen, one was of the Frog family, a water family, the other was of the Squirrel, a terrestrial family.[6] This is suggestive of a dual social grouping in the tribe and will be taken up again. The origin legend of the aquatic group referred to is found in the Water Famine myth, which relates how the culture hero, Gluskɑ'be, killed the monster frog who had retained all the water of the world in his stomach, and freed the rivers to relieve the world drought. The people were so impatient to quench their thirst that many of them rushed into the water and were transformed into the various fish and marine creatures. Whereupon their human relatives who escaped the transformation assumed the name of their transformed relatives. Those survivors became the founders of the different human families who thereafter partitioned the country among themselves into hunting districts. In the subsequent history of these families, we find the Penobscot believing that the descendants of the original founders gradually assumed some of the peculiarities of their relatives transformed into animals, on the native theory of cross-inheritance. The sculpin,

absence of anything corresponding to it among the culturally related Wabanaki and Labradorean tribes. The notes collected were at first also somewhat unorganized in form and sequence. Although not without harmony in spirit both in internal values and in respect to conditions of life among hunting peoples, the suspicion of fictitiousness was soon dispelled by further penetration of the topic with the aid of Newell Lion.

[6] Dr. Siebert offers the following on family hegemony and succession of chiefs. "The famous Penobscot chief, Joseph Orono, who died in 1801, was of the Beaver family. This fact has been ascertained from two independent sources. One of my informants, an Orono descendant, remembers her grandmother referring to him as kəmohsoməs ktcitəmahkwe, "Our grandfather, the Great Beaver." Mrs. Fannie Eckstorm, of Brewer, Maine, in a personal communication, informs me that Chief Orono signed several deeds with a beaver as his mark. Two of my informants state that the Otter sib furnished several important Penobscot chiefs in the past.

"homely head," family for example, was regarded as possessing the characteristic of facial homeliness.   The toad, "dirty,
smelly," family bore the stigma of their name, and the yellow
perch, "old foot wrapper, sock," held a low social rank, again
through sharing association with its eponym.   As will be
seen, personal names in the family groups were also often
nicknames of the original animal.

Hence an affinal relationship was established between
human families and existing animals, resulting in the use of
a term *ndo'dem*, "my co-relative," in referring to the animals
related through ancestry.   The Penobscot employ this term
with its classical meaning in social parlance.

The grouping of the mammal-named families, as opposed
to those bearing names of sea creatures, and their location in
the interior forests, is also significant as contrasted with the
territorial grouping of the salt-water groups.   In some of the
former we encounter secondary origin legends quite different
from the common legend of the latter.   Unfortunately, in the
case of these animal families, some of the legends are wanting.
Here also the older Indians thought that the families shared
some of the temperamental traits of their associated animals,
some being stealthy, others sluggish, others active, and others
timid and poor.   It is also stated that in the case of each
family division the diet consisted largely of the animal whose
name it bore, and that this particular creature was most
abundant in the territory of that group.

The matter of taboo in relation to behavior between the
human family groups and their animal eponyms also comes
up as one of the complexes of the family institution here.   In
the history of the Mitchell family (no. 3), a taboo against the
killing of the female bear develops as a family proscription.
The interpretation of this feature must, however, take into
consideration the fact that a similar ruling results through
the artificial relationship between an individual hunter and
the deer, as related in a tale, but for some reason it does not
become a family taboo.

Out of justice to the powers of discernment, or whatever
else it may have been in the dynamics of social change among

preliterate peoples, shown by the old Indians in giving the animal nicknames to their family groups, it cannot be denied that the characterizations are ludicrously apt in many cases. The inherited expectation, for instance, that members of the Whale Family (Stanislaus)[7] be large and dark is apparently realized in the present descendants, and the lazy characteristics of the Hare (Newell) family are still to be remarked in the behavior of some members of this group. So the Atteans of the Squirrel family are actually held to be a bright, active folk, all of which traits the people regard as true and persistently surviving marks of totemic heredity. More than one outside observer has become somewhat credulous of the alleged physical family characteristics of today when these have been suggested in the village talk of the Indians.

A most peculiar intimacy is apparent in all the social and economic associations between the family group itself and this animal "totem," but this is not true as regards religion. The historical, territorial, naming, dietary, pseudo-physical, and social coördination noted as forming the imaginary bonds between the animal and human groups seems to offer a new type of social complex. Although hitherto unreported in this area, this might, I suspect, be found to be more prevalent than has been thought among other nomadic hunting tribes in the north—the "game totem" idea of Haddon.

Mythically the aquatic families seem to be the oldest. This, together with the generally denser population, smaller size of the hunting districts, and more sedentary life of these down-river families might indicate that the Penobscot drifted into their present habitat from southern New England, following the line of the coast and working their way up the large rivers toward the interior. On the other hand, this evidence may be offset by the resemblances in language and culture between the Wabanaki populations and those immediately north of the St. Lawrence River.

[7] No exposition of the social history of an unlettered people, if discretely handled, can evade the issue of conflicting opinion upon points of family genealogy when different informants are consulted. Accordingly I make entry of the notes of Dr. Siebert concerning the Stanislas line. He recorded that all the recent members of the Stanislas family belonged to the Squirrel "gens," although they told him that they did have defunct relations who belonged to the Whale family group.

The family group, or family band, is called *si'wenawɑk*, another term *ndalnɑ'bemɑk*, "my people," denoting practically the same thing, that is "my family group."

I give below the list of family groups, the numbering of each corresponding to the numbering which marks the territory in the map on page 6, the family name, the modern one adopted after the era of Christianity, the appropriated hunting territory, and mention of the family legend of origin or association following in order.

The bands of the northern part of the country assembled usually at the northern villages, "where the current piles up sand," *Madawɑ'mkik* (Mattawamkeag), and *Tcimski'tegukʷ*, "big dead water" (Kingman). The central bands held their gatherings often at *Matna'guk*, "Long Island" (Lincoln), where there is still a dwindling village. All however had Indian Island (*Panawa'pskik*) for the central tribal headquarters where they held elections and ceremonies as at a capital.

Dr. Siebert's studies substantiate the listing in the tabulation beginning on facing page, except that he was "unable to identify the Sculpin family among the Penobscot." He also obtained the names of four family units of which I was not informed, namely, Porcupine, Turtle, Owl, and Dragon Fly.

FAMILY ORIGIN LEGENDS, HISTORIES, AND SOCIAL PECULIARITIES

We now come to consideration of family origin legends explaining the associations occurring back in the legendary era between human groups and animal prototypes. Tales of animal association of a type similar to those invented among the Northwest Coast tribes in explanation of the family social and physical traits have come down in Penobscot social tradition for some of the families, but not all. It is not easy to explain this trait occurrence in a detached, limited location in the far northeast. Nowhere thus far among the other Wabanaki or the Labradorean Algonkian are similar family and animal associations reported. And the now almost complete survey of social organization in the far northeast leaves

Number on Map	Name	Analysis	English Name	Modern (1910) Christian Family Names	Territory	Origin	Remarks (for further details see next topic)
1 2	Saŋge Nɑmɑdjeno's·es·u	(?) "side walker"	Lobster, Crab	Mitchell (Day-ligi·t) Gusup	Shores of Penobscot Bay. Territories not differentiated. Headquarters at Madjibigwa'das·ik (Castine) and E's·ik, "clam place" (Stockton).	(See Water Famine Myth) Originated from people transformed into crabs and lobsters.	Said to have always lived "near the lobsters and crabs", catching them in quantities and being expert seamen and salt-water canoemen.
3	Awe's·us	"roaming creature"	Bear	Mitchell (Bear), Denis	Lower western banks of Penobscot River, around Belfast.	Ancestor abducted by Bear (see Bear Abduction Myth).	A family high in rank. Taboo against killing Bear. Nicknamed "Bear."
4	Sɑngwa'dekwe	"homely head"	Sculpin	Francis (Joe)	Lower east country from Penobscot River, around Bucksport, east to Union River.	(Cf. Water Famine Myth)	Nickname, "Rockhead," said to be a homely family.
5	Nɑha'mu		Eel	Neptune	Valley of Kenduskeag (Kɑnde's·ki·k "overgrown eel place") River north to and including Bɪ·gwa'dɐk, "abundance of game" (Pushaw).	do.	This family had the reputation of being magicians, with eels for helpers. They lived extensively upon eels which are abundant in the district.
6	Ma'ske	"smelly, dirty"	Toad	Glossian (Pete)	East shore and country from Penobscot River including valley of Sunkhaze River.	do. (?)	A family of low caste, slovenly.
7	Awha'n·dos	"creeping insect"	Insect	Newell, Nelson	West of Penobscot River north of Pushaw Lake, around Dead Stream and Birch Stream.	(?)	
8	Pagɑ'mke	"Pops up and down suddenly" (on account of stealth).	Fisher	Newell Francis Sabat Francis	Shores of Passadumkeag Stream.	(?)	

Continued on next page

Number on Map	Name	Analysis	English Name	Modern (1910) Christian Family Names	Territory	Origin	Remarks (For further details see next topic)
9	Pode'be	"monster"	Whale	Stanislaus	Territory uncertain. Thought to be west of Penobscot River adjoining Insect family, north from Piscataquis River to Millinocket Lake.	(Cf. Water Famine Myth) There is also a family tale of transformation of relatives into whales	Said to be a family of large, dark people.
10	Tama'kwe	"cuts wood"	Beaver	(None)	Territory uncertain. Thought to be east of Penobscot River, north of Fisher territory.	(?)	This family is extinct. Nicknamed "Beaver."
11	Kaba' se	"driven out of water by light of torch."	Sturgeon	Sockalexis	From Ragged Lake west to Moosehead Lake.	(Cf. Water Famine Myth)	A family high in rank.
12	Ma'lsam	"(?)-dog"	Wolf	Polis, Susup	Territory around Nahmakanta, Pemadumcook, and North Twin Lakes.	(Cf. Dog Ancestor Story)	
13	Tcigwa'lus		Frog	Orson	Spencer Lake, Lobster Lake, and Pine Stream.	(Cf. Water Famine Myth)	One of the two highest bands. Chief chosen from this.
14	Mik'we		Squirrel	Attean	Caribou, Ragged Lakes west of Chesuncook to Black Brook Pond.	(?)	The corresponding highest band; chief chosen from this also.
15	Ezəba'nas		Raccoon		Salmon River from mouth to the mouth of Mud Brook on east branch of Penobscot River.	(?)	Family is extinct. Julie Newell last member.
16	Ala'ŋksu	"(long?) tail"	Wolverine	Lewis	From Mattawamkeag northward, east of Mattawamkeag River, Headquarters at Tcimski'tegukʷ, (Kingman).	(?)	

NUMBER ON MAP	NAME	ANALYSIS	ENGLISH NAME	MODERN (1910) CHRISTIAN FAMILY NAMES	TERRITORY	ORIGIN	REMARKS (FOR FURTHER DETAILS SEE NEXT TOPIC)
17	Wana'gɑmes"·u	"addle-headed creature" (with narrow face and foolish ways).	Water Nymph	Coley, Nicola	Russell Stream and Pond	(Cf. Origin of Water Nymph.)	A much respected family, descended from illustrious founder. A warrior family.
18	Ki'uni'ge	"Wandering about with load on back" (like a hunter in traveling).	Otter	Saul, Nicola	Ripogenus, Sourdnahunk Streams, Telos and Harrington Lakes, between Chesuncook Lake and Mt. Katahdin.	(?)	
19	Kc̄cipesu' Abi·gwe'si·gan	"big cat, foot wrappings, socks" (on account of big padded feet).	Wildcat	Fransway Penus	Around Musungum Stream, Mooseleuk Streams, and Seboois Lakes.	(?)	
20	Matagwe's·u		Rabbit (Hare)	Newell	Masardis waters		A band of poor hunters, with a small territory. Said to be feeble and poor, like the rabbits.
21	Asiga'nas	"old foot wrapper, sock"	Yellow perch	Penewit	Caucomgomoc and Russell Pond	(Cf. "Water Famine Myth.")	Lowest band of all. Said to be lazy and shiftless, after manner of yellow perch.
22	Kc̄c̄iga'gago	"big crow"	Raven	Swassion, Susup	The largest territory in tribe, embraces district north of territories all the way to St. John River, and east to Little Madawaska.	Derived from the Passamaquoddy (Siebert)	An active band of hunters who owned the whole northern wilderness. Originally seven brothers.
23				Denis	A medium sized tract, east of Union River to Frenchman's Bay.		A mixed Penobscot and Passamaquoddy family which did not figure regularly in Penobscot grouping.

almost nil any future expectation for such a possibility. In Penobscot, the family-association complex assumes, indeed, a totemistic color. The discussion invited by this perplexing case will, however, be left untouched at present to make way for what is more essential to our purpose now, namely, presentation of the material itself relating to Penobscot family narrative history. In reference to some of the families there is nothing to offer beyond the name and some generalized suppositions; the theories of social and physical attributes previously referred to. For those family groups, however, possessing associated legends as their specific property, there are data now to be presented under the numbers and names assigned to them on the chart and summarized tables. The myth of the water famine, in which the transformer Gluskabe changes certain human beings into races of aquatic creatures, has a bearing upon the origin of those families whose identity is connected with creatures residing in the water. Since this tale applies to families numbered 1, 2, 3, 4, 5, 6 (?), 9, 11, 13, 21, it may be given in translation.

The Water Famine, Origin of Aquatic Creatures and Their Families

From this the origin of fish, frogs and turtles. A long time ago they settled the Indians, up the river. A monster frog, Aglǝbe′mu, forbade them water, these Indians. Some even died on account of the thirst for water. The Gluskɑ′be came there. He saw his people looking sickly. He asked them, "What is the trouble?" They told him, "Aglǝbe′mu has almost killed us all. He is making us die of thirst. He forbids us water." The Gluskɑ′be said, "I will make him give you water." Then they went with Gluskɑ′be their chief to where Aglǝbe′mu is. Then he said to him, "Why do you abuse our grandchildren? Now you will be sorry for this, for abusing our grandchildren. Now I will give them water so that all will get an equal share of the water. The benefit will be shared." Then he grabbed him and broke his back. From thenceforth now all bullfrogs are broken-backed. Even then he did not give up the water. So Gluskɑ′be took his axe and cut down a big tree, a yellow birch, cutting it so that, upon Aglǝbe′mu, when it fell down, the yellow birch, it killed Aglǝbe′mu. That's how the Penobscot River originated. The water flowed from him. All the branches of the tree became rivers, all emptied into the main river. From this came the big river. Now all the Indians were so thirsty, nearly dying, that they all jumped into the river. Some turned into fish, some turned to frogs, some turned to turtles. A few survived. Now that's why they inhabit the length of the Penobscot River. Thence, now, they took their names. Some took fish names, since their departed relatives turned into fish. Now, thence, they took in this way their family names, from all kinds of fish and turtles.

1. Mitchell (Lobster).

This was one of the important old Penobscot families. One of the last to subsist entirely upon the products of the sea in its own territory. Among the last of its conservative members was old Dr. Mitchell, a professional herbalist. The nickname, Dje'kwadis, "early riser," or Daylight, has remained attached to the men. Its origin is embraced in the Water Famine legend.

2. Susup (Crab).

We have no information to differentiate this group from the preceding, except the name.

3. Mitchell (Bear).

One of the families highest in rank. Early known, and even today possessing a reputation for good behavior and dignity in the tribe. Tradition states that its hunting territory was apportioned from part of that held by the Lobster family. That there was some unassigned territory in these environs makes these family connections seem plausible, for we learn that below the Mitchell tract, on the shores of the upper bay and some of the islands, rested a tract recognized as public territory to be occupied in the summer by any of the families who desired to go to salt water to replenish their supply of seal oil.

A family under the patronym of Sabatis Denis, of mixed Penobscot and Passamaquoddy descent, occupying a tract east of Union River, seems to have had affiliations with the Bear family. I have not included this among the twenty-two original Penobscot families.

The legendary association of the Mitchell, Bear family, is most distinctive, and accounts for the imposition of a hunting

taboo upon it in relation to the Bear.   Several versions of this
story are given.

Origin of the Bear Family

Perhaps the most interesting feature in the social organization of the Penobscot is the data we have concerning the
family known as the Bears.   The facts regarding this group
primarily have nothing to do with the origin of any of the
previously discussed groups.   They refer only to an ancestor,
in one of the families, who was abducted by bears and treated
as one of their cubs.   Afterwards, being recovered by his
human relatives, this man and his descendants became known
as bears, and the circumstances of his life with the bears
developed the idea that he had acquired some of their characteristics.   Subsequently his descendants never killed bears,
but held them in a sort of supernatural kinship reverence.
More than this, in pictographic carvings, these offshoots of the
legendary ancestor represented themselves as bears.   A feeling of a different identity seems to have grown up among
them, emphasized no doubt by the legend told their ancestor,
and, following the idea of kinship, they ordinarily seem to
have married outside of the family.

Judging from material available among informants, some
of them the descendants of the original hero, we seem to have
here a family group in the process of metamorphosis into a
typical gentile group, with a common, mythical, half-animal
ancestor and a family historical legend, a common name, a
tendency towards exogamy, a taboo against harming the
animal concerned in their myth, a crest, as it were, and a
separate and superior group identity in public estimation.

The major portion of the data concerning the Bear family
was brought to light through a descendant of the original hero
of the ensuing tale, who owned a very old powder horn
bearing an incised representation of his mother, who was a
Bear, seated in the bow of a canoe traveling to the hunting
grounds with her husband.   This interesting legend as recorded from the translator is as follows.

The Story of the Bear Family

Many generations ago there was a man, his wife, and a little son, who started out from the village to go to Canada. They were bound for a great council and dance to be held at Caughnawaga. They went up river to a certain place where they had to make a carry of twenty miles to reach the headquarters of another river which leads to the St. Lawrence. When they came to this carry, the man started ahead with the canoe on his back, leaving his wife to pack part of the luggage to the first halting place, and the little boy to run alongside of her.[8] But while she was busy arranging her pack the little boy started off and ran to catch up with his father. But the man had gone on so far that the little boy did not find him, and so the child got lost. Meanwhile the mother thought the little boy had reached his father, and so bothered no more about it. The child strayed from the trail and was lost. When the mother arrived at the halting place, she asked her husband where the boy was. And he asked her the same. She told him what had taken place, and they at once started back to search. But they could not find him. On account of this, the pair turned back and went home to tell their story. All the men of the village turned out, and for months they hunted everywhere for the little boy; but they did not find him. All the next winter they searched, until in March they discovered a place where some sharpened sticks lay near the water. They then concluded that the boy was alive somewhere and had been spearing fish. There were footprints of bears about. They then concluded that the little boy had been adopted by bears. But no one in the band could trace him any further, and they were almost ready to give up the search. Now there was a lazy man in the village who did not take much part in the searching, but lay around idly. Everybody kicked and abused him and said, "Why don't you hunt for the boy? You are good for nothing." Says he, "Very well, I will." And he started off. He goes right to the bear's den and knocks with his bow on the rocks at the entrance. There arises a great noise inside, where the father, mother, and baby bear live with their adopted little boy. The father goes to the entrance and holds out a birch-bark vessel. The lazy man shoots it and kills the bear. The mother bear says, "Now, I will go," and takes another bark vessel and holds it out of the entrance and is killed too. Then the cub does the same, and

[8] In making long portages the Indians stopped part way and camped over night. The route they were traveling was an old well-known trail from Penobscot Bay to the Iroquois village at Caughnawaga.

is killed. All the bears are laid out dead in the cave. Then the lazy man enters the cave and sees the little boy, all afraid, huddled up in a dark corner, crying for his relatives, and trying to hide. The lazy hunter now carries him home to the village, and gives him to his parents. So everybody gives the lazy man presents: two blankets, a canoe, ammunition, and other things, he gets. He gets rich. Now the little boy was turning into a bear. Already bristles were beginning to show on his upper back and his shoulders, and his manners were changed. But finally they got him back like a person again, and he grew up to be an Indian. He got married and had children. But they and all his descendants were called Bears. They always drew a picture of a bear on a piece of birch bark with charcoal and left it at their camps wherever they went. All his descendants did this, too, and they drew the picture on their possessions. I am one of the Bear family. My mother was one, and her husband drew the bear picture on his powder horn. There were many descendants in different families, and people called them bears.

In the history of this bear family, whether or not it embraces the whole of the Bear hunting family group of later times, I am tempted to think that we are in the presence of a comparatively recent process similar to what might have occurred among the more highly organized central Algonkian. Outside European influences, unfortunately, checked its development before it became well established. In short, it seems to me tentatively that this feature of Penobscot social life is not without considerable illustrative significance in its bearing upon social life of the Algonkian in general. The Penobscot, indeed, seem in many respects to represent an early formative pattern of Algonkian culture.

A sequel to this tale tells us that the old bear mother told the boy when he grew up never to kill a female bear. She told him how to distinguish between the sexes at a distance, by going to high ground and looking over the country for his game. Where he would discern a thin stream of vapor rising, there would be the den of a female bear. He was not to go there. But where the vapor from the den rose in a big streak it was a male bear and he could go for it. (The vapor is believed to come from the concentration of the breath of the animal while hibernating.)

4. Francis (Sculpin).

No specific information obtained. Origin included in Water Famine story.

5. Neptune (Eel).

A family that frequented salt-water districts, subsisting, by repute, largely upon eels which were extremely abundant in its waters, and also producing magicians who derived their power and vitality from eel helpers. The Water Famine Myth is said to cover the origin of this family.

We have, nevertheless, a concurrent tale of ancestral association with dogs. Duplication in family stories occur. Several tales of dog association are given. Before glancing at them, however, it may be noted that sexual appetite seems to be assigned to its earlier members, and several instances of misconduct, besides the association with dogs, reveal themselves, as ethics are judged from the Penobscot point of view.

One of its prominent ancestors, old John Neptune, a former lieutenant-governor of the tribe, acquired among the Malecite a sobriquet for his fondness for women. Among the Malecite the occasion must have been extreme, to have produced such a result. Another instance is related of one of the earlier women of this family who ran away with her first cousin and bore a son who died young; a social crime in Penobscot behavior which is thought to have left its mark on the family. Another of its members, who died about 1870, is said to have kept a herd of from fifteen to twenty dogs. Her children "had long pendant ears." It is added that when strange dogs came to their camp the children would attack them and she would join in. This was the wife of old Padjo Susup (Padjo, probably a corruption of "Poor Joe") who was likewise reputed to have been of "canine mixture" through having long ears. The family history seems fraught with similar confused allusions. Even in recent years, quarrels have taken place between its descendants and others through these unpleasant accusations when they were intoxicated.

Another example of the elementary formation of a family group with mythical animal associations is explained in the following tradition.

The Dog Ancestor

Long ago, a hunter started out on his hunting excursion alone except for a large bitch which he owned. When he returned he had with him a baby girl. He would not tell by whom the child was born, and from its peculiar appearance and manners rumor spread that he had cohabited with his bitch which had given birth to the child. The child, it is said, before lying down, would turn around three times as dogs do. From the creature there were many descendants who eventually married, and there are still those in the tribe who trace their ancestry to it. They are reputed to have rather large flapping ears, as a trace of this descent.

The above is fairly self-explanatory. It may be added that the descendants of the supposed dog-woman are locally well known, and show resentment towards any mention of it. No conventional totemistic attitude, however, has developed in the case.

A Neptune family of different extraction, without definite territory or totemic association, is remembered. Informants thought that this group was not even related to number 5. Captain Swassion Neptune and Sockabesin Neptune, brothers, were earlier prominent men of this line. That there is a Neptune family prominent among the Wawenock of Becancour, formerly neighbors of the Penobscot on the coast westward, may presumably have some bearing upon the confusion of family names. François Neptune, a Wawenock informant (1914), told me of the existence of a related branch of his family among the Penobscot.

6. Glossian (Toad).

Information on mythical associations here is meager. The group was held in low social esteem, and irregular social behavior is attributed to some of its members. It is said that one of them, who had intercourse with his brother's wife, had been obliged to marry her upon the birth of a child that died young out of punishment. Two other members of this generation it was said had no children for similar reasons. Another instance of concubinage is cited. Members of the family also seem to have earned the sobriquet Maske, "Toad-like" (Moll Maske, Mary Glossian and Maskises, "Little

Toad," Sebat Glossian). As to origin, the only statement obtained was that the family was allied with the Frog (no. 13) in the Water Famine legend.

7. Newell, Nelson (Insect).

There is practically no historical information concerning this family, which is largely Passamaquoddy by mixture; whence comes the later family name of Nelson.

8. Francis (Fisher).

For this family we have no social or historical facts of particular significance to offer. Some of the men have carried the aboriginal patronym, Paga′mke, "Fisher," as nicknames down to the present. No origin tale or associations have been brought to light.

9. Stanislas (Whale).

The physical attributes of large size, dark skin, dignified manner, and longevity are given by popular tradition to the men of the Whale family. Curiously enough this impression is borne out by several of them living in 1915. The origin legend goes back to the Water Famine event. The following short narrative, relative to the transformation of members of this family into whales, can hardly be given the prominence of an origin legend in view of the literary emphasis assumed in this connection by the Water Famine legend. It shows, however, a definite tendency to create association and collateral relationship with a totemistic animal.

People Transformed into Whales

There was a man who had two daughters. One time, the family was abandoned by the rest of the tribe, and the three tried to follow and overtake them. Traces of the departure of the people led down to the sea. When the man and his daughters reached the shore, however, they gave up the effort to go farther. They walked right into the water and became transformed into whales, being seen later blowing off shore.

Origin of the Name of the Water Nymph Family
(Second Version)

Mandoa′mek𝓌, "Spirit (Devil) Fish," was so named for his cruelty. As a boy he used to catch catfish and cut off their heads to show his valor. He was very brave. One time, when still young, he ran away from home to escape being punished by his father. With some other boys he went up the river and camped in hiding. While there he met two strange persons in a stone canoe with a high bow. They had "hatchet faces" with eyes, nose and mouth close together. One of them said to the boys that he would help them find a party of enemy Mohawk in hiding and camping up the river. They went to the place and surprised the Mohawk while they were asleep, and the Water Nymphs, for such they were, helped them by pouring water over the Mohawk's fire to create steam to add to the enemy's confusion. The boys cut the throats of the Mohawk and scalped them. Then they came downstream and reached the village (Oldtown), surprising the people by displaying the scalps from their canoe. Madokʷha'ndo, "Strange, Queer Spirit," was a descendant of Mandoa'mekʷ.

10. Beaver (no European family name).

There is no information to give in respect to this family, which died out with Joe Təma'hkwe (Beaver) many years ago.

11. Sockalexis (Sturgeon).

This is another family of high standing in the tribe. The men of three generations ago all bore the surname Kaba'hse, "Sturgeon," or an equivalent. For instance, Kwuna'kwədun, "Long mouth" (Attean Kwuna'kwədun, one of the family patriarchs). Among the missing links, through which possible relationship between Penobscot families and the now dispersed tribes adjacent to them on the west may be traced, we have a fragment of evidence in the following:

A traveler, Kendall, about 1807 reported the existence of a family of Indians residing at Cabbasseecontee (*Kaba'sikanti*, "sturgeon fishing") lake, near the Kennebec River, along the direct route of travel leading from Moosehead Lake to the sea. The Sockalexis (Sturgeon) family hunting grounds were located on Moosehead Lake. What affinity exists between the extant Sockalexis (Sturgeon) and the long-forgotten Sturgeon band of Kendall's time can only be conjectured. Kendall recorded an interesting legend of the origin of the Indians he met as being transformed sturgeons—an episode suggestive of the usual local transformation pattern.

Cabbassagunti Version of the Family Origin Myth [9]

In Winthrop is part of a lake, six miles in length, called till lately, Lake Cobbeseconte, but now Winthrop Pond. From the lake, a small stream runs southeastward into the Kennebec and is known by the name of Cobbeseconte, as the English pronounce it; but by the Indians called Cobisseconteag, which in their language, is "the land where sturgeon are taken." A very trifling number of the Indians of this river are still in existence and belong to the village of St. Francais, where they bear the name of Cabbassagunti-quoke, that is, "people of Cabbassaguntiquoke." Cabbassa signifies a sturgeon. . . . However, the Cabbassagunties were not only inhabitants of Cabbassaguntiquoke, but Cabbassas or sturgeons themselves. They relate, that in days of yore, a certain man, their progenitor, standing on the banks of the river stripped himself, and having made formal declaration that he was a sturgeon, leaped into.it. He never returned out of the water in human shape, but a sturgeon, into which he was supposed to have changed himself, or to have been changed, was seen playing in the stream immediately after his disappearance; and, upon this evidence, in addition to his own declaration, all the nation professed themselves ever after to be sturgeons. Another fable of the Cabbassagunties respects the outlet in the lake by which the stream below escapes, and at which they represent the rock as having been cut by the ax of a mighty manitou, standing with a foot on either bank of the outlet.

Interpretation seems to make it clear that here we have a version of the common human transformation myth related by a small band, probably constituting a family group, living on a family hunting territory located about Cabbasseconte Lake. This version, it would seem, explains their own concern in the general myth, and attributes their family ancestry to the sturgeon in a manner completely reconcilable with the Penobscot family legends.

12. Polis (Wolf).

From existing sources of information, the confusion reigning between this, the Mitchell (Bear), and the Susup-Neptune families, no positive identity can be given it. The bear ancestor story, previously given with history of family number

[9] E. A. Kendall, *Travels through the Northern Parts of the United States in the Years 1807 and 1808* (3 vols.) New York. 1809. Vol. 3, pp. 123–125.

3, is extended also to this family. The time is too late to clarify the obscure connections.

13. Orson (Frog).

This is one of the two families highest in esteem, from which in early times the hereditary chief of the moiety with water creatures in totemistic associations was chosen. Family statistics show high mortality among children here, one of the families (Attean Orson) having lost thirteen or fourteen children at early ages; his brother (Nicola) having had four children married, three of them without issue. Its origin springs from the Water Famine episode. The prominent position of the frog in this myth seems to have extended some glory over the human co-relatives. The frog is, moreover, the bringer of babies in Penobscot fable.

14. Attean (Squirrel).

Here is a family of high social rank equal to that of the several groups previously mentioned. This family group furnished the hereditary chief of the moiety in the tribe comprising families derived or associated with land animals (p. 234).

15. Raccoon (no English name).

This family died out some years ago. No noteworthy facts in reference to social history were obtained. Its sterility, however, is a remembered feature. My notes show that the last two married women of the line, sisters (Elizabeth and Sulian), lost thirteen or fourteen and four babies respectively in recent years—infant mortality with a vengeance!

16. Lewis (Wolverine).

No specific traditions are available beyond the name, some marriage statistics, reference to the abundance of wolverines in the district, and the use of the wolverine nickname among men.

17. Coley, Nicola (Water Nymph).

Our earliest note of family history points to Piel Mali who died over a hundred years ago. His proper name was that of the family, Wanagαme's'u, denoting the water fairy prominent in folklore, characterized by its peculiar conformation of face. Genealogy has nothing of interest to add, except that his wife was a Micmac. Social attributes, however, accord the family a high reputation as warriors, a name borne out by its men through a long span of tribal history beginning in legendary times and maintained through the Civil War period. Medicines and practices insuring protection against injury were handed down in this family. Among them may be mentioned eating the head of a living terrapin, which protected one of its members (Lola Coley) from injury through the entire Civil War. The legendary origin of the family association with the water nymph, and the determination of its warlike characteristics and valor are covered in several versions of a tale pertaining to the Mohawk wars, as follows:

The Origin of the Water Nymph Family

Once upon a time, a long time ago, boys went up the river to fish. They went above the islands and caught a lot of black chubs (*awu'skhowak*, "spies"). The boys cut off their heads, stuck them on pointed sticks and stood them upright in the bow of their canoe. When they came down the river and neared the island they began singing a war song. An old man heard them and told the people in the village that the boys were coming home with enemies' heads on poles in their canoes. When they got nearer, the people saw they were nothing but fish heads, and to avert misfortune they made them stop singing. Now, one of these boys was named *Mandowa'mek*, "Devil fish." [10] He gathered the boys and told them they would all go back and this time they would have better luck. So they again ascended the river. Before they had gone far they met two creatures paddling a canoe toward them. These men had very narrow faces and very large noses which they covered with their hands as they came near the boys, shy because they were so ugly. When they came close they said, "Mohawk are camped up the river," and passed on. These two creatures were *Wanagame'swak*, "water nymphs." Now the boys, led by Devil Fish, ascended quietly and made camp for the night up the river near the Mohawk camp. They waited till night, when the Mohawk were asleep; then went in and cut off their heads. The next morning they returned to the village, this time with heads of the Mohawk on poles in the bow of their canoe. They sang their war song. But this time no one told them to stop. For this deed Devil Fish

[10] In another version his name is given as *Ma'dokwaha'ndo*, by which he is known in history.

became the founder of a family. His descendants formed the water nymph family and band."

18. Nicola (Otter).

This family seems to be of Norridgewock extraction. The family legend refers to the period about 1723, when the Abenaki Mission was demolished by an English force, and the missionary Rasles lost his life.[11] The story runs that one of the Indian fugitives lost a hand in the encounter (from which he derived a name, Temi'ptinat, "Hand Cut Off"). He escaped by swimming a rapids, afterwards known as Bomazeen Rips, on the Kennebec River. From this event he acquired the additional title of Bamǝzi', "If all";—by popular etymology, "If we were all there we should have been massacred." This family was closely intermarried with the Sturgeon family (no. 11).

19. Penus (Wildcat).

Information is lacking beyond the statement that the oldest remembered sire (François Penus (Phineas)) had married a St. Francis Abenaki, bringing it into connection with that tribe.

20. Newell (Rabbit (Hare)).

A family of Malecite extraction known as Wa'bus, "Hare," incorporated with the Penobscot since about 1870. We learn that they were wanderers through the country, settling at last at Oldtown, and for a long time subsisting by charity. The family head of this group was an old man, Ktciwabu's, "Old Rabbit." He was so dubbed because he limped. As may be seen in the list of family intermarriages, the Rabbits soon became blended with the Penobscot. Their hunting territory remained on the eastern frontier of the Penobscot, bordering Malecite territory.

21. Penewit (Yellow Perch).

This is a small and insignificant group tracing origin from the Water Famine episode. Its social attributes, to quote popular saying, seem to be defined by the translation of its

---

[11] A thorough discussion of records of this event is given by Mrs. Eckstorm, "The Attack on Norridgewock (1794)," *New England Quarterly*, Sept. 1934, pp. 541–78.

animal sobriquet Asiga′nəs, "Old foot wrapper," or sock, denoting likewise the worthlessness of the yellow perch.

22. Swassion, Susup (Raven).

This was perhaps the largest and most active family of hunters in the tribe. Seven brothers were the last to maintain the hunting territory farthest north, reaching to the Canadian boundary. They acquired the nickname, "White-squaw." Unfortunately, no legendary associations were obtained. Its active marriage history is shown in the table of intermarriages.

FAMILY INTERMARRIAGE AND RESIDENCE

Restrictions of marriage between families, and the equally important question of residence of the married couple with the husband's or the wife's family group (patrilocality or matrilocality), have been accorded some attention by investigators collecting social data in the northeast.[12] Penobscot habits falling within these categories, and reasons for them, illustrate types of occurrence in the unstabilized bilateral society of an eastern tribe living under the economic dominance of hunting.

That there were no restrictions as to marriage in or out of the family group has been previously mentioned. The feeling against union between those of close kinship, however, led to more frequent marriages between members of different family groups. It is understood that men did marry women of their own group, but not if they were as close as first cousins, who, in this case, bore the same designation in kinship terminology as sister, that is, bəhe′nəmum. When marriage took place between persons of different families—the dominant habit as investigation shows—the husband was free to choose his own location of domicile, unless he had been induced to agree upon marriage to take up residence with the woman's family, sharing her family ties and her father's territory. Father-right was the tendency in respect to name and personal identity, except in the second generation of

[12] For comprehensive survey of marriage regulations in this area, see A. I. Hallowell, *American Anthropologist*, Vol. 34, No. 2, 1932, pp. 171–99.

matrilocal cases. The man usually chose to live with his wife's people. This was frequently stipulated in the marriage agreement between the parents of the couple. It is explained that a man who had many daughters would press this point to secure help in his hunting, and we are told that circumstances of population and richness of game in the parental districts largely determined such moves.[13] The children in either case were a part of the group into which they were born, although when they grew up they could go with the family of the other parent, if hunting prospects were more favorable there. After a generation or two in one group, however, claims upon the other related groups faded out.

Owing to lack of prescribed regulations, each family group, being made up of representatives married in from others as well as those directly inheriting descent in it, must of necessity have been greatly involved as to ancestral identity. Moreover, a part of the group could, on account of overgrowth or disputes, withdraw and join another connected with it by marriage or descent, even though remote. They were in reality small hordes only arbitrarily united, composed of shifting elements claiming a loose unity in territory, name, and food interests. We are also informed of change of residence of sons and daughters according to economic opportunities as hunting conditions changed year by year. To what extent the spirit of coherence formerly existed, it is hazardous to say now. Further than this it must be taken into consideration— and it is quite plain to anyone who has associated with Indians living under similarly loose conditions—how irregular and confused the record of descent becomes after a few generations. In every concern they are primarily centered in the present. Hence, it is easy to conceive how, in the hunting days when family unity was an element of existence, their momentary group of affiliations would be the potent ones, and knowledge of attachments dating back over two generations would tend to be forgotten. After the change from hunting to industrial life in the past three generations, concentration of the families in the permanent villages has

[13] Two sons of a Passamaquoddy chief, Newell and Joe Francis, both promised to live with their wives' parents, and did so.

further acted to obliterate the bonds of family solidarity developed under the isolation of a hunting period.

A glance over the information assembled in the subjoined list of intermarriages between families will show that the generalized statements of informants are supported by statistics and that there are no specific restrictions or choice-limitations among the families; no inclinations to marry with those derived from similar classification among the animal forerunners; no endogamic preferences, nor those leading to reciprocal marriage; in short no stated grounds for marriage control.

What we should like most to know, however, by reference to actual cases, is whether it was more frequent for the married man to join his father-in-law's hunting crew, or to take his wife and remain upon his paternal grounds. This, apparently, cannot be ascertained for the Penobscot at so late a day. While most of the men over sixty years of age in 1910 remembered the family locations, it was nevertheless impossible to secure marriage-residence statistics for the period when the tenure system was strictly observed. Consequently the much-desired check upon the information deposed in the following marriage census cannot be made.

By way of explanation: The readings are to be made horizontally. The numbering of the families corresponds with that given them on the tabulation previously made, and also upon the map showing the locations of the hunting territories. The family designations are the European patronyms with the animal associates beneath. In the squares, the larger figures show the number of marriages between the groups, while the small superior figures denote the generation in which it occurred, numbered backward from the contemporary generation. Thus 2^1 means that two marriages occurred between the families designated among the youngest living married adults of the group in 1915, when the list was prepared, 1^2 that one case occurred in their parents' generation, and 1^3 one in the generation of their grandparents. The list represents the minimum of intermarriages within the period covered in every family questioned, many cases being forgotten or not known.

PENOBSCOT FAMILY INTERMARRIAGES (PERIOD ABOUT 1845–1915) AND MARRIAGES OUT OF TRIBE

| | PENOBSCOT FAMILIES | | | | | | | | | | | | | | | | | Passama-quoddy | Malecite | Micmac | St. Francis Abenaki | Iroquois | White | Half-blood identity (?) |
	1,2	3	5	X	6	7	8	9	11	13	14	16	17	18	20	21	22							
1. Mitchell (Lobster) / 2. Susup (Crab)		1³			1²	1³	1²					1¹			1²		2¹	1^{1,2}	1²	1²	1²			3¹ 1²
3. Mitchell (Bear)	1³		1^{1,2}											1³			1¹	2¹ 1^{1,3}						
5. Neptune (Eel)	1²			2²		1²	1²	1³	1²		1²			1³	2²		1²	2²	1²				1³	
X. Neptune (?)			2²		1²	1²	1²					1²		1²			1³	3²	2³					
6. Glossian (Toad)	1²			1²					1²	1²	1²			1³	2²		1³	3³	1²		1³		1³ 2³	1²
7. Newell] Nelson] (Insect)	1³			1²						1³			1¹	1³	1³		1^{1,2}	2² 1³	2³		1²		3² 2³	3²
8. Francis (Fisher)	1²			1²							1²		1¹	1²	1³		1^{1,2}	2² 1³	3²		1³		1²	1² 2³
9. Stanislas (Whale)			1³	1^{1,2}												1²		2² 1³						1² 2³
11. Sockalexis (Sturgeon)	1¹				1²						1¹		1²				1^{1,3} 2²	1^{1,3} 2²	1³	1³	1¹		1^{1,3}	1^{1,2}
13. Orson (Frog)	1²			1²	1²	1³	1²		1¹						2²		1³	1³	1²	1³			1³	1²
14. Attean (Squirrel)			1²	1²	1²	1³	1²										2²	1³	1¹	1³			1²	1²
16. Lewis (Wolverine)	1¹						1¹							1¹			1²	1²		1²				
17. Coley (Water Nymph)				1²		1³	1¹			1²				1¹			1^{2,3}	1²			1¹			
18. Nicola (Otter)	1²	1³		1²		1³	1³					1¹					1^{2,3}	1³	1¹				1²	
20. Newell (Hare, Rabbit)	1²				2²													1³	1¹				1³	1^{1,2}
21. Penewit (Yellow Perch)																		1³				1³		
22. Swassion (Raven)	2¹	1¹		1²	1³		1^{1,2}		1^{1,3} 2²		2²			1^{2,3}			1²		1^{2,3}				1³	
Totals within tribe and with aliens																		10³ 17² 3¹ = 30	4³ 8² 2¹ = 14	2³ 2² = 4	1³ 2² 1¹ = 4	1³ = 1	7³ 5² 1¹ = 13	3³ 9² 4¹ = 16

In comparing this list with the family enumeration given in the table referred to, some numbers and names will be found missing. Families number 4 (Francis [Sculpin]), 10 (Beaver), 12 (Susup, Polis [Wolf]), 15 (Raccoon), and 19 (Penus, Fransway [Lynx]) lost their identity as units long ago, wherefore marriage details were confused in the memories of informants.

Marriages with Aliens

In 1915 there were more family surnames in the Penobscot tribe than are given in the preceding list. The others are of alien origin, having no share in the land tenure scheme of the tribe. They are derived mostly from Passamaquoddy and Malecite. I have limited the information to Penobscot groups only, those considered to be of long standing as social units of the tribe. The intermarriage of Penobscot with immigrant Passamaquoddy and Malecite has been very marked in the past, as in the present, as will appear from data arranged in the second part of the table. No attempt has been made to list those marriage cases by families, the tribal identity only being indicated. A visitor to the tribe today would, however, find the Penobscot population abounding in descendants of Passamaquoddy families (Sockabesin, Solomon, Mitchell, Denis, Sapiel, Lola) and Malecite families (Paul, Polchis, Tomah, Joseph, Francis, Nicholas, Saulis).

Among the alien unions—those with other Wabanaki tribes —in the period covered the Passamaquoddy exceed in number with a total of 30 (in the 1st, 2nd, 3rd generations counting backward, 3, 17, 10 respectively); the Malecite total 14 (2, 8, 4 by generations); the Micmac and St. Francis Abenaki, 4 each. Within the span of the records, there were 53 Penobscot marriages within the tribe, 52 with other Wabanaki peoples. What would this mean in respect to the constituency of tribal blood if the proportion held good for earlier periods? For we see that the Penobscot have married as frequently with the other Wabanaki tribes as among themselves.

Regarding marriages with whites and half-bloods, little can be said that would apply to tribal history as a whole. The 13 unions with whites during the period covered would be put in shadow by the marriages and removals I have learned of since.   By half-bloods, in the last column, is meant individuals of Penobscot or other extraction who did not inherit the tribal territories.

Some of the unlisted families are descended from half-bloods who inherited neither the ancestral animal associations nor territories, or from illegitimate offspring of the hunter proprietors who fared similarly, or from Indians of other tribes whose social positions were somewhat anomalous according to the Penobscot fashion of looking upon *pi'ləwi a'lnαbak*, "strange Indians."   None of these have been entered on the list as units unless, as in some instances, after the second generation, when the descendants had married into landed Penobscot families and had become incorporated with the exclusive group.   The leading families of direct European descent by recent mixture, French and Irish chiefly, are Ranco, Shay, Basset,[14] Loring,[15] Lewis (1912).   The question of blood mixture among the Wabanaki tribes is one fraught with interesting possibilities, and may be commended as topic for investigation.

THE QUESTION OF MOIETY GROUPINGS

The problem of a dichotomous grouping in the earlier eras of Penobscot social history calls for passing attention. Beneath the surface, as revealed in the tales and in the data on family privileges, recurring indications of a dual partition of the tribe are met.   To quote from some of the culture-hero episodes:

Again he left, and in seven days' time he came to another village, and again he went into the first wigwam.   In this village one side was quiet and the other side was uproarious. . . . The latter were tormenting the other people across the village (because they were afraid).

. . . He came to the other side of the mountains.   He saw a village and said, "Now then, soon I shall see my people."   Looking

[14] A family of supposed Micmac extraction, having come from Mohegan, Conn., by some vagary of migration, though not of Mohegan connection.

[15] The ancestor of this family early in the nineteenth century established himself with the tribe, the children marrying into the Francis (Fisher, no. 8) family.   He is remembered as having been of Portuguese descent mixed with Indian, from eastern Massachusetts, possibly Mashpee or Gay Head.

he saw half the village quiet, and the other half noisy, and many
there together playing ball, and others dancing. He entered from
the quiet direction, and in the first wigwam he entered was Woodchuck. . . . She began to cry and said, "Poor grandson! we suffer
very much because we are all slaves." [16]

The preceding passages are taken from the tale of Long
Hair, a myth hero who effected certain transformations as did
Gluska'be. He then defeats the men of the malicious faction
in games and hunt-tests. Another hero is Snowy Owl. His
adventures likewise begin amid the strife of opposed village
factions.

"There were two camps of the people. One was inhabited
by people who were rough and abusive. The latter persecuted
the former. In the quiet camp lived a family with a son
named Snowy Owl. . . ." Snowy Owl destroys some monsters, for doing which he is later honored by the abusive
people, and is made their chief. In a tale recounting the
adventures of White Weasel, a similar implication is contained
in the sense of the story.

What this means in respect to former types of social subdivision may be left to the imagination of the theorist. By
analogy with other areas in eastern North America, some of
them Algonkian, such indications may be construed without
too much guessing, as being vestiges of the peculiar feature of
the half-tribe or moiety. Also, by including certain allega-
tions in the information dealing with the relative standings
of families and hereditary chieftaincy pointing to a similar
idea, we may build up an appropriate concept of duality for
early Penobscot social organization. To use native designations taken from the myth texts, the half-tribe abahso'dene,
"half village," and agamo'dene, "across, opposite, other side,
village," are the usual terms, while isiga'ni, "one side," is
used for one, agamo'dene for the other side. They were parti-
tions of the villages as well as the tribe, marked off from each
other by opposed characteristics. And these, fortunately for
our purpose, may be classified to aid in understanding the
principle involved in the division.

[16] "Penobscot Transformer Tales," *International Journal of American Linguistics*,
Vol. 1, no. 3 (1918), p. 228, 243.

The opposed characteristics presented by the two groupings are as follows: residence at some distance from each other
in the camping or village grounds; peacefulness versus war-
likeness; quietude versus boisterousness; hospitality toward
strangers versus hostility; opposed teaming in games and
contests; fair play in village or tribal games (ball, hunting
contests) versus foul play; humility versus arrogance; cruelty
versus kindness.   And finally, we have noted that the family
groups derived from or associated through traditional events
with aquatic animals have a common origin tale and a hereditary chief chosen from a certain high-caste family of the
genus, while those families possessing associations with terrestrial creatures have theirs apart.

From Penobscot sources, I am unable to bring more information to bear upon this discussion of an important feature
in American ethnology.   Such will have to be sought among
the neighboring Wabanaki bands, in the memories of whose
older men something of interest may still be treasured.

In recognition of the importance of this whole question in
the area considered, I am glad to quote Dr. Siebert's views of
the points brought out in the foregoing discussion.

Persistent inquiry has failed to reveal any evidence to support
the idea that the Penobscot had any dual division or moiety organization.   However, certain facts point towards some sort of an
embryo dichotomy.   The twenty-four gentes fall about half into
aquatic and half into terrestrial groups.   There is also the old
schism of the Penobscot tribe into Old Party and New Party
factions, which dates back to the early nineteenth century and has
not yet entirely disappeared after many bitter fights.   Perhaps if
the Penobscot had been permitted to develop their culture for
several more centuries without European interference, they would
have developed a moiety complex by contact modification with the
more intricate social organization of the tribes in the south and east.

REGULATION OF CRIME, INDIGENCE, AND ORPHANAGE

Fortunately for our purpose, Penobscot tradition is specific
enough in regard to punishment of crime to add some facts
to our knowledge of northern Algonkian customs of right.
We are told that in cases of murder, the family of the victim

assumed the right to pursue and take the offender. Then
they tortured him to death. The right to such transaction
was given by the chief, after he had been informed of the
crime and the intended retaliation. The securing of the
chief's consent seems to have been the sole appeal to higher
authority in the process of adjustment. His words were
generally to the effect that the offender be punished by torture
in any way that would satisfy the victim's family. And the
informant likened the procedure to the liberty and disposition
that animals have in torturing their victims. It is remembered that the cutting off of ears was practised in some
instances, but for what misdemeanor was not specified. Emphasis was laid upon the idea of satisfying the feelings of the
victim's family—no limits were recognized. This was called
enawilawe''ta'hozu, "satisfying the grief of the bereaved."
In the tales we have one case, that of Gluskabe whipping the
fox to the point of death for tormenting his poor grandmother.

It has always been customary for the children and grandchildren to take care of and support their elders. Forbear-
ance in matters of this sort must have been great in olden
times, as one hears of some aged folk who were too feeble to
perform necessary physical duties for themselves. Others
bedridden, were infested with vermin, yet all such were the
objects of pity and care. There are several blind and bedridden old people in the village today, who, though great
burdens to their families, are well treated. It should not be
forgotten, however, that instances appear in narratives pointing to abandonment of the aged. The apparent cruelty of
this custom is mitigated by knowledge of the fact that in the
past whole communities were plunged into famine, and were
forced to move from time to time in search of victuals. To
linger in behalf of some helpless persons would mean starvation to the whole band of children and women.

The poor were in general the burden of their relatives.
Orphans fell to the charge of their uncles and aunts, but most
characteristically to their grandparents.

The frequency of reference in the tales to adoption of
orphans by old women called "grandmother" is a suggestion

worthy of attention in viewing the social life of the forest people. The tales represent real conditions in Penobscot society. To cite some cases of the sort within recent times, we have Nick and John Andrew, orphans cared for until grown up by their maternal grandmother, Cecile Barker; Francis Neptune raised by his maternal grandmother, Clara Neptune; three boys of the Denis family raised by the paternal grandfather, Frank Denis, when their father died and their mother remarried; and Joe Balls Susup raised by his maternal grandmother when his mother died at his birth. Gabe Paul has likewise raised two nieces and three children of nephews and nieces. It was usual for the dying parent to entrust his children to a sister or brother, and such a wish was held sacred.

Illegitimates, if not recognized and supported by one of the parents, were, and still are, generally taken care of by an uncle until they became of age. Widows, if they had no sons old enough to support them, lived with either their own, or their husband's family until the children grew up or they married again. Women who did not marry usually remained with their parents or their mothers and sisters-in-law. Men who would not support themselves suffered at their own expense, a few sometimes banding together as loafers and living from hand to mouth or visiting their relatives. For the alleviation of aged or disabled families during the winter, the other members of the camp or village voluntarily contributed food, clothing, and firewood. All of the above regulations are still largely followed.

PARTNERSHIP

A close personal relationship often developed, it is said, between two young men who would pledge mutual support in all matters of life and share each other's property and fortunes. This relationship is expressed by the before-mentioned term *ni·da'be* (*ni·da'be, ni·da'mbe*), "my partner." This was irrespective of kinship, and is the closest term of address outside of the family kinship names. As among other Algonkians, this institution may have had a more formal aspect in the days gone by. I suspect, indeed, that some connection was involved between the partnership of youths and the young men's communal house remembered in some villages, and to be mentioned shortly.

CHIEFS AND OTHER OFFICERS

Formerly the office of head chief, *sa'ngama*, "strong man," was held for life. It would seem that about the year 1875 the hereditary chieftainship was discontinued. To a certain extent only this was hereditary in the Squirrel family and in the Frog family. In later times the term was shortened until, as now, it is an elective position held for only two years. The loose political organization of early times permitted little importance to develop in the office of chief. The Penobscot were at best only weakly governed. From the derivation of the name, "strong man," "hard man," we learn something of the chief's qualities in the old days. Few details regarding the office and its duties have come down through tradition. We know briefly that cases of dispute, even of crime, were occasionally referred to the chief for adjustment. Perhaps his office was principally one of dignified representation at ceremonies either at home or at intertribal festivities. The festive formalities of the chief's election itself, and the honor of having been chosen as the head of a people, seem to have constituted, as they do in the tribe today, the main feature of the office in times of peace. The chief seems to have posed more as a chosen "leader" of the people, their representative in dealings with outsiders, their chief councilor and leader in times of war. So far as is known, the chieftaincy was not necessarily hereditary, though in several cases history records son succeeding father in office among the Maine Indians.

To support the dignity of the chief, and to form his staff and council (*mani'skassu*), lesser chiefs to the number of seven were appointed, sometimes for life, sometimes to be replaced by others. While honorifically classed as *san'gamak*, "chiefs," their usual title in colonial times was *ge'ptinak*, "captains" (from the French or English).[16a] Upon special occasions they had particular duties assigned to them by the chief. The place where the chief and council gathered was

[16a] Wabanaki memories of King James I (1566–1625) have introduced the term *Kin djames* as a designation for "King."

called *gwunda'wun*, "assembly." The place of the chief was at the center of a semicircle formed by his councilors. Those of the people who chose to be present sat in a body facing them. All were permitted to attend.

Another minor office of the tribal council was, and still is, the *nodjin'adji'pta'sit*, "one who goes about and gets (them)," messenger or notifier. He informed the people of meetings, announced appointments of committees, and the like.

One of the most characteristic rulings connected with the chieftainship of the Wabanaki was the custom of a tribe's not electing its own chief. The Penobscot first chose their own candidate from consideration of his prestige in the community, his personal prowess, and other meritorious qualities; then they dispatched messengers to the neighboring tribes inviting them to attend the election. The ceremony of installation was most elaborate, and ordinarily lasted many days, celebrated with dancing, feasting, sports, and games. The visiting tribes were formally received in bands, upon the shores of the river facing the village. They were escorted to their assigned quarters, their canoes were carried up, and they were feasted as lords. The celebration was called *Ska'wehe*, nearest rendered in English by "greeting." A general description of this important ceremony is given under the heading of ceremonies. A special account of one which took place in Oldtown a number of years ago is, however, appended here, with also a modern election ceremony witnessed by the writer in 1910, for comparison.

Chief's Installation Ceremony

Impressive and protracted installation rites were marked features of Wabanaki civil life. Only fragments of the procedures have come down through memory among the living, yet we have a succinct and graphic description of the Penobscot ceremony to quote from Dillingham,[17] its author unknown.

On the 19th of September, 1816, at Oldtown village, Sagamore Atteon, John Neptune, next in grade and command, and two captains were inducted into the office, with the customary ceremonies. To assist in these, the chiefs and fifteen or twenty other

[17] Cf. Dillingham, p. 16.

principal men from each of the tribes at the St. John river [Malecite and Passamaquoddy] had previously arrived, appearing in neat and becoming dresses, all in Indian fashion.

Early in the forenoon, the men from the Tarratine [Penobscot] tribe, convening in the great wigwam called the camp, seated themselves on the side platform according to seniority, Atteon, Neptune, and the select captains at the head, near the door; the former two being clad in coats of scarlet broadcloth and decorated with silver brooches, collars, arm-clasps, jewels and other ornaments. Upon a spread before them, of blue cloth, an ell square, were exhibited four silver medals, three of which were circular and twice the size of a silver dollar, the other was larger, in the form of a crescent. All these were emblematically inscribed with curious devices, and suspended by parti-colored ribbons, a yard in length with ends tied. Aware of the gentlemen's wishes to be spectators of the ceremonies, they directed the Indian acting the part of a marshal, to invite them to the camp. The admission of the female visitants was also requested, but he replied as directed by the chiefs: "Never our squaws, nor yours sit with us in the council!"

The spectators being seated below the tribe, upon the platform or benches, covered with blankets, the Marechite [Malecite] delegation, preceded by their chief, entered the camp in true Indian file, and sat down, according to individual rank, directly before the Tarratines [Penobscots]. These now uncovered their heads and laid aside their caps and hats, 'til the ceremonies were closed.

Four belts of wampum, brought into the camp by a stately Merechite, were unfolded and placed in the area upon a piece of broadcloth, which enclosed them; when his Sagamore, presently rising took and held one of them in his hands and addressed Atteon, from five to ten minutes, in a courtly speech, laying the belt at his feet. Three others in rotation, and next in rank of the same tribe, addressed in a similar manner the Tarratine candidates of comparative grades; all of which were tokens of unchanging friendship and sanctions of perpetual union. The Sagamore then taking the medal nearest Atteon, addressed him and his tribe in another speech of the same length as the former, in the course of which he came to momentary pauses, when the Tarratines collectively uttered deep guttural sounds, like "aye." These were evident expressions of assent to have Atteon, Neptune, Francis and others their first and second Sagamores, and two senior captains. The speaker, closing his remarks, advanced and placed the suspended medal, as a badge of investure, about Atteon's neck, the act by which he was formally induced into office and constituted Sagamore for life. Neptune and the two captains in their turns, after being shortly addressed by the other Marechite actors, were invested by them with the ensigns in the same way.

During these ceremonies, the Quoddy Indians without stood around a standard, twenty feet in height, to and from the top of which, they alternately hoisted and lowered a flag, as each Tarratine was induced into office; at the same time and afterwards, firing salutes from a well-loaded swivel near the same place.

Mr. Romaigne, the Catholic Priest, attired in a white robe and long scarf, having seated himself among the Tarratines, before the ceremonies were commenced, now rising, read appropriate passages from the Scripture in Latin, and expounded them in Indian dialect; and next a psalm, which he and the Marechites chanted with considerable harmony. In the midst of the Sacred song, the whole of them moved slowly out of the camp, preceded by the priest, leaving the Tarratines seated, and forming a circle in union with the 'Quoddy Indians, stood and sang devoutely for a few minutes, and closed with a "Te Deum."

The priest then departed to his house, and the Indians entering the camp, took their seats—the 'Quoddy Indians in the lower place, abreast the sitting spectators, when they commenced their tangible salutations. In this form of civility, each of the two delegations rising in turn, literally embraced, cheek and lip, the four new made officers, and shook heartily by the hand all the others of the tribe.[18]

The spectators, at the marchals' request, now withdrew, to be spectators only about the doors and apertures; when the Tarratine females, clad in their best dresses and fancifully ornamented joined for the first time the Indian assemblage, and the whole formed an elliptical for dancers. In close Indian file they moved forward in successive order, with a kind of a double shuffle, to their former places, animated by the music of a light beat upon a drum, in the midst of the circle, well accompanied by vocal tune. [Formerly their chief instruments were the rattles, made of small gourds, and pumpkin seeds.] The female dancers then retired, the Indians took their seats, and the spectators were re-admitted.

To close the ceremonies, four chief men of the Marechites severally rose in succession and sang short songs; somewhat entertaining, which were duly responded by others from the new made

---

[18] This possibly refers to the Ska'wintowagan, Greeting Dance, see p. 288.

officers, through which, the whole assemblage uttered, at almost every breath, a low-toned, emphatic guttural sound, not unlike a hic-cough—[he', the sign of assent] the singular way they expressed their plaudits and pleasures.

More than three hours were consumed in these ceremonies, which were succeeded by a feast already prepared. Two fatted oxen, slaughtered and served into pieces, were roasting; rice, beans and garden vegetables were boiling, and bread-loaves and crackers were abundant. If the cookery, neatness and order were unworthy of modern imitation, the defects were counterbalanced by the hearty invitations and welcomes with which all the visitants, equally with the natives, were urged to become partakers, both of the repast and the festive scenes. The regularities of the day relaxed to rude dances and wild sports in the evening, which were by no means free from extravagance and excess.

The circumstances are evincive of the cordial fraternity and political union of these tribes. Never have they been known on any emergency, to act otherwise than in concert.

Peter Nicolar's tradition adds several features to the civil ceremony procedure.

A dance ceremony called *mowia'wegan*, "Chief's Dance," serving as a prelude to the installation dance, was remembered in outline by several of the oldest informants. It was enacted by chosen women. One old woman carrying a walking cane led a file of dancers, all women. We are not told what other prerogatives these women enjoyed. They circled only once around the council room. This done, the chief to be inaugurated went to the leader and placed a good broadcloth blanket upon the old woman leader's shoulders, and the seven council men placed similar gifts upon the seven women dancers. These gifts were kept by the women as presents. None of the songs were remembered, but their word burdens were in praise of the new chief. This dance has evidently not been performed since some time prior to 1870. The appearance of the matrons of the tribe in the chief's ceremony and the favor done them by the officers are reminders of Iroquois political sentiment toward women.

These elaborate rites have degenerated into a shrunken ceremony. On January 1, 1910, at the biennial tribal installation, the procedure witnessed was as follows. I only give the election rites here, leaving the dancing, which was the aboriginal part of the performance, to be described later (p. 358).

The tribe—men, women, and children—assembled in the dance hall, *gwunda'wun*, early in the afternoon, a general invitation having been given out by the chief-elect for all to attend the installation rites and the ensuing dance, to be given, according to the custom, at his expense. The chief elect (Piel Nicolar) was seated in the center of the platform, with the newly elected officers and also those of the departing administration about him. At the proper time one of the old councilors, a leading man of the tribe, addressed the assemblage, stating the purpose of the occasion in a speech intended to direct the thoughts of his auditors to the history and the government of the tribe. Two other speeches by ex-officers were of the same import. The ex-chief next arose, carrying the chief's medal (a silver medal bearing a facsimile of Andrew Jackson and dated 1827) attached to a ribbon, which he solemnly placed over the new chief's neck after delivering a speech. He stood by the side of the new chief, with one hand upon his shoulder and the other upon the medal. The import of his speech was that he had tried to serve his people faithfully. The medal having been placed upon his neck, the new chief arose and made an impressive speech, full of promises and native patriotism, thanking the tribe for the honor, and asking help and coöperation. The ensuing speech was delivered by the lieutenant governor (Louis Ketcham), the second highest in office. After these formal addresses a number of the councilors made others, some containing comical allusions, all, however, tending towards encouragement and replete with promises. The furtherance of the Catholic religion and the development of friendliness and coöperation with the whites figured largely as topics in the speeches. After the bestowing of the medal upon the new chief, I counted and made notes of eight such addresses varying only in the personality of the speaker. Two of these were delivered in faulty English. The final speech was delivered in English by the Roman Catholic priest then officiating at Oldtown. With a few trite remarks regarding duty to office, divine appointment, and responsibilities to the church and school, he brought the assembled people to their knees and closed the meeting with a prayer.

The above account is more interesting as a contemporary record than as an example of native ceremonial. When the people had had time for supper, however, the dance hall was lighted and they gathered again to enjoy the dancing which preserves its native character intact. Young people at an early hour filled the hall, and the children began dancing before the elders arrived. When enough had gathered, the present principal dance leader (Joe Solomon) started, shaking his rattle and singing a "round dance" song. Subsequently dancing was incessant until past midnight. Many of the men and women wore native costumes in whole or in part. Some of the young men were painted. A visiting Sioux (Sherman Hawk), in his native garb, lent additional color to the occasion. He learned the Penobscot dances readily. As the guest of the new chief, I was escorted in the center of a group, comprising the chief or governor, lieutenant governor and leader, through many dances with interlocked arms. A feast provided by the new chief concluded this part of the ceremony, and some European dances were introduced by the younger men of the Indian Island orchestra. The details of Penobscot dances witnessed upon this and other occasions are reserved for special treatment further on.

RELATIONSHIP RESTRICTIONS

Within certain limits of relationship, restrictions exist against the use of obscenity, suggestive joking, teasing, insulting remarks, and above all against breaking wind in presence. The lack of freedom as to these particulars in the presence of certain relatives of the opposite sex, without regard to others, brings certain of them within the bounds of conduct taboos. Naturally the observance of the taboo falls chiefly upon the men who are perhaps more prone to obscenity, yet I have observed plenty of cases where women do, and need to follow similar restraints. Those who come within the taboo group are, in the case of men, their sisters most emphatically, female cousins and aunts, though the restraint weakens much with the latter. So it is in reciprocal cases with the women. Not only a person who is related to those present, but also a stranger must observe the same propriety when associating with his friends and their female relations. It will be seen, then, that a man may indulge in obscenity and the like in the presence of his wife, children, and his mother or any of his wife's relatives. The sister taboo, however, seems to be the most strictly observed. There are cases of quarrels arising between friends over the violation of this peculiar taboo. Moreover, it still remains a strong emotion, the mere mention of crepitus before one's sister, for instance, coming as a shock. On the other hand, it occasions little concern before others not of the proscribed group.

Stories are current explaining this feeling, where as a final thrust of revenge someone will insult his enemy's sister, even if by nothing more than some deprecatory remark about her person. In another tale, a man falls dead from shame after accidentally breaking wind before his sister.

As one of the old men tersely phrased it, one may not say any "misbeholding word" before his own or another's sister, nor even indulge in boisterous laughter or joking. A brother takes it as an affront. I recall the chagrin of a Penobscot visitor to a white man's home in seeing a brother and sister dance together and, after what was to his senses such a bold display of moral laxity (no exaggeration), the former occupy a lounge at her side.

The closest intimacy, confidence, and coöperation existed between girls and their maternal aunts, boys and their paternal uncles, sometimes even exceeding that of the parental relationship. The young man was normally "apprenticed" to his paternal uncle to learn his woodcraft.

Segregation of the "Pure Men," or Runners

In each family group were some young men who acted as runners, to cover large tracts of country, run down moose, deer, and other game, and kill them in their tracks. These young men, of whom there might be a small number, two, three, or four, were closely guarded by some old men lest defiling influences weaken their endurance and fleetness or cause the game by magic to escape being overtaken. Such a young man was called *k^wsiwa'mbe*, "pure man." The "pure men" were chosen for their fleetness of foot. As soon as one of them could be outstripped by a younger candidate, the latter would take his place. To have served as a runner or "pure man" was considered a social honor.

The members of this group were under surveillance all the time. They could not marry, sexual intercourse was forbidden them, they had to use only certain kinds of food, and the like. Some of their prescriptions are interesting. The young runners worked for the community at large. When they would run down and kill moose or deer, they would only bleed the carcasses and leave them for the other hunters to find by the tracks and carry back to the village. When a runner became superseded he was released from his ascetic obligations and could then marry and settle down to ordinary life.

The old custodian watched them at night to see that they did not sleep with their legs outstretched, as this, it was thought with good reason, would mar their running qualities. To make them draw up their knees, the custodian would strike the runners' soles with a stick. When sitting they always had to keep their knees drawn up, which kept their tendons stretched.

They were not allowed to chew spruce gum as this would impair their breathing. To account for this they explain how the spruce gum originated from scabs from a myth woman's [19] crotch. Should they chew the gum, it would make their testicles clack when they ran, and so forewarn the game.

Boys in general, it is claimed, after the age of puberty were accustomed to live in separate dwellings in the larger communities or villages. Here, until they married, their life

---

[19] *Pukdjin'skwe'ssu*, "Jug Woman," a hag-like personification which roams the woods, uttering weird cries and often seducing children. She figures prominently in the myths. On one occasion some young men began twitting her for her scabs and ugly looks. She became angry and declared that thereafter they would chew her scabs. Then she climbed up a spruce tree and scraped off her scabs against the bark. They now appear in the gum exuding from the tree.

was largely spent in a communal sphere. The men too, it is said, had a separate lodge in the village, where they held dances and gatherings. This was, in all probability, the council hall, *gwunda'wun*.

Naming [20]

Names (*wiza·wɑ'ngan*) were of two sorts, although no particular system was followed. The family groups with inherited territories, and having an animal for a brand or totem mark, were known to outsiders by the name of that animal; a generic classifier. Among themselves, however, and to their intimates in the family or village, men and women had special nicknames or sobriquets which were acquired from personal peculiarities or odd experiences during life, or from a word or expression, often baby-talk, much uttered in childhood. Cravings seem to have figured also as bases for names.

In regard to the generic names, it seems that some association, weak though it might be, was felt between the animal orders and the people bearing their names. The older members of the bear group, for example, were known as "old bears," the younger as "little bears," and the women the "bear women." Other individual names would become "bear woman, young" or "bear widow, young," and so on for the different groups.

Regarding the category of names, the sobriquets, I subjoin a list as remembered. Some, indeed, still persist as nicknames. They are somewhat arbitrary in nature, with no apparent underlying system. They were acquired in several ways, however, for example, by the eating of too much of this, or by doing too much of that, or by stealing something. So we find "Smoke Fish" as a nickname for a man who was once caught stealing smoked fish from a neighbor. Some men habitually used certain profane expressions; such expressions becoming characteristic, nicknames ensued. So we have Joe "Clean," Joe *Tapni'mɑk*, "Testicles," as recent personages.

Adamhi'gan, "Cut with an axe." A hero in the early wars with the Mohawk, mentioned in the stories. He was

---

[20] Vetromile (*Indian Prayer Book*, p. 443) has some pertinent remarks on Penobscot names.

so named because during infancy, while attached to the cradle-board, an enemy tried to kill him, but only struck the board with his tomahawk.

Adjɔssa'tegwe, "Dragon fly," an ancestor of the Bear family, so called because he was extremely thin.

Sankɔde'lak, "Stream emptying into a river." This man was named after the Sagadahoc River, across which his mother escaped with him on her back when their camp was attacked in the Rasles attack.

Ami'knak⁽ʷ⁾, "Sharp borer" (?) (a species of insect). A woman spoken of in traditions.

Samu'sit, "One who walks along the edge of something, Line-walker." A traditional name, appearing also as Samoset in Massachusetts history.

Tcekhuwe'skit, "One who is looking for an easy time." This has an obscene tinge.

Maska'mbe, "Bad person."

O'lɔno, "Man" (Micmac). A chief, famous in Maine history, who died in 1802.

Ma'djaha'ndo, "Evil Spirit." A Penobscot chief who died in 1698.

Awa'tawe'ssu, "Star," a feminine name.

Sɔ'bɔdis (Sabattis?), "Jean Baptiste."

Dj'ekwat, "Daylight," so named from the owner's habit of rising with the sun.

Di'diɑs, "Blue jay," a feminine name; in another case given by a husband to his wife.

Ma'ndoām'ek⁽ʷ⁾, "Spirit fish." Another hero of the early Mohawk wars.

Eliwi'tamɑk, "They call him a nickname," applied to a St. Francis Indian who came to Oldtown and said he was going away because they called him a name (Indian humor).

Misel wa'i, "Mitchell wine," derived from his declared fondness for wine.

Nona'nis, "Little teat," a female name.

Po'djo, "Poor Joe (Neptune)."

Joe Tɔma'kwe, "Joe Beaver," derived from his fondness for beaver meat.

Pka'has, baby-talk for *ketɑ'nk* ʷ*zu*, "ghost," derived from a childhood fear of ghosts (Piel Nicola).

Po'tcalɘwes, from Passamaquoddy *amotca'lɘwes*, "fly," which he, Sebattis Mohawk, mispronounced.

Si'ktepsu, "Died from inhaling a bad odor" (Joe Solomon's father), a saying that became attached to him as a sobriquet.

Ba'dos, from French *bateau* so named because he got in a fight over a boat.

Malko'ke, "Lazy one."

Setate'kit, "Dancing backward (in going forward)," (Piel Nicola), derived from his style of dancing.

Tcɘgwa'lɘs, "Frog" (Etienne Attean), the name of his reputed spirit-helper.

Nɑ'phis, "Louse nit" (Sebattis Susup's grandfather), so called from his affliction.

Podebe'sis, "Little whale" (Steve Stanislas), derived from his size and dark color. He also belonged to the Whale family group.

Mali me'sakwɘdjɑn, "Mary big-faeces" (identity omitted), derived from advertising her ability to surpass the tribal cannon [21] in capacity of discharge.

Muskwe'ssu, "Muskrat" (John Francis), derived from recklessness in crawling about and running logs as a lumberjack.

Pa'kwaekasia'sit, "Arrowhead finger." A mythical maiden whose fingers were burned to a crisp by Mohawk captors.

Wula'mbes, "Pretty face," a man's name.

Nata'nis, "Dragon-fly."

Sawana'ki, "South."

Oba'gɑn, "Springs-up," referring to the spring-stick of a snare.

Persons might have more than one name and be known under different ones in different villages or districts. Again, an offensive sobriquet might become attached to a person which he might not himself hear very often, and which after

---

[21] At feast days and elections an old iron cannon is discharged, one acquired by the Penobscot in Colonial times.

a time he might outgrow. It seems, in general, in the matter
of names, that the extreme looseness noted was a true characteristic, no particular function or rank having been connected with them. One customary rule was, however, for
the eldest and next eldest son and daughter, in case there were
many children, to inherit the name, with the termination -sīs,
"little," until the parents' demise, after which the termination would be dropped. In large families the children, after
the first two, would acquire different names.

At the earliest age the children were called *awa'ssis*,
"baby," next young men are hailed as *skino'sis*, "young
man," and girls as *nakskwe'ssis*, "young woman." Men
generally address each other as *nida'be*, "my partner." An
old woman goes under the term *wino'sis*, "old woman," and
an old man, *ketca'wit*, "old one."

These appellatives serve in general as names for all persons
not otherwise designated. The kinship terms are also frequently used as vocatives.

For the sake of those interested in transitional customs, I
give below the later Penobscot family names after the French
priests had begun to convert and christen them. The following became adopted as surnames and first names.

Pla'nsway	Francis	*A'ttean*	Etienne
Su'sup	Joseph	*Po'lis*	Little Paul
Pi'el	Pierre	*Lo'la*	Laurent
Nico'la	Nicholas	*Pe'nus*	Phineas
To'mah	Thomas	*Glo'ssian*	Gros Jean
Saba'ttis	Jean Baptiste	*Mi'sel, Misa*	Michele
Sa'piel	Jean Pierre	*Swa'ssion*	Joachim
Sockale'xis	Jacques Alex	*Tcisala'pin*	Big Sylvia
Sockabe'sin	Jacques Bastian	*Ma'li*	Marie
Sa'ksis	Jacques	*Si'sul*	Cecile
Sa'kus	Jacques	*Ka'tlin*	Catherine

The above are written as used in the tribe. I have added
the accents.

Mitchell (Michele), Newell (Noël), Francis, Lewis (Louis),
Dana (Denis), and Solomon are common as modernized family
surnames. Some others of doubtful derivation are Neptune,
Bowit, and Holit.

A quaint custom was until recently observed, that of visiting around and bringing presents to the homes of the different families on the Catholic feast days of the saints whose names they bore. For instance at Christmas time, *Nibaya'mia'wi*, "Birthday Eve," they would bring presents to, and wish blessings upon, the family and persons whose names were Noël or Newell (French, Christmas).

Care of Children and Growing Up

When a woman was approaching delivery she required constant attention. Anything she wanted was given her to eat, lest the child be "marked" with the article craved. She was also careful not to look at anything ugly lest the child be born so. After delivery she was given a decoction of yellow ash leaves boiled very bitter and strong. This cleansed her.

The navel cord was cut, wrapped up and burnt or buried. If this was not done the child might grow up with a tendency to snoop, habitually prying as if searching for something. The afterbirth was buried.

Sometimes, in the old days as tradition says, bastard or deformed infants were killed. There is a story of how a man, some years ago, stopped two women from throwing a bastard girl baby into the river. They gave him the baby to bring up, and she is now living in the tribe.

In and about the camp, when not on the cradle-board, the baby was kept in the baby hammock, *alœbegia'zudi*, "swinging receptacle," of suitable size for the occupant. It is still in use among practically all the northern Algonkian. It is made either of buckskin or of a blanket. Two thongs or ropes are rove through the sides, while spreading sticks at the head and foot complete the sack. In fine weather, the hammock is hung out of doors from trees, at other times indoors, suspended from tent poles or posts. The padding for infants was sphagnum moss which was also used as a cleaning swab for children and women.

During teething time babies were given a bit of smooth bone or preferably gristle, to chew on. This was tied to the wrist by a string lest it be swallowed.

A boy at any early age might be given a little bow and arrows and taught to shoot small birds and animals. Some of the old people remember how cruel they used to be with little birds, parties of them, and even grown-ups with them, pelting to death some creature they had cornered. The idea was evidently to develop the hunting instinct in the young.

The periods of the life cycle are recognized as follows:

dji′djis	newly born infant	senɑ′be	man (adult)
awɑ′ssis	young child	phe′nɑm	woman (adult)
skino′sis	boy	ktciphe′nɑm	old woman
nɑkskwe′sis	girl	ktcialnɑ′be	old man
skino′s	young man	wine′sosis	very old woman
nɑ′kskwe	young woman	pəlu′səssis	very old man

The following terms should be noted, *pmauzwi′no*, "person" (lit. "living man-person"), and the general name for Indian, *alnɑ′be*.

An observer of child life among the northern forest tribes will notice how influences tend to induce silence in their play and conduct. Penobscot children's games lack boisterousness; there are relatively few singing games, lullabies and rompings. Crying children are promptly quieted by soothing. In child life silence is enjoined; the reason given was not to betray the presence of camps to the Mohawk and also not to alarm game in the neighborhood.

Marriage Procedures

The institution of marriage, *niba′wɑgan*, was an important event in Wabanaki life. It was attended before and after by relatively numerous obligations and rites. The ceremonies seem to have developed through the idea of advertising the union of the couple before the eyes of the people at large. By means of the long-remembered wedding dance and feast, this purpose was accomplished. The obligations devolving upon the man seem directed toward proving his ability as a family provider and guardian. As before noted, there were no exogamous groups, the only restriction against mating being those of kinship. It was not considered proper for cousins on either side to marry. Anciently polygamy was not fre-

quent but optional, as was also the sororate (marriage with the
sister of a deceased wife).   After their contact with the more
complex Mohawk, the Penobscot claim to have adopted a
more elaborate system of proposal and marriage.   So they
tell of two customs, the old style and the later.[22]

The old form of proposal and marriage was extremely
simple, so they say.   It is indeed spoken of jocularly nowadays.   After a young man had decided on the girl of his
choice he would take occasion at some convenient time, when
no one was looking, to toss something, a chip of wood perhaps,
near where she was sitting.   Should the girl pick up the
object he could take it as a sign of her acceptance.   This
scheme is known today in mild love-making.   In the oldest
times it is said to have constituted marriage.

The more typical later proposal, however, was as follows,
though premarital courtship became more lengthy than before.
The young man, when he had settled his mind upon marrying
some special girl, would appoint an uncle, or some elderly
man to be his go-between.   Extra dignity was lent to the
occasion by having two old men for negotiators.   He would
then procure some wampum, if he were rich enough a collar
or necklace, if not, just a string (Fig. 79).   Next he would
compose a message, the main points of which would be represented by the arrangement of white and purple beads.   This
message, accompanied by the mnemonic wampum, would be
forthwith entrusted to the go-between's care, and he would
go to the home of the girl's parents carrying the wampum in
a rolled-up red handkerchief or other gaudy cloth.   Here his
message would be delivered, and the wampum left, to be
debated upon by the girl's family.   The negotiator would
depart for a while to allow time for deliberation.   Before
long he would return for an answer.   Now should the girl's
family have decided negatively, the wampum would be returned to the old man, who would deliver it to the sender.
And the matter was dropped.   But should the suitor be
favorably regarded, the wampum would be retained and upon
the negotiator's next visit he would be answered in the affirmative or asked to defer a little longer.   The retention of the

[22] The same is true of the Passamaquoddy.   Cf. Prince, (a) p. 493.

wampum was considered a sign of consent. It often happened that the husband, after the wedding, would buy back the wampum. According to accounts, marriage negotiations were often wearily prolonged by dallying. The favorable report delivered, both families met and fixed upon a night for the wedding dance. This constituted the marriage ceremony. In the meantime matters rested, the betrothed pair not enjoying any association with each other. The ceremony just described is called *Ke'lulwewa'ngan*, "negotiation."

It was invariably expected at this juncture that the couple-to-be would agree to "live together always" in fulfillment of the ethical ideal cherished by the Wabanaki. The son-in-law was expected, also, to take up his residence with the wife's father and family, sharing and working his father-in-law's hunting territory until the latter died. The elders attribute this in part to sentiment, saying that daughters are pets and cannot be relinquished, "even left out of sight."

The marriage wampum itself, either a necklace or string used in this capacity, was known as *kelulwe'mkewi*, or *kel-ku'lwewi*, the same as the ceremony. It should be recalled, as noted before, that among the Penobscot, wampum never came to be used as currency nor was it a medium of bride-purchase. It was made to be used in ornamentation, as a rare gem, or to be used in a formal capacity as a reminder of pledges, compacts of different forms and ceremonies.

The marriage ceremony proper, to resume, although culminating the event did not, under the old régime, close the obligations of the bridegroom, as will be seen. Upon the night arranged by the families of the couple, a social dance took place in the dance hall, the expenses being met by the groom. This dance, to which the whole village was invited, was virtually the publication of the union, after which, in the eyes of the community, the couple was considered bound together. The wedding dance actively survived until at least 1910. The description to follow is based upon repeated observation and participation in the festivity.

Those attending are dressed in their best, the older people in Indian garb, by early evening assembling in the dance hall of the village. The dances which constitute the major part of the rite, i.e., its aboriginal element,[23] are performed first in the evening. They comprise a group of separate dances, the songs of each being different but the manner of dancing the same. Just how many distinct songs were known I never could determine. Upon the occasions observed, however, they numbered almost a score. A leader who shakes the cow's horn rattle sings the burdens of mostly meaningless syllables interspersed here and there with exclamations and sentences. The dance movement is that of the ordinary social dance. Examples of the music will be presented later. The stations of the principal performers of the Wedding Dance are as follows. The groom is flanked on one side by the leader and a companion while another friend takes position at his other side. Facing these are four women, one of them the bride opposite to and facing the leader, another her chosen friend facing the groom. Or perhaps instead of women facing the four men there may be a quartet of male friends and relatives. This is the leading squad. The next squad behind this is formed of four females facing four males in the same way. It may happen that the bride is not a member of the first squad, preferring to take her place opposite a man in the second. The number of partners in each squad may also vary from three or four to as many more as can conveniently circle abreast inside the hall. Following these squads of dancers are more in the same formation, depending upon how many join in. They then circle about the hall contraclockwise, until the leader brings the song to a close by a series of high cries (ta ho—) taken up by all the men. Then the dancers in broken order headed by the leader, stroll leisurely about in the same direction, talking and laughing with the bystanders until the leader assumes his position, sounds his rattle and begins the next song, when all behave in the same manner as before. The step of the men during the dance is an alternating step and shuffle, although there is much individual variation. At certain changes in the song the facing lines reverse their positions, those advancing forward thenceforth moving backward, and vice versa. The

[23] It is understood that the formal marriage rite has been previously performed by the Roman Catholic priest.

distinctive feature of these dances is that at the end of each song the leader shouts "*matama'l yəhe'*" echoed by the rest, which cry symbolizes "marriage." It is asserted jokingly that the cry is a corruption of French, *madame mariée!* Except for this, and the part taken in it by the bride and groom, there are no particular differences between wedding dances and the ordinary round dances performed on all social occasions. The wedding dance itself means more an occasion for performing a group of dances rather than any one particular dance. From its prominence in the marriage rite, however, the round dance of the above type has come to be regarded as the more characteristic of wedding festivities.

The night of the wedding is consumed with round dances, and is concluded with such others as the *Matagi'posi*, "Twisting on the Ground," commonly known as Snake Dance, and the *Nawa'dawe* "Old Time" (?) or Micmac Dance (see p. 285).

By morning the affair is over and all make for home. The newly wedded pair also separate, going to their respective abodes. For the period of about a week the two do not live together, and a strict watch is kept over the groom by his comrades lest he steal an interview at the home of his bride. Should he be discovered even so much as coming from the parents' dwelling, where she stays, he is apprehended and forced to promise that he will give a dance to the village as a forfeit. This means that he must provide eatables, hire the singer and dance leader, and in short stand for the full expense of a night of pleasure dancing.

Now, at the termination of this period of continence, another ceremony called *Nada'buna*, "carrying the bed," took place. This is generally preceded by another night dance similar to the first. The groom, accompanied by his friends, then carries his bedding, *abo'nu*, over to the bride's dwelling. They then are left alone in each other's company for the first time, and the wedding rites are over. An additional rite in which the couple bow seven times to the noon-day sun is also mentioned by Nicolar,[24] but of this I could learn nothing.

It was the rule in the old days for the husband, after a short sojourn with his wife, to embark on a hunting trip

[24] Nicolar, p. 145.

alone in the northern interior. This trip was supposed to cover about a year, although longer periods are remembered. The object was to accumulate wealth in peltries, to gain experience and to prove ability as a family provider, as well as to demonstrate self-continence in the husband. The journey often took the hunter so far away that he came into touch with parties of Mohawk, so there was an added incentive for the groom to secure some scalps to display upon his return home. The season of separation was also a test of the young wife's fidelity. After the husband's return, the pair would reside with one or the other's family and share their hunting territory.

The Penobscot have, however, long given up such rigorous measures. They speak in admiring terms of the old days when marital fidelity, virginity, and continence were supposed to be the invariable rules of life. Adultery is said to have been punished by death. Girls are said to have been reared in innocence, and marriage was desired at an early age. Switching was sometimes resorted to by husbands who wanted to punish troublesome wives.

The term *ni'zwiak*, wife or husband, is derived from the numeral *nis*, "two." From consulting the kinship terms, it would seem that marriage had the effect of uniting the husband's and wife's family in a reciprocal relationship secondary to, but separate from, the blood kinship bond. And the family was the seat of honor, the soul of society.

Menstrual Seclusion

The Penobscot are to be included among the tribes which, over a widespread area in America, had the practice of isolating women during their menstrual periods. We learn of this only through the memory of the older people who testify that in a shelter apart from the dwellings the women at such times were obliged to remain alone, attending to their own wants. Lest the men be weakened by contact with them, the women did not cook for them nor come into touch with them. Young girls, particularly those just arriving at puberty, had to take care not to cross a young man's path, lest the act sap him of some of his vigor. An idea prevailed that a menstruating woman could involuntarily poison a man, either through food or by touch. So a neighbor came in to cook for a man while his wife was ill. Also, for her own good, a menstruating woman must not touch cold things. Menstruation is called *bedənaswe'wak*, "haulings."

Burial

When a death occurred in the village everything became very quiet as the people were notified. If festivities were going on they were peremptorily checked. The deceased was dressed in his best clothes, and ornaments were placed upon him. If the deceased were a man, a bow and some arrows, in later days a gun, were placed with him, and, as tradition asserts, in early times also a stone gouge or the like. The body was wrapped in a roll of birch bark, *buskəni'gan*, and buried several feet deep in the burying-ground, *buskəni'gamik*, "grave habitation." Near each village a place was located where dead were buried, preferably a sandy place where excavation was easy. High commanding hills or bluffs near the river were liked on account of their solemn dignity. A curious tradition is recorded about the cemetery at Indian Island. The Indians would not enlarge their overcrowded graveyard, for they thought they would die to fill it up again if they did so.[25] If people died away from home, or in the distant hunting grounds, every effort was made to bring the remains home for interment near the village.

A short time before the body was buried, however, a mourning or funeral ceremony was performed. The relatives and friends gathered at the house and demonstrated their grief. Some elderly men standing near the corpse chanted the following dirge for a while, the assemblage joining in. Some say that it was the office of the head chief to sing this song shortly after the death of a villager, and to do so again when the body in its bark wrapping was interred. The song is said to be a prayer to the soul. "Now our aged man is going to sing a 'dead song,' *me'tcīnayintowa'gan*," was the introduction phrase.

[25] Vetromile, p. 68.

Death Song

(P. R. 20)

ya ni go we ya   ni go we ya   ni go we

Another version is

(P. R. 69)

Mourning

If the deceased person left a spouse, a company of old women, consisting mostly of relatives of the departed, visited the widow or widower and placed the mourning upon him. This consists in modern times, the custom still being practised, of a suit or dress of black. It is presumed to have been formerly paint or perhaps ashes. This mourning was imposed upon the bereaved for a year or, if advisable, perhaps half a year. During this time a strict watch was kept on the mourner's conduct, because it was tabooed for him to indulge in any of the following acts: sexual intercourse, joyful festivities of any kind, the use of liquor, and incidentally anything which would be irreverent to the memory of the deceased. From what we gather, in the nature of popular opinion, the mourner was under a ban, hedged about with criticism and the appearance of conventional behavior for the specified time. Should a lapse of conduct reach the ears of the old women, they took off the mourning and left the mourner in profound disgrace. Popular sentiment was strong enough to provide sufficient punishment for the offense, the disgrace being considered ample.

When, however, the set time had passed, the same old women visited the widow or widower and removed the black garb. That evening a dance rite was held in which the participants, including the mourner, were daubed with red

paint on the forehead by an old woman, the occasion being
the signal for abandoning grief. The dances were of the
ordinary round type though the first song was a special one.
When this dance was over, the mourner was free, and could
marry again or associate without restraint amongst his friends.
The rite was called *gatsiwe'ndimak*, "mourning removed."

Mourning removal

(P. R. 109)

The burden is he ya we *ya he* + he nī ya we *ya he* + he
ya we ho *ya he* + ga hyo *no* + *ya he* + skīnosīs'tuk ("boys")
ya he he ne no *ya he* + etc.

DIVISION OF TIME

The formal divisions of time were, like other natural phenomena, regarded as spiritual personifications, especially the
seasons of the year, which also figure in mythology. The

days, too, are personified, often being spoken of, according to the weather, as *wu'legi'skak*, "good day," or *ma'djigiskak*, "bad day." The day personifications seem, however, to become merely weather beings, forces to be reckoned with as disease or ill fortune would be.

The year period is *eliga'duk*, a term embodying the idea "frozen-over time," and indicating that years are reckoned by winters. The ordinary concept of the year is denoted by that for winter, *pəbu'n*, when considered as a unit of time in narrative. The year period begins with January, *piliga'dən*, "new, strange, year."

Four seasons of the year were recognized, *si'gwan*, spring (March until May); *ni'bən*, summer (May until September); *dagwo'gəwi'*, fall, "double (?) finished," referring to the ending of summer (September until December); *pəbo'ni*, winter (December until March).

At the beginning of these periods, the term *mɑdje'-* "commencing" is prefixed; *mɑdje'sigwan*, "opening of spring."

The term for month, *gizu's*, is the same as that for sun and moon, or night-sun.

A vague understanding of the solstitial epoch was grasped by the early Penobscot—one evidently quite independent of European teaching, as is shown by the folklore associated with it. After the close of the "Great Moon" (December) they knew that the days began to lengthen by regular degrees and that the nights began to shorten. The following observation translated expresses the seasonal climax in the poetical imagery of the natives. "Days commence to lengthen as the footsteps of a bird; nights commence to shorten as the footsteps of a bird." Which means figuratively that the days begin to lengthen one after another by an increase of time equal to the step of a bird walking over the snow. To visualize this one must have seen the measured footprints of the partridge upon the snow surface. By July the saying is reversed to indicate the shortening of the days and lengthening of nights in similar stages.

The names of the twelve months, divided as we divide them, given by several old men, are as follows. The month begins with the appearance of the new moon and lasts until the end of the full moon. They knew of no way to adjust the unequal lengths.

{angəlosa′mwe′sit or	"hard times"	January
pəbu′ni gizu′s	"winter moon"	
{bo′bioda′genis	"wind scattering leaves over crust of snow"	February
tagwo′skəni gi′zus	"crust on snow moon"	
pənoda′mwi gizus	"egg-laying moon"	March
{sigwənəme′gwi gizus	"spring fish (alewife) moon" or	April
aməso′ gizus	"spear fish moon"	
kik'ai′ gizus	"planting moon"	May
muskhogi′ gizus	"(seals) rise on the water, moon"	June
ɑdji'tae′ gizus	"berry ripe moon"	July
{wikge′ gizus	"(seals) fattening moon"	August
skamu′ni gizus	"corn moon"	
{madjewado''ki gizus	"animal rutting moon"	September
pkwiptesi′ gizus	"reddening of leaves moon"	
{pəninibial gizus	"leaf falling moon"	October
azəbɑ′skwa′djəs	"ice forms on shores"	
pɛbʊ′naməswi gizus	"winter-fish (rock-cod) moon"	November
{ktci′ gizus,	"big moon, winter coming moon"	December
pəbona′mwi gizus		
nibaya′mia′wi gizus	"Christmas-eve moon"	

Most of these deserve further comment. They say that January was their hard month. February's name refers to the wind blowing the leaves. The name of March is thought by some to refer to hens. April's name may denote the alewife-spawning period. June's name has reference to young seals growing fat and resting upon their mothers' backs off shore. July received a Catholic designation as well, *skwude-besk'hɑ′zik*, "shooting fire out." They developed the custom of assembling about a fire with guns and shooting at it until it was extinguished. This was connected with a Pentecostal ideal instituted by the missionaries. An early author, Vetromile, erroneously thought this to be a native solstitial ceremony. The name for August denoted an important season to the Penobscot, when the young seals were fat enough to remain floating when they were shot.   November acquired also a church designation, *pa'tamawe'ndimɑk*, "praying for souls in purgatory," from the Roman calendar.   November is named from the frost fish or tomcod (?) (Microgadus tomcod (?)) called *ɑbona'mes*, "winter fish," which throng the Penobscot waters in the late fall.   December, "big moon," refers to the long nights when the moon is so prominent.

If the lunar divisions are to be regarded with any certainty as being native in origin, no doubt need be felt concerning the antiquity of the seasonal divisions described under the topic of Hunting (pages 35–6).   These are founded upon the seasonal activities of aboriginal life, which may mean an initial step in the evolution of chronology.   Enumeration is lacking.

The month itself is subdivided as follows:

piligi'zoʻs	"new, strange moon"
pkəniha'do	"filling-up," first quarter
məza'kɑnnahazu	"reaching end of horizon (so it can just be seen)," second quarter
gizɑ'gizoʻs	"finished moon," third quarter

The missionary author Vetromile [26] gives a list of months and a nine-fold division of the month according to phases of the moon.   Though inaccurately recorded, his facts, judging from phonetics, are from the St. Francis Abenaki rather than from the Penobscot.

The day, *gi'zoʻk*, "during sun," and night, *təbo'ʻk*, "during dark," are roughly divided into the following periods which form the shortest time units in Penobscot reckoning:

a'ləmi dje"kwat	early morning before daybreak, "going towards dawn"
dje"kwatʻ	dawn, about sunrise
gisdje"kwat	early morning after the sun is up, "past dawn"
spoʻzwi	morning, until nearly noon
baʻskwe	noon
giziba'skwe	afternoon, "past noon'
adlǫ'gəwi	evening, about sunset
niba'wi	night time

[26] Vetromile, p. 79.

| e'ləmi təbo'kik | late at night, "going on in darkness" |
| eba''si təba''gak | midnight, "half or middle in the darkness" |

Besides these are

pemgi'sga,	today, "crossing day"
se'ba,	tomorrow, *awa's·eba*, day after tomorrow, "across tomorrow"
wlǫ'gwe,	yesterday

The Penobscot had a device for noting the time of day by putting a dial stick upright in the ground or snow and observing the length and direction of the shadow it cast.

A list of the days of the week originating with the missionaries is:

sɑ'ndi	Sunday
kizsɑndi	Monday, "after Sunday"
nīsəda'lok·ɑn	Tuesday, "second work day"
tsəda'lok·ɑn	Wednesday, "third work day"
yewa'lokʻ·ɑn	Thursday, "fourth work day"
skewatukʷ	Friday, "fresh day," referring to taboo on meat probably having reference to "fresh fish"
kada'usɑndi	Saturday, "going to be Sunday"

COUNTING AND MEASURING

The Penobscot system of counting presents some interesting points of distinction in regard to the classes of objects enumerated. Seven classified series of enumerators comprise the following groupings: independent numerals, dependent numerical prefixes, enumerators for persons and animate creatures, enumerators for inanimate objects—all cardinal numerals. The ordinal series comprises enumerators for concrete objects (i.e., the "first in position") for abstract ideas (the "first in space"), and the distributives ("one by one," etc.).[27]

As employed in crafts and techniques, the measurement unit is chiefly the flat palm with thumb extended, placing the ends of the thumbs together for two hand-breadths. This, the one- and two-hand span, is customary in gross measure-

[27] Further discussion of the characteristics of enumeration would require several pages of vocabulary and grammatical comments. The field of mensuration is, however, a rich and important one in respect to the word content and concepts of time and space relationship. The material is fertile enough to justify treatment in a separate paper which it is my intention to prepare in due time.

ment as a standard for manufacture of objects such as baskets, arrows, tool handles, snowshoes, traps, canoe parts, paddles, and such. Instruction in crafts is also given by these gauges. It is employed in horizontal dimensioning. Smaller spaces and openings are measured by the extended closed fingers of one hand, thumb down. This is for vertical spacing. A smaller standard is the single finger width. The smallest gauge is the tip of the finger nail.

In reckoning bulk, the number of four or five appears to be a commonly used unit. Small quantities are counted out in groups of two, as frequent observation revealed.

Turning from the more pragmatic aspects of mensuration we encounter a custom as much fraught with imagination as anything to be expected from the viewpoint of uncivilized man. It is the familiar and ancient measure for distance on water, in the forest, or along the shore and from the mountain top, redundant in myth and in the present vernacular of hunters; namely the "look," called *tegaga'bi·muk*, "as far as one can see." Its significance is only apparently unreal. A trial in the wilderness is convincing in its favor when following directions given by a guide.

Aside from the data given in the preceding paragraphs, occasional notices of methods known for denoting relationships in time and space will be found in other sections of the volume.

So far as can be determined the cultural number seems to be seven.

FIGURATIVE SAYINGS, EXPRESSIONS, AND ETIQUETTE

The arrangement in allegorical form of humor and thought between man and animals is a marked feature of Penobscot behavior. In the translations to follow are given current sayings and expressions illustrative of a vein of informal humor never far below the surface. It would not be possible to indicate which of the examples are flashes of individual talent, and which are repetitions of common stock in sayings. One may discern in them simple phases of wisdom, didactic lessons or satirical observations on human behavior and etiquette.

"You are indeed like a fly, hurrying off when finished eating." This is said when a guest takes his departure too soon after a meal.

"Hidden is your paddle. You cannot depart now." This is said to postpone the departure of a guest and is, of course, derived from the manner of traveling entirely by canoe.

"I camp on your trail." Such is said by a person intimating that he will not give up the pursuit of another. It is commonly used to signify persistence, the expression being derived from the hunter's custom of camping, when overtaken by night, on the trail of a moose.

"Playing raccoon" is a saying used when referring to a person who feigns sleep or indifference. It seems to correspond to the expression "playing 'possum."

"(Like a) chub quick biting" denotes the action of a person who impulsively jumps at a suggestion, as one would say of another being "played for a sucker."

"Pitch hand" is a term applied to one who steals. Whatever he touches sticks to his hand.

"Resembling an eel being slippery." Literally, "as slippery as an eel." Eels were very important in the old Indian régime, furnishing a ready allusion for an unreliability; or a wavering personal habit. It was common to allude to some animal when rehearsing the characteristics of a person. The intimate knowledge of animal life, an observation to be constantly borne in mind, explains this tendency.

"Resembling partridge so wild." This is said of a shy, retiring, or bashful person. "(As nimble) as a squirrel" is another saying of the same class.

"The fox is smart but he gets caught in the trap just the same." This is said of a person who is sly and tricky. They think a man of this sort always gets his own medicine in the end.

"You must tell a story because you ate the rabbit's (hare's) head." When hares are eaten whoever takes the head to eat the soft parts, considered tidbits, is said to owe a story to those present.

"He will have to suck his paw for the winter." Thus said the ant to the locust, referring to his own industry and thrift.

It is said of lazy men in the village, and alludes to a belief concerning the hibernating bears.

"Do not pare your fingernails because before next Sunday your hand will smell." This is explained as meaning that long fingernails are a protection to the fingers when put in a "soft place." It leaves something to the imagination.

"He causes a noise by striking his feet on the ground." The reference is to the habit of the hare stamping its feet as an alarm. It applies to persons who have the same habit.

"He worries it. He cooks it." A saying alluding to the cruelty of the carnivorous animal teasing his prey before killing it. The teasing, it is thought, is to render the victim unmindful of its pain, or by another opinion to make the victim tender.

Crepitus evokes several exclamations, among which is "So-and-So is going to spread a feast." And this individual, if he is a good fellow and financially able, would do so for the company.

One preparing a special dish for himself is said to do so because "his anus orders it."

"Hare sitting there counting snowflakes, (saying) 'Coming down, coming down, coming down.'" A saying alluding to snowy weather, depicting the hare squatting in his "form" or "set" in the snow beneath a tree-trunk, it may be, counting the descending snowflakes. It is also observed how the hare has pellets in his intestines resembling a series of beads. Each time he counts "Coming down" (*pe'mihak*) he passes one of these pellets.

A long time ago, they say, a young man got married and the pair went far into the woods. As they did not return, the people set out to hunt for them. At last the two were found dead, locked in embrace, the man upon the woman with his elbows worn to the bone, the woman with the skin worn off the back of her head. That is a puzzle story they tell to young married couples.

"(It is) hungry, moccasin," is said of a moccasin that is torn out at the toe. They think the rent resembles a gaping mouth. "It reeks" (*maski'mate*) is the expression ordinarily elicited by unwelcome flattery, patronage, or insincerity.

There is a pun on this word, "it smells like a vulva (*masi'-ma'te*)." This is a common form of Indian humor.

Puzzle making was a regular feature to a certain class of old folks who were known in the village as *nəba'ulinowak*, "riddle-men." They passed their time in composing riddles not only to be used for amusement in general but also to be employed by the speech makers in the council meetings. The feature of riddle-speech is said to have been prominent among orators. It was thought to be a mark of skill to conceal one's meanings in parables and subtle sayings.

An example may be given of the light riddle. One of the old riddle-men came hobbling down through the village holding something behind his back out of sight. He stops a young man passing and says, "I have overcome a man with no arms or legs but a big head and mouth." "Who is that, for Heaven's sake?" exclaims the young fellow. "Why, I have brought him along," adds the old man. "*Kii!* where is he?" "Here he is now," and the old man produces a dead snake.

A'ləmus walade'sis, "little dog dish," is an exclamation of extreme surprise; lone equivalent to the profane repertoire of the white lumberjacks. It serves every purpose as an expression, but its application to the situation seems to baffle inquiry. Among both men and women the common exclamation of surprise is *ki·i·!* or *i·i·*, when combined with disgust, *ee!*. Sudden disgust and discomfiture brings forth *ma'k·ətcis*, "vulva," from women for the most part. An equivalent to the expression "the devil!" is Penobscot *alagi'tdis*, a rhetorical extreme. Rhetorical pauses and polite assents are varied, *a'eada*, "Well, so!" *gwi'na*, "really?" *gehel·a*, "indeed, truly," *ehe'*, the dulcet affirmative, lead up to *anda'* or *nda'*, and *a'ha*, the emphatic negative and positive; "no" and "yes."

Formal etiquette has its phrases, few but gentle. *Pa'-kwenɑ'gsi·an*, "Long may you live," is said pleasantly by persons when meeting (note that the Labrador Eskimo greet each other with the same sentiment). The expression is accompanied with hand-shaking. A symbol of warmer affection is the kiss, denoted by the native term, *ba'sis* (diminutive). When entering the dwelling the visitor is told "*a'bi*," "sit down." Formerly when bark wigwams were used the visitor's

place was at the right, just inside the entrance. Here his
place was assigned by the salutation *a'bi aga'mɑdek*, "sit
down at the side." A more intimate or honored guest would
be told *a'bi na'udek*, "sit down at the rear." At the back of
the lodge fire opposite the entrance was the host's place and
that of his close friends. Smoking together ordinarily follows
when people meet. At parting a host says, *Mi'na gǝbe'djose*,
"Again come back."

A social gathering in the town hall and a dance was sometimes held to welcome visitors of importance or bands from
other tribes. At leave taking, friends shake hands and say,
a'diyo (French *adieu*).

DANCES AND CEREMONIES

I have already had occasion to describe some special
dances, and ceremonies which include dancing. While it may
seem extraordinary for eastern North America, where dance
and song usually have magical and religious import, we nevertheless face the evidence that dancing in this region does not
reveal discernible religious aspects. Its function was secular;
to furnish the choral display of social gatherings on occasions
such as marriage, feasts, elections, formal greeting, games,
war, trading, rejoicing after the hunt, and mourning. To the
Algonkian ethnologist these dances, without holy purpose,
may seem like a body of art lacking soul. I have little hesita-
tion in offering as an explanation of this condition the influences of Christian control; the substitution of the "holy
songs," the Indianized church liturgies, for the original prayer-
appeals in song and dance which we may imagine to have
existed before conversion several centuries ago. The change
from sacred to strictly social dancing and singing may have
transpired without coercion on the part of the priesthood,
rather by free adoption of hymns through fondness for their
soft melodies. The holy songs, I believe, have usurped the
function of an original spiritual repertory, leaving the social
dances to survive.[28] The last phase of Penobscot dance his-

---

[28] A similar transition has taken place among most tribes of eastern North America. Modified Christian chants with native words have exerted an irresistible lure
upon Indian musical fancies, from the Eskimo and Montagnais-Naskapi of the Labra-

tory has closed its cycle. Not for the last eight years or more has the old council hall resounded to the dance rattle and tramping of feet. The singings heritage is passing without succession after the last two living song leaders shall have died.[29]

In the Penobscot categories, there are five or six types of dance defined according to movement and song; one of them, the predominating round-dance cycle, embracing a large enough series of weakly differentiated songs to last through a night of dancing. During the period of association with the people, opportunity frequently arose for witnessing and taking part in dance performances—the sources of the ensuing descriptions.

The dance, in general, is called *alnaba'gan*,[30] "common, original, human dance," or *pəma'gan*, "crossing(?)." They are night performances, in recent times enacted in the village dance hall. Formerly, we are told, an enclosure, within a breast-high fence or brush, was erected for dancing.

The instrument used is the cow-horn rattle. Formerly it was a gourd containing pumpkin seeds. Drumming accompaniment in the Micmac Dance was provided by the singer beating on the floor or ground with rattle or a baton. The drum has never been used in dance performances within memory. As to regalia in days gone by, a few observations may be added here to what has been treated under Dress. It is customary to dress up with ornaments and beadwork as much as possible. As late as 1914 some dancers wore costumes, in part at least, consisting of beaded collars, cuffs, coats, moccasins, sometimes feather headdresses and paint.

dor region to the Creek and Cherokee of the southeast. Collections of church ritual chants are waiting to be made. These will, I foresee, provide material for a still unrealized phase of evolution in native music. They form the latest phase. These later historic trends of change have, however, only affected dance history by strangling the religious ceremonial meanings and throwing all dances into the category of social festivities. This seems to explain the condition at Penobscot and accounts, at the same time, for the disappearance of the drum, another pagan instrument-medium in the eyes of the clergy.

[29] Even the Indian Island orchestra has dissolved and dispersed. The reasons given are lack of interest and the cankerous ridicule directed upon native interests by some of the modernistic parvenus.

[30] Another stem *ginte'* occurs; its wide distribution in Algonkian languages I have discussed in *A Study of the Delaware Indian Big House Ceremony*, Harrisburg, 1931, f. n. 2, p. 12.

The old women appeared in calico waists, short decorated skirts and pointed caps. Penobscot art I have dealt with in a separate paper, giving its symbolical aspects which developed here as a particular trait-instance among Algonkian of the East. (See bibliography, Symbolism in Penobscot Art.)

An incidental feature of the ceremonies and songs should not be overlooked. In reading the accounts of explorers along the north Atlantic coast, one meets mention of how the natives received them with series of "terrifying" yells and shouts. These were intended as evidence of friendship and rejoicing, as they afterwards learned when uttered at certain intervals during other ceremonies of greeting. Jacques Cartier mentions the yelling custom a number of times. In this practice we have what is known among the Penobscot as conventional yells, forming a species of acclamation during ceremonies and dances. The voice pitch of individual men being different, an accidental harmonious effect is produced, weird and thrilling to alien ears—a feature, so far as I know, peculiar to the region. Examples of these conventional cries are as follows:

ta ho′ +   ta ho′ +   ye hye^c hye +

It should be borne in mind that these outbursts seem spontaneous. Some criers will cry above or below others, and so produce a peculiar, perhaps accidental, musical coordination.

In some of the dance songs there is a discernible element of composition, the leader varying his cadences with the different syllables and also arbitrarily repeating, raising, or lowering the tones of certain bars. Individuality among dance leaders is not only betrayed in the singing, but also in mannerisms, especially in starting a dance.

The Penobscot, Malecite and Passamaquoddy have been copartners in dances for a long period. Between singers in

[31] + indicates approximate tone value.

these tribes, however, there are greater differences in detail of syllables and melodies than are observed between singers of the same tribe; sufficient for the Penobscot generally to distinguish their own songs among others. I also find them able to identify Malecite and Passamaquoddy songs. In some cases they can readily tell by certain peculiarities which of the Penobscot singers have sung into the phonograph. The Micmac dance is, however, distinctly recognized as a borrowed one, and distinct in motions and tempo. Not all of those who know the round-dance songs can sing the Micmac dance.

The musical transcriptions to follow were written by Mr. Jacob D. Sapir from wax cylinder records made by myself before 1916, now in the University Museum, referred to by numbers in parentheses. Dr. George Herzog has been kind enough to offer advice in the handling of the scores written so many years ago by Mr. Sapir.

Round or Wedding Dances

The characteristic Penobscot dances are those which we term round dances, from the manner in which the company circles about the dance hall. They bear the designation *alnīga'n* or *alnɑba'gan*, "common dance" or "person's dance."

The different songs form a set of dances, all the same in form and manner of dancing, and differentiated during the performance only by intervals of rest or promenading. How many songs may have originally formed the complete set it is impossible to say. At least a dozen have been recorded collectively from Joe Solomon, Piel Sakus, Joe Thibaudeau, Piel Nicola, Louis Nicholas, and the rest in twos or threes from other singers. Some free play is also displayed by the different leaders. As to function, I may mention again, these dances are purely social, and are used for such occasions as weddings, elections, visits, and feasts, to make up the festivities of the night.

In the round dances, the rattle, which is shaken by the leader, is the indispensable musical instrument. The leader strikes the rattle against the palm of his free hand, sometimes holding it on a level with his face, again lowering it almost to his knees. The beat of the rattle is in one-two time, the accent being on the first beat. The step is a simple alternating step and scuff with each foot. Stamping with the heel during the step is also common. In the same dance, some men merely tramp hard in time with the others, bringing out individual fancies in step; all, however, in unison. Nevertheless it becomes apparent that the rattling, the singing, and the foot beats are not in the same rhythm; the effect not being discordant but so uniform to the ear that it is with difficulty that one is brought to realize that all three are moving in independent rhythms. Other interesting features occur in these dances, the cries of the participants, for example, the comic postures of the leader, and the intervals of intermission. The singing is a two-part performance, like that of other eastern and Atlantic coast tribes, the leader singing the burden syllables, which have no meaning, and the participants responding with a choral burden, a feature which has been discussed previously. In arranging the song burdens, I have followed the scheme of putting the chorus portion in italics. The order of sequence of the songs both in the dancing and as given below is purely arbitrary.

Before presenting the music itself, something should be said about the round dance formation. The movement of the dancers is contra-clockwise within the ambit of the village dance hall. The arrangement is as follows: The leader, flanked on each side by one or two men, faces a line opposite consisting of the same number. The facing rows form a squad which retains its relative position throughout the song. Following behind this squad are as many more like it as there are dancers to form them, women composing the rear squads, and children the last. In the first with the leader are the chief, or governor if he chooses to dance, and other dignitaries, as well as honored guests. Nearest to the leader, especially opposite and facing him, is the most honored place. Often the men in the rows lock arms, and during the dance all bend low together and yell. In this manner the column of dancers, the squads varying from three to five abreast, move around the dance hall, some advancing forward, some backward. However, at the option of the leader, at certain intervals which are largely determined by a sudden rise of tone in the song and by yells, the facing squads reverse, the individuals passing around each other singly, so that those who the moment before were going forward are now dancing backward. At these junctures they all whoop, and some cry "^{h}ye^{c} ^{h}ye^c ^{h}ye^c+" on different notes, producing a barbaric and stirring harmony. Then, when the leader has continued the song to his satisfaction, he brings it to a close by stopping rattling, and shouting "taho'+" which, repeated by the men, concludes the song. When performed at weddings, this cry is reinforced with "matama'lyəhe'," which signifies marriage. For a short period of rest the leader marches about relaxed

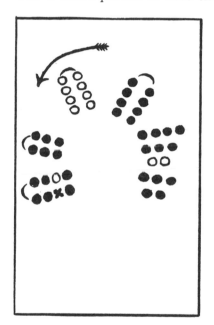 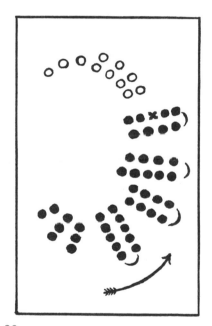

FIG. 80

DIAGRAMS SHOWING MOVEMENT OF TYPICAL
ROUND DANCE

X leader

o women

● men

Bracket Indicates Dancers Facing Each Other Who Reverse
Their Position at Intervals During Song

and mopping his brow, exchanging friendly banter with the bystanders. He may be accompanied by those who have been dancing, unless they are too fatigued. After circling the hall leisurely once or twice the leader calls his followers, resuming the song as they form in squads as before. This procedure is repeated until they have had enough, or until the feasting is started.

Several typical round-dance formations are diagrammed in figure 80, as observed during a former election ceremony. The legend underneath explains what is necessary. The three women at the head of the column in the first diagram were, at the time noted (1912), attired in full native garb, and being the three oldest women in the tribe they took the leading position. They advanced with a short shuffling step, arms at their sides, and they took no part in the singing.

(P. R. 68)

The burden is: he wi yu hwa *ha ne hi ahihe;* ho hyu we hi *ahiho;* widjokemine ("help us out") *ahihe;* ho hyo we hi *ahiho:* repeated indefinitely, generally omitting "help us out" addressed to bystanders, not to spirits. At end, ta ho.

(P. R. 27)

The burden is: he' hai gwa' *ni ho;* ho' hai gwa' *ne hi;* he' hai gwa' *ni ho;* he' hai gwa' *ne hi.*

(P. R. 28)

The burden is: hai ya ni ho *a hi he;* he ni ya *a hi ho.*

(a)

(P. R. 16)

The burden is: yau' ni' ho yau' ni ho (repeated).

This is a version of a popular and common type of Round dance song. It is interspersed with exclamations urging the bystanders to join in the dance and telling the participants from time to time to yell.

(b) Another version of the same song is:

(P. R. 15)

The burden is: yau' ni ho yau' ni he (repeated).

(P. R. 11)

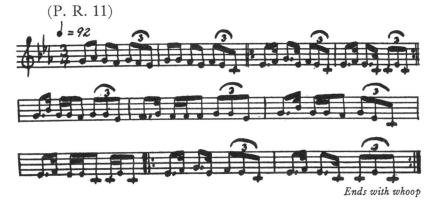

Ends with whoop

The burden is: ka' yu wa' ni *ya' hya he* (repeated).

(P. R. 19)

Ends with whoop

The burden is: he' yo ga *he na* (repeated).

(P. R. 14)

Ends with whoop

The burden and words are:

a	kwe' hai wa' ni he	*a hi he*
	yo' hai wa' ni ho	*a hī he*
	ski'nosistuk	*a hi he*
	"boys"	
	widjo' ke'mine	*a hi he*
	"help us out"	

(Repeat *a*)

gadu'smɑn sa'yizɑm	*a hi he*
"drunk (is) my comrade"	
no'delda'mɑŋga	*a hi he*
"I am sorry"	
eligɑdu'smit	*a hi he*
"he has been drinking so"	

(Return to *a*, again repeating)

In this dance, two girls were selected by the chief to dance alongside several guests. The singer remembered the occasion, as it took place once when they visited the Passama-

quoddy.   The two girls had silk shawls over their shoulders.
With the shawls they covered their own and their partners'
heads.   After dancing awhile thus, the two couples withdrew
and sat down side by side for a while among the spectators.
The men so favored regarded their partners as temporary
sweethearts.

(P. R. 13)

Ends with whoop

The burden is: (*a*) *ya' hya he'* (repeated); (*b*) kwe' yu wa' ne
kwe' yu ne (repeated).   The first part of this is purely a chorus
part.

(P. R. 108)

The burden is: kwe hai wa *ni ho* (repeated).

(P. R. 70)

The burden is:

wi yu fa'ne hi	*a hi ho*
ye+hai yu'we hi	*a hi ho*
ye wi ya wa'ne hi	*a hi ye*
ga ya wa'ne hi	*a hi ye*

ya widjo'ke'mine' skinosi'stuk ("help out, boys")

(Note the *f*, the only occurrence of this sound in Penobscot. I believe that it is a result of labial closure in pronouncing quickly *hyu-hwa*.)

(P. R. 71)

Ends with whoop

The burden is: kwe' hai gwa' *ne hi'*; he' hai' gwa' *ni ho'* (repeated).

(P. R. 66)

The burden is: gwe ya' *wa he no'*; hi ya' *wa he no*; ga ya' *wa he no*; gwe ya *wa he no.*   Ends with "*matamalyəhe*" (p. 257).

(P. R. 12)

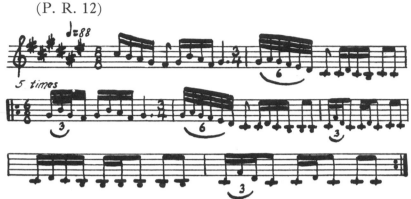

Ends with whoop and rattle

The burden is: kwe hai' *wa' ne ho*; kwe yu *wa' ne ho*; ko yu *wa' ne ho* (repeated); kwe hya *wa' ne ho*; ko hai *gwa' ne.*

(P. R. 12, b)

The burden is: kwe' hai gwe *ha' yu we*; ho' hai gwe *ha' yu we*; he' hai gwe *ha' yu we* [32] (repeated).

Wedding Dance

(P. R. 8)

[32] "With great energy, a very peculiar and beautiful form."—J. D. Sapir.

The burden is: kwe′ hai wa′ ni ho *a hi ho′;* ho′ hyu we′ hi ho
a hi he′ (repeated alternately, indefinitely). The last bar is
the concluding cry "*ta ho′*."

Wedding Dance

The burden is: kwe′ hai wa′ *ni ho′;* ho′ hyu wa′ *ni he′*
(repeated with variations).

The song burden here is the same as the preceding.

Snake or Creeping Dance

The dance known as *Pəmatagi′posi*, literally "coming twisting along on the ground," is commonly designated the Snake
Dance on account of the motion taken by the line of dancers.
Another name is *Yune′ha*, taken from the predominating
syllables of the song. It is a social dance performed on
festive occasions. A leader, carrying the rattle which he

shakes vertically or sideways, sings the song loudly, the rest
of the dancers forming a continuous line behind him, either
with interlocked arms or holding hands and joining in the
song as they may. Men and adults are usually nearest the
head of the line, and girls and children at the tail end. The
step is a simple, short, rapid trot. The line, guided by the
leader, generally circles the area once or twice, and then
begins making closer circles toward the center and unwinding
again. The end of the line of dancers is swung about like
the lash of a whip, as in the country "snap the whip" game.
They sometimes make it very rough.

Anciently when the Penobscot lived in villages or camps
of closely clustered wigwams, they used to start this dance
and wind in and out among the lodges, those last in the line
grabbing hold of bystanders (and even the sleeping occupants
of wigwams) by arms or hands and dragging them into the
line. The trick is still practised upon the spectators in the
dance hall.

Newell Lion had heard that the dance anciently represented the movements of a serpent (constellation) in the sky,
but he could give no further connection with it.

The rattle is shaken in one-two time, the accent being on
the first downward stroke. Some attempt seems to be made
by the leader, as I have observed when watching him, to
keep the rattle and step coincident in time. The song, however, is entirely independent, in time, of the rattling and
stamping.

The burden is: yu ne' ha *yu ne* (repeated, leader alternating
with chorus as indicated by italics). At the end of the first
song the leader cries, "Help us out everybody."

Another example;

(P. R. 9)

The burden is carried by leader. he+ he hai yu′ ya; he+ gwe hai yu′ ya; he+ gwe′ ya ho yu ya; he+ gwe′ hai ho yu ya; ho+ he hai ho′ ya. At the end "ta ho!"

Micmac Dance

The Micmac Dance, *Nawa′dawe*, "Old time, Ancient (?)," is most energetic in movement. It is thought to have been brought originally from the Micmac, though there is no other evidence beyond the report that such dances were common among the latter. This is usually the last dance to be performed at the gatherings.

The music is furnished by one man (or two as once observed) who either squats or sits with extended legs at one end of the dance hall and beats the rattle vigorously upon the floor. A baton of ordinary firewood may be used instead of the rattle. When danced out of doors, a birch-bark basket or properly the drum, it is said of earlier times, was beaten upon with the rattle. This man, of course, does not take part in the dancing. He is also the only one who sings. In this respect the Micmac Dance differs from the others. So much for the one- or two-man orchestra which furnishes the accompaniment.

The performance itself is usually begun shortly after the song has started, two men running out into the center of the dance area, giving a few yells and stooping low, facing each other with arms spread and crooked. Keeping the crouching posture, they circle about one another. Other pairs or even single dancers join in as they feel inclined. Only men take part. The step is very energetic, consisting of an outward scrape with the ball of one foot and a stamp with the other flat, the two alternating regularly on one side until a transfer is made to motions on the other. Performers vary the step to produce more noise by stamping with all their weight on one foot and shuffling with the other. Although I have never seen women take any part, I was told that sometimes they did by standing outside the men, making short sideways steps and slowly waving their outstretched arms level with the shoulder.

The dance seems to be purely for amusement, a conclusion to festivities; the noise and exuberance of the occasion culminating in a grand finale. Stamping and yelling on the part of the dancers is a feature. One might add that sweating is another, because endurance and sweating are much discussed by the assemblage when all is over. The singing, and hammering with the rattle, are usually continued until the last dancer has stopped through fatigue.

An element of the songs for the Micmac Dance is their vigor and general wildness. The syllables are, as might be expected, meaningless. The several men who are known as leaders of the Micmac Dance have somewhat different songs, though they agree closely when theirs are compared with dance songs of the other types. There were, to my knowledge, only four of these leaders at Oldtown in 1912, the leaders of the other dances not knowing the songs for the Micmac Dance. As to time-beat of the drumming with the rattle: beginning with a regular staccato it gradually accelerates to the limit of speed, then slows down, and accelerates again in time with the singing or stamping.

The following are versions recorded:

(P. R. 10)

Ends with whoop

The burden is: ho+ka ni' ya ho'; he+ka no' ya ho'; ka ni ya ho+hai+ (much varied and syllables prolonged).

(P. R. 107)

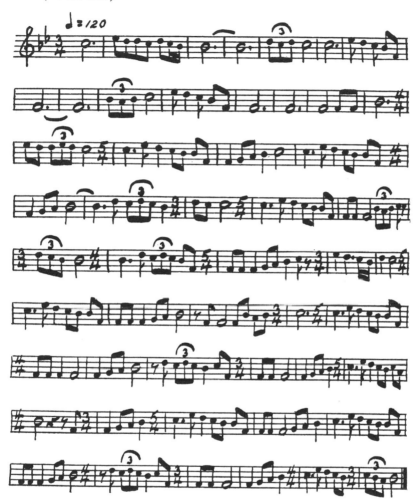

The burden is: ha ni ya he+na+; he+no+; he ya+ ha ni ya no+; ha ya+ ha na ho+; he ya+ ha ni ya ho+ (with drum, or beating on floor).

(P. R. 22)

Ends with whoop

The burden is: he na, hu yo he, he ya na (very much repeated, the different syllables prolonged and the groupings varied without order).

Still another version is:

(P. R. 4)

Greeting or Election Dance

This is perhaps the most solemn of the ceremonies. It is called *Ska'wəhe*, "Greeting," or *Ska'wintowa'gan*, "Greeting Song." [33]   The dance itself was only a part of the complex

[33] The name *Skauhi'gan*, "Means of Greeting" is also used.

ceremony which was performed when the tribes of the Wabanaki confederacy met together for the installation of a chief
for one of them, or for councils. The songs and syllables are
claimed to be practically the same among the Penobscot,
Passamaquoddy, and Malecite,[34] yet each had its own method
of procedure in its own dialect.

In the old days when it was customary to assemble upon
summons to inaugurate each other's chiefs, much intertribal
visiting was carried on. These visits were formally carried
out according to traditional usages. They constituted the
principal political functions of the loose alliance maintained
among these tribes and are discussed in an essay on the
Wabanaki confederacy listed in the Introduction.

The visiting band always arrived by canoe. When the
Passamaquoddy visited at Oldtown, they appeared either
coming up or down the Penobscot River, the Malecite always
down. When the Penobscot went to visit the others, they
went up river to the Malecite, or down by way of the bay to
reach the Passamaquoddy, at their main village at Pleasant
Point in Passamaquoddy bay.

There are two aspects of the ceremony; according to
whether the Penobscot were visiting others, or whether they
were hosts receiving visitors. Since the home tribe is most
concerned with the latter, we may narrate this procedure first.
As soon as the visiting tribe was sighted on the river, the
people of the village gathered on the beach. The men stood
in the foreground, while the visitors halted their canoes in
front of the assembly with flags flying from bow and stern.
Then, in an even line, the canoes were slowly paddled ashore,
the occupants singing their Greeting Song.

Then the men of the village formed in two rows leading
up from the water's edge to the village, armed with loaded
guns. Upon the approach of the canoes the guns were fired,
the act symbolizing the reception of an enemy, as well as
being a salute. When the chief of the visitors landed from
the foremost canoe, his band singing their chant, he walked
up, also chanting, between the rows of hosts while they fired

[34] For a Passamaquoddy version, see J. D. Prince, ref. 2.

their guns again. Then he returned to his canoe and the flag in front of the chief's house in the village was lowered and raised again. When the visiting chief reached his canoe, the chiefs next in rank, one by one, went through the same procedure. I profess to find in this symbol of the well-known rite of "running the gauntlet" a dramatic gesture of hostility and peace summarizing the periods of Wabanaki contact before and after foundation of the confederacy.

Next the chiefs of the village escorted the chief of the visitors to a special lodge, or to the home chief's lodge, and the *gepti'nak*, captains, of the village carried the visitors' canoes from the water and laid them down before the guests' house. When this was done and the flag had again been lowered and raised, both people mingled freely and exchanged greetings informally, and shook hands with each other. The rest of the day, until night-time, was spent in visiting friends in the village, and in feasting. The big dance was generally held during the afternoon.

During the celebration, until the new chief had been fully installed, the home people all wore an oblique bar of black paint across their faces as a sign of mourning for the last chief.

That night the dancing began early. In the dance hall a row of vessels, or caldrons, brimful of stew filled the center of the floor. Generally a whole moose, or later a cow, was barbecued for this feast and served in big vessels in the open over a long fire. On both sides of the row of steaming vessels sat the men of the village ranged in their proper rank. Between these rows, as at the first reception on the beach, the visitors, one by one in order of rank, entered the hall and danced around the pots.

As each danced up and down the hall, circling the vessels once, he shook hands with each of the hosts seated at the side, saying, "Shake hands, my relatives!" No rattle was used in this dance, the accompaniment being furnished by the men of the village who shouted, "*he' he' he'*" in regular rhythm. Considerable time was taken up by the dancing, especially if the visiting company was large.

When the dancing and handshaking were over, birch-bark or wooden dishes were provided, one for each person present. When all was ready, the village chief shouted the well-known cry "*Kəwalade'wal*," "Your dishes," the signal for every man present, host and visitor, to help himself from the row of vessels. Then followed the feast and informal social intercourse.

The ensuing night was spent in dancing, the following days with games and contests between men of the tribes present who formed opposing sides. The time between council meeting was filled in with dancing and merrymaking, until the visitors departed, their mission accomplished. It is said that the guests often wore out their welcome on these occasions, but that the debt would be evened up by a return visit before many months.

When the Penobscot visited the Passamaquoddy, they approached the shore at Pleasant Point in their canoes, singing on the beach and awaiting their guests who, when they had landed, formed in an opposite line and one at a time, the chiefs first, shook hands with those opposite, saying *kolasi·'-kolba ki·ga'wasnowa'k*, "We salute you, our mothers," but arbitrarily meaning "our brothers and sisters."

The above account of the Greeting Ceremony is generalized from the statements offered by old informants, some of whom had participated in such events in their youth.

During the occasion, capes or collars (Figs. 58, 60, 65) and wristbands of red cloth decorated with white beadwork scroll designs were worn by the chief to be elected, and by the other officers of his council. The symbolism of the designs on these articles of regalia has been discussed under Art (p. 160). Something remains to be added in reference to the specific meaning of colors and designs worn at the council and installation ceremonies. The red background has the significance of war, while the white beadwork is emblematic of peace. The dualism corresponds to the meaning of the ceremony, its object being to promote peace relationship where lurks the possibility of war between the tribes represented in the gathering. Thus the quasi-hostile demonstrations in the formal reception of the chiefs. The salutes and the marching up from the beach between armed files, all simulate latent hostility. The symbolism, in brief, denotes, "Here, no matter what might exist to provoke enmity between us, let us be embraced by the ties of peace." This is the ideography of the inturned curves of the designs. As explained previously, the regalia, capes, cuffs, coats, and other articles of dress have the scroll and double-curve designs, the curve enclosures denoting the tribal units within which the various villages, chiefs, officers, and families are represented by the ornaments inside the scrolls, all pictured in contact with one another. Some of these articles have been figured. Figure 58 shows a chief's cape embroidered in white beads and ribbon appliqué. It was called a mourning cape, and was worn by one of the tribal officers during the ceremony while the assembly was still mourning for the defunct chief and until the new chief had been installed in office. On the narrow ends of the cape, and around the inner border are scrolls signifying the bonds of unity encompassing the assembled parties. The lower central figure denotes the place of mourning indicated by the filling of dark ribbon work between the beaded lines. The little ornamented embellishments inside the scrolls of this large central area, which are also filled with ribbon, denote the tribal officers and the family members of the dead chief wearing mourning. The fact that it is a mourning article is shown by the absence, in the central area, of the cross which is the sign of a chief.

Greeting Dance Songs

From several sources, I obtained song records of the Greeting dances. There are said to have been originally ten songs or parts to the whole procedure, of which the ensuing transcriptions are remembered portions. There were two forms, an older, slower and more impressive version, and a later or, as the singer stated, a "new style," more rapid and less stately, which seems to have replaced the other some time ago.

The words "*Kolasiko'lba kigawa'snowa'k*," "we greet you, our mothers," occur at intervals during the singing of this approach-ceremony. The syllables of the above have been lost.

The formal Penobscot Greeting Song follows, being given in several versions.

(P. R. 66 b)

(*a*) The syllables of this are:

  he ga hwa nu de
  he ga hwa nu da   (repeat)
  gwɑn ha li ya ho
  gwɑn ha li ya he   (repeat)
      (Repeat the entire score)

(P. R. 72)

(*b*) Another chant is:

The syllables are the same as the preceding.

(P. R. 18)

(*c*) Still a third rendition of the preceding chant in the "old style" is the following:

After several repetitions of his chant, the host chief stopped and pronounced the following welcome at the conclusion of the song. Then came the handshaking referred to in the account of the ceremony.

"Welcome to you, my good people. I am glad to meet with you who are coming to visit us. Much do I rejoice that you have come to visit us, my kinfolk."

Here the Greeting Song was repeated several times and the address was continued.

"Much do I rejoice that you have come to visit us."

Hereupon the formalities proceeded as explained in the account.

Another song belonging to the second part of the Greeting Ceremony is the following. This was sung for the dancing which took place subsequent to the first solemn introduction. As the Greeting Ceremony began to decline in formality among the Penobscot, this song came into more general use for the reception of guests, and so came to be called the "New Style" Greeting Dance.

(P. R. 74)

Ends with whoop

The burden is: kwe' hai yu wa ne', *hai' yu we'* (repeated over and over).

Malecite Dances

Peddler's Dance. A popular amusement dance introduced long ago from the Malecite was the *Pe'dlɑs be'djose*, "Peddler is coming." It was danced the same as the ordinary Round dances, only differing in music and words. It humorously pantomined the coming of a peddler loaded with such goods as the Indians liked. Its origin probably dates back to the arrival of some peddler in first-contact days, when the natives were impressed with his amusing appearance and conduct. A version by one of the Malecite intermarried with the Penobscot at Oldtown is given, as well as one rendered in the Penobscot language by a Penobscot, showing how the song has become adapted.

(Malecite version)

The words of the song are a play upon the character of the peddler, as the translation shows. "Peddler is coming, *ya hi ye*. You can tell by his looks, *ya hi ye*, he wants money, *ya hi ye*. Help him along, *ya hi ye*." (Repeated.) The phrases are by the leader, the burden sung by the dancers. The entire part was repeated enough to cover sufficient time for the dance. Minor changes were made according to the ability of the leader.

A Penobscot version of the same song-cycle is:

(P. R. 17)

The words, with the syllabic burden, are translated as follows: "Peddler is coming, *ya hi ho*, ho yu hwa ne ho *ya hi ho*, ho hyu we hi *ahi ho*. He has money, *ya hi ho*, (repeat syllable burden). Rubbers, he wants to buy, *ya hi ho*, (repeat burden). Old shirts (rags) he is going to buy, *ya hi ho*, (repeat burden). A bag he wants to fill, *ya hi ho*, (repeat burden). He desires (help) when his bag is full, *ya hi ho*, (repeat burden). So well he knows how to dance, *ya hi ho*," (repeat burden).

Trading or Clown Dance

This is a gaming ceremony, obsolete now for upward of fifty years, called *Noləma'higan* "(Acting like) clown," also translated as "Risking Dance" (*nolə'mi*, "risk"). It was performed by two detachments of people located in separate houses or lodges. It was a night-time performance, and popular enough to be played two or three times a week. Each party chose a trader or clown (*nolma'hamɑt*), dressed in outlandish garb. A mask made of the head-skin and antlers of a deer is also mentioned (Fig. 30). Again, they attired him in women's clothing, or stuffed out his back like a hump. Then one of the clowns was sent forth by his own party, carrying in a bag some object to barter, such as a hat, knife, basket, or the like, called *pə'modigan*, "offering." He went to the other house where the people were waiting. He was obliged to remember who had sent each article he carried. As the clown or messenger reached the door he gave several

cries, 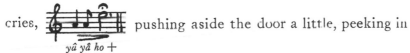 pushing aside the door a little, peeking in

yâ yâ ho +

and stamping on the threshold like some animal. Then letting go the door and pausing a few moments, he repeated his weird cries, those within answering with shouts, "he' he'," and

crying, 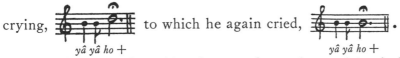 to which he again cried,

yâ yâ ho +   *yâ yâ ho +*

Then he entered, making faces and carrying on in a droll manner, parading up and down the floor and displaying the article he wished to trade, praising its value, and shouting improvised challenges, jibes, and jokes at the assemblage. Sometimes the messenger had an assistant at his side.

After some moments of strutting up and down, the messenger began to dance, stooping forward, arms akimbo, then straightening up and twisting his back, singing the trading song while the assembled spectators accompanied him with regular repetitions of *hega hega hega* or *he' he' he'*.

During the intervals of singing and dancing, the clown tried to induce some one to trade with him; to exchange something of equal value, if possible, for the object which he offered. He first usually approached the head of the house. Naturally a great amount of comic, wordy abuse took place between the spectators and the clown. But it had always to end in barter, otherwise the clown would not leave the place. Sometimes the company worked itself up into great heat over the deal. One clown is remembered to have pursued a man, who tried to get away from the dance, across the river to the middle of Oldtown village, and at last to have forced him in the public streets to make a trade. On another occasion it is related that Old Raccoon, who was a famous performer, actually brought a canoe right into the room where the company had gathered, and there drove a trade. Years ago old Sakis Nelson exchanged a fishing rod for a vest.

A masterpiece of dramatic fiction, however, produced by the Trading Dance ceremony is the following:

One night there was a large crowd gathered in a house. Suddenly the signals of the trading-dance performer notified the group that the procedure had started. He soon made his customary entry, when behold, he was garbed in a shroud! He began his antics, and some of those present responded with the usual answers, *he' he'*, and consummated trades with him. Everything seemed to be all right. Certain ones, notwithstanding, cast jibes at the clown trader saying, "He stinks." Whereupon the mysterious performer cried, *He ga kǝni'yo he ga di' gǝna*, "Hega, look out you. Soon you will all smell like that." And before spring came those who said that were all dead. (The ghost had been insulted and had "poisoned" them.)

When the trade had been concluded, the clown returned to his own party, where the coming of the clown-trader from the other party was awaited. Upon his arrival the same procedure, or practically the same in effect, was repeated until he made a trade. This amusing performance was continued through the best part of the night, often to be taken up through several ensuing nights.

Sometimes upon more serious occasions, the trader from each party would have an assistant who would remain with the opposite party to attend to the real business of the players, and each trader would go the rounds. The traders or clowns were usually the spokesmen for their party. From all accounts, the Trading Dance must formerly have been an important and popular ceremonial pastime involving the whole village for several nights.

The clown regalia of the trader was an important characteristic feature of the performance. One disguise is shown in figure 30. Again, we learn from others that a mask of birch bark was seen, and in winter often a hunter's horned cape-hat (see page 44 and Fig. 9). The disguise is termed *tcabote'-swiye*, "clown-like." No rattle was used. What connection could be traced between this dance and the Iroquois False-Face Begging Dance is something to think of, as Dr. W. N. Fenton points out to me.

The following trading dance melody was obtained at Oldtown.

(P. R. 21)

Ends with whoop

Pine Dance

The Pine Dance, *do'toweziga'mɑk*, was an old-fashioned, woman's performance. It was essentially a test of skill and endurance or, as they say, "smartness," combined with amusement. A singer provided music with the *Nawa'dawe*, or Micmac dance songs, while the women, as many who desired, dressed in their best, hopped and shuffled in the center of the floor amid shouts of encouragement from the assemblage. It is a dance quite without form, the steps and motions being determined by individual fancy or ability.

Hunters' Rejoicing Dance

The return from the hunt was the occasion for a dance of rejoicing. In this the men performed the movements of the ordinary Round dances, but there was a particular song for it, which was supposed to convey an expression of thankfulness for success in the forest and a safe return.

This is the one Penobscot song and dance which resembles the common dances of the Montagnais. The latter have special dances for the different animals, performed before and after the hunt.

(P. R. 110)

The burden is: yo ho+ ho+ ho he no+ hu wa+ ho+ yo ho+ ho ha yo+ ho+ ya he+. (The song is tremulous, the notes much prolonged, as indicated by the +.)

POSTSCRIPT [35]

CHANGING currents have by now altered the course of life of the Penobscot Indians through modifications brought about in their environment, and economic subjection to demands of the age incident upon the coming of the white man. The matter presented in the foregoing monograph is intended to draw a cultural picture in historic times of an Algonkian tribe of the northern New England forest—the Canadian zone of the biologist. Its time-span is confined to horizons lying within the limits of the latter half of the nineteenth century. Within this time-span the framework of native culture retained its independence and most of its traditional characteristics. It was still distinctly Indian. My material and sources should accordingly not be misunderstood in respect to their historical setting. It is no attempted reconstruction of the prehistoric past, rather a record of the historic era of transition when native institutions in the area were even then midway in transition to European forms, under predominating influences of the French first, then the English. Within the latter the northeastern Indian has finally become almost completely submerged. And there is much to point to the conclusion that the people we now designate as Penobscot are in reality an ethnic composite, the tribe itself a political unit, its culture a blending of native New England elements derived through a course of some centuries from perhaps wider horizons than we know of as yet.

But, after all, the ethnology of the past century is now merely a memory in Penobscot life. The new era is well under way. Improvements of the age have filtered into homes on Indian Island, and new ways have transformed the habits and the very ideals of community life even in the twenty years' lapse of time since the records here preserved

[35] This section reproduces the substance of an essay prepared as a culmination to a short term of fieldwork among the Penobscot in 1936 under a grant from the Faculty Research Fund, University of Pennsylvania. (*The General Magazine*, Vol. XXXIX, No. IIII, 1937.)

were made and finished. The same old river sweeps past the
island and tumbles over the rocks a few hundred feet below
the still-water where the batteau-ferry crosses in its leisurely
passage to and from the "landin'" on the Oldtown side as it
carries the constant flow of brown-skinned basket sellers on
missions of peddling or shopping for groceries in the still
dingy stores on Main Street. And the ferrymen are still

FIG. 81

OLD PENOBSCOT COUNCIL HOUSE

Home of Newell Lion in Later Times

brawny Indian youths who collect five cents for the round
trip from their restless tribesmen and ten from the curiosity-
haunted "tourists" whose cars roll over the vacationland
highways of Maine. The distant low mountain domes to
the south and east still raise their forest slopes tempting the
hunters of the tribe from the din of radios, going all day and
until late at night in the houses of the village, to the chase of
moose and deer. But the lure is more than ever the five
and seven dollars a day they earn as guides, not so much the

irresistible lure of the silent woods and the splash of the ash paddle. Graded and paved highways have opened up the forest lands. Outboard motors noise up the river reaches. And many of the men whose fathers knew chiefly the mysteries of the woods now know better the intricacies of the Oldtown Woolen Mill whose five-hundred-foot sweep of brick wall has, since its erection in 1889, been a shadow on the horizon of Indian Island and a factor in breaking the morale of the "people (of the river) of white rocky slopes." The white-water anciently boiling over the ledges below the island is now diverted into the sluiceway of the monstrous mills, and the clatter of looms by day and many nights pervades the silence where the howling of wolves in the boyhood days of Newell Lion, only ninety years since, proclaimed the rule of the wilderness. Where salmon formerly abounded the sluice dam stands as a barrier.

There are still a few old men and women with the ineffaceable stamp of the forest aboriginal on their faces and bearing, the stooped and in-toed march and step of hunters and canoemen in their youth and middle age now reduced to aimless peregrination on the new cement sidewalk of their village. The tattered remnant, some now senile, of the score of robust hunters and rovers who contributed to the study now behind us, from whose ranks in a period of six years, from 1927 to 1933, the then priest of the band buried fifty-five as his records showed, now could be numbered on the fingers. Of more than a dozen able dance leaders, upon whose knowledge and energies I drew in 1914, only two survive. From these men, Joe Thibedeau, estimated to be ninety-seven, and Louis Nicholas, eighty-five years of age, the last offerings of dance songs were recorded in 1936—the finale of Penobscot choral art. Behold old Joe, deaf and feeble, confined to his dooryard beyond the little bridge crossing to Oak Hill, the elevated suburb of the main village, taciturn but affectionately friendly and pleased with the honor of being asked to rehearse his repertory of songs to which we danced in the council house some twenty-five years ago. Then his voice was strong and his body rugged, when he taught the young folks to dance the Indian as well as square dances; and a great ladies' man to boot.

The case of poor Louis Nicholas, *alige* Louis as they say, is more difficult to treat. A rugged man he was thirty years ago, hunter, canoeman, guide and axeman known the length and breadth of Maine. A silent-mannered man of the poise that one finds among his kind. Look now who is coming up the road, uncertain of step, one eye closed, talking to himself in an undertone. He stops before a group of children conducting some tourists from the mainland. "Would you like see Injun dance? I can dahnce fo' you gib me few cents." And out from an inside pocket comes a hollow cow horn containing a handful of shot; his *ahalnan* or dance leader's rattle. A preliminary shake or two and he begins a wedding-dance song in a voice yet strong and clear, tapping the rattle in time upon his palm. He commences to short-step one of the ancient social dance measures, which not so many years ago thrilled the crowds in the Indian dance hall. And the little group of onlookers smiles, nods and looks wise. "Poor childish old fellow," and they move on to be shown by the children the next curiosities of the "Indian Reservation" as the signs along the road proclaim. But the children "tour conductors" get the pennies, not Louis. This is indeed the end of Penobscot musical history. The grand opera of a tribe of forest folk has dwindled to the status of a senile, beggar joke bleated in the gutters of his own village. There are no tears in the eyes of the restless tourists, but there are in the eye of Louis Nicholas. He is offering them a sample of what he treasures as the swan-song of the formerly abundant musical art of his tribe. He knows in his muddled brain that it will fade out with his breath. Another offering he makes; his "holy songs" chanting his comforting prayer-book litanies, "Oh you Jesus," "Jesus crucified," "Regina coeli," "Magnificat." And the tourists wonder how much longer they will have to tarry to hear the finish before they may move along to the next curiosity on show, and if they will be taxed for pennies by any more Indian antics. But why this irony? No one tells them that Louis performs daily devotions, without fail singing fifteen of the litanies in Indian. No one interprets

the low-voiced prayers he utters between them standing in
the roadway while they laugh, as fervent supplications to
Mali, Saisos, and Ketchi Niwesk (Mary, Jesus and Great
Spirit), to take him to heaven, soon to be with his family and
friends.   Louis is eighty-five.

With much inner satisfaction I find now upon returning
to Indian Island after over fifteen years of absence that
Indian is still spoken in many homes, despite a prophecy of
thirty years ago.   As I remember, Charley Daylight's wife
was one of a class of women on the Island speaking no English;
Charley for his part speaking no Indian, yet living successfully enough to raise a family under these outwardly ill-suited
conditions.   The circumstances governing the non-use of
English of such women were not those of low intelligence.
The reason lay in their attitude toward white people and
toward their own heritage of pride of tongue.   So I still find
in 1936 the two married women of my host's family group
speaking no English during my stay, but understanding it.
And one of them successfully runs a grocery store, basket
souvenir shop and poolroom combined.   Moreover, most of
her customers, the younger generation of Indians, do not use
Indian in their transactions with her.   Yet I cannot forget
that most of what Indian speech one does hear on the island
is Malecite, brought in from St. John river across the Maine-
New Brunswick border through intermarriage between the
two tribes.   The pure Penobscot language may be used now
by but twelve out of the total of some five hundred Indians
on the island, as Dr. Frank Siebert has estimated it.

And then, too, the clangor of the mills across the river and
the hum of traffic on the busy highway winding toward the
northern woods have not deafened the ears of all Maine
Indians to the pleasant whisperings of the evergreens or to
the thrilling bellow of the moose in the fall, when, as the
legend runs, the blood of the celestial Great Bear now slain
by the star-huntsmen following in his wake has begun to dye
the leaves of the hardwoods in scarlet hues.   Despite our
lament over the passing of old Wabanaki modes of life and
thought, much remains beneath the surface of commercialism.
I found again, as of yore, the canoe-man companion indicating

the distances yet to be covered on the winding river course by "looks." That is to say, "The mouth of Birch Stream where we turn in is *two looks* ahead," meaning that when we get as far as we can see from here, namely *one look*, our destination will be as far as we can see from there, *another look*. All this for miles in the estimation of the "white eyes," which I still find them calling the white man.

Indian behavior still persists. My recent comrade of the paddle irresistibly fell into discourse on the topic of his last moose hunting with the gusto of hunters of the fathers' times. He produced the birch-bark moose call and moaned forth the "love" call of the cow moose in the rutting season then drawing near, and next the answer of the eager bull, the whining "hurry-up" of the cow again; indeed the whole gamut of the love vocabulary of these monsters of the spruces. Even did again the pouring of water from the birch moose-horn imitating the urination of the cow moose under the excitement of the coming encounter. And how strongly I was reminded by this of the problem confronting the psychologist of animal and human reactions in genito-urinary responses under sex-emotional stimuli. This Indian carried out his dramatic forest pantomime of his own accord and with the art of a veteran of the woods. And that was all Indian! Far away then in those hours the basket-shop, the peddling truck, the canoe factory, the Five-and-Ten, the cinema, the snappy story magazines, as the sun went down in a prismatic blaze of glory. Perhaps Indian nature is still nearly uppermost in the make-up of these Indian islanders with the white blood in their veins.

And now a word more before blotting this thumbnail sketch of impressions as they came to me after almost two decades of time, with its changes, and after turning from the ethnology of the virile period of native culture which prevailed in the latter half of the century just passed.

I confess with pleasure that I still find the native inhabitants of Indian Island delightful company. With these men one can still play at being back in the colonial days. Lurking memories of Jesuit mission times, of the French and the colonial struggle for supremacy, of the Tarratine wars are there. How we all, like the financier of Detroit, suffer the pleasant malady of nostalgia for the ancient! The diversion seems never to grow stale. Lore and legend are still topics of talk, and even of rationalization, in the kitchen and front rooms of Indian homes though the radio crooner's voice may exceed in vehemence. And for those moods when weary of the past and its nuances; when to enjoy the pulsations of living social contacts is needed, there is likewise something waiting. Some of the men, unconventionally friendly and delightfully intimate, induce one like myself to "bathe one's spirit, after struggles of cleverness, in rich silences like coming home to truth and beauty," using the phrases of Daniel Gregory Mason. They are apt to bring us directly to the essence of what human democracy really is apart from its code of teachings by the masters of social theory. In such men, genuinely and unaffectedly natural, like my distant associates of the forests of Canada and the summits of the Great Smokies, I find a naïve contagious sense of the "infinite mystery and richness of life." The closing recollection of my last sojourn on the river with one of them is framed in a vision of sunset over the unforgettable river, far-stretching woods and a soothing crepuscule with the whippoorwills.

And yet, perhaps, I have dwelt overlong on the portrayal of life in the village in a tone of pathos. One slips imperceptibly into that vein of treatment when dealing with native life in its ever changing and generally decadent state. Nevertheless, there are other sides to be enjoyed as one would enjoy the company of the living rather than that of the senile or the embalmed. It is true indeed that each day sees some of the men embarking for an "up river" trip in canvas canoes equipped with hardware store outfit for trapping or fishing and grocery store provisions, to cruise, to hunt, fish, or to secure sticks of ash for basket-making wives or daughters. The old feeling for the bush is still there though perchance diluted with a yearning for the movies at Oldtown, the Saturday afternoon and evening hustle of shopping in the Five-and-Ten on Main Street. Newell will go for a few days up-river to camp alone. It may be at any time of the year, even though at seventy years of age he is suffering with angina and has the agency doctor's advice not to exert himself by paddling ten miles against current and head wind. That's Indian!

Frank, and there are many of his name and temperament in the village, like the guides of the past generation, is always ready to take out a party up-country whether the urge be for moose hunting or botanizing, whether its personnel be doctors, judges, or bartenders, landed families, *nouveaux riches*, or neither. He and his kind know the waterways from Ellswirth and Eastport to the Restigouche and the St. Francis across the northern border in Canada. They know the lurking places of moose—bulls, cows, and calves—the "yards" of deer, and pools where the big "lakers" lurk; where eagles may be seen, where medicine herbs may be identified, where the flies are bad or not so bad. That's Indian too.

Knowledge does not stop there. They even profess to exceed the learning of dendrologists by "proving" the existence of two species of balsam in the Maine woods by the taste of the pitch and the color of the bark. They will distinguish a "strong" variety with pungent pitch and black bark, a "sweet" or medicinal one with white spots in its bark, to the amazement of the tree experts whom they are guiding.

The Indian Island guide knows by "magic revelation" where the big fish may be found. A wise and curious-minded "sport" fisherman wants to test his guide's knowledge of the coveted places. The guide claims to know it by the taste of the fish in the water. Not believed? Question, "Are there fish here?" The guide tastes the water. "No, not right here." More questions as they paddle on. Here at last is a good place for fishing. The Indian again tastes the water and says he can now taste fish. After several tastes to test the evidence the "sport" decides it is a mystery; the water tastes the same as anywhere else. Urged by the Indian to try a cast, he casts a fly and gets a big trout. That's an Indian trick too.

And the silent, smoky Indian guide from the village will refuse to heat water and wash the feet of his tired boss in the evening when in camp after a hard day's hunt, even though the boss be an English gentleman, and discharge imminent upon refusal. The Indian guide will then abandon him in the woods to find his way out as best he may. That's Indian too, very! Nor will he stand for too much patronizing familiarity on the part of his "sport" when perpetrated in the manner of dealing with "Injuns" according to the popular significance of the term. So the following reminiscence. One of the light-skinned natives of the Island hired an exceedingly dark and Indian-looking relative to aid him on a fishing trip with a sport from Boston. Both of them had a parochial school education. The dark man had little to say the first day and the sport watched him askance with a manifest sense of distrust. He looked too dark. The two guides noticed the sport's uneasiness and, conversing in Indian, decided that it would be fun for the dark man to play up his part as a "savage" who knew little of white man's ways. Thenceforth he spoke in monosyllables and grunts as he had read that wild Indians do. The sport kept watching furtively to see what he might do next. When dinner was cooked the dark man took one of the hot potatoes from the pan with his fingers. Sportsman looks on in disgust and says something to the other Indian about it, complaining of serving oneself with fingers and not using a fork like decent people. When the light-skinned man interprets it the other grunts, seizes a fork, sticks it into a potato and begins chewing it off like a monkey, to the utmost, undisguised, and unspeakable scorn of the sport and corresponding amusement of the Indian guides. That's Indian, too! Humor and teasing are traits of Wabanaki character.

The "bush" still lures the villagers of Indian Island up river, exerting a pull upon interests and activities. And while we are witnessing the decay of the native social order, its external form is preserved somewhere withal, appearing sometimes, it may be only in outline, and then to a degree surprising to an observer who, wandering through the byways, sees so little to remind him of Penobscot man as being a reality.

I must not forget to do credit to the persistence of native knowledge of the woods and its animal life which I feared had passed away with the several score old folks who had gone to the "land above" since my contact with the tribe ceased. Once having recorded some seventy bird identities in an essay into ethno-ornithology, I still find my Indian Island host discussing bird names and giving observations on their habits with the same old familiarity and assurance of source knowledge as of yore. The art of moose-calling with the birch-bark horn is renewed with the gusto of three decades ago, the habits of the bull and cow in the fall rutting season, the jealous rages of rival bulls and their onslaughts, are just as much the engrossing topics of conversation at the midday or evening meal today as they were then, even while now the radio in an adjoining room is giving twice-daily broadcasts of political crises in Europe. Indian will, it seems, be Indian in some aspects.

My Indian Island host reminds me how he has learned that the frightened bull or cow will urinate or defecate when startled by dogs or hunters—evidence indeed of correct observation and deduction of animal psychology and behavior. How many of us can cite offhand as good an instance of emotional stress affecting the control of enterogenital functions in either man or animal? It took a hunter-guide of the Indian Island village to do it. And yet the same Indian peddles ash-splint and sweet-grass baskets in a car, has an electric metered ice box, a radio, and reads detective magazines in bed under an electric globe. Another has accompanied a Geodetic Survey party to Alaska as woodsman, been 140 feet below water in a caisson building the Bath Bridge, defied the "bends," scrambled along four-inch steel girders two hundred feet above the river as a riveter, spent four years with the Canadian forces on the German front, carpenters, and is now awaiting a date to guide sportsmen on the Allegash and St. John rivers as an all-around woodsman. Not only this but he speaks Indian (Malecite) and English as a bilinguist and can find himself in Canadian-French—he also claims Swedish through association with Swedish ironworkers. He, Peter Paul by name, who can pass as a white man anywhere, is an Indian! A human culture amphibian! So they come and go.

The older Indians of the region as I knew them possessed a deep streak of humor, and an attitude toward their surroundings which constantly turned up the funny side of almost everything. It ran from dry laconic sayings and comments in Indian or in broken English to ribaldry and obscenity, not infrequently tempered with a kind of guilty shame which we expect to find in countrymen anywhere. This faculty has not departed from the present generation of the changing Indian Islanders either. Their streak of humor flows on. Only lately it happened, and still causes a real laugh in the true vein of Wabanaki comedy: Molly spoke both English and Indian, but she stammered atrociously. Old "Auntie" could neither understand English well nor read, but she enjoyed intensely seeing the movies at Oldtown's center of art. Paying Molly's admission she took her to interpret the descriptive legends thrown upon the screen. Poor Molly tried her best but could only stammer "k, k, k, k, k" as the legends were quickly flashed on and off, to her own and "Auntie's" chagrin.

The purpose of the foreword has, I trust, been in some measure accomplished in showing that a study of this character treating the life of a contemporaneous tribe of the northern hunting zone must be accepted with its obvious limitations as covering only a relatively short span of time in cultural history. This span is now about closed. We cannot validly reconstruct the cultural picture of an earlier period. The next study to be made will be one of acculturation. Finally it is my idea that from this will emerge a concept, it may still be but a vague one, suggestive of the degree of intimacy with the workings of nature achieved by the northern Algonkian, through long living experience in the cold evergreen forests. They will not reveal themselves as a people planted in an inimical environment but as the denizens of a zone well provided with the means of enjoying that state of well-being and satisfaction which a Father-Creator affords for his children—as the Wabanaki claim to be. A case, indeed, to delight the mind of Rousseau could he have known and admitted them to classification as even crude examples of monism! Equipped from the beginning with powers of discovery and an ingenuity to avail themselves of examples set before their eyes in the economical workings of nature, they progressed with a genius to invent and to pattern their own society and mental life; then to gratify their senses aesthetically through consciousness of unity with nature and its laws, and to improve inventions through imitating the arts and cunning of the beasts as observed in their everyday life. Theirs was a cultural destiny thwarted by the interruptions of an alien civilization—the end of a primitive Utopia.

LIST OF PUBLICATIONS QUOTED

THE following list gives the works referred to in footnotes in the text under author's names. It does not, however, pretend to cover completely the references to the ethnology of the Wabanaki. Titles marked with an asterisk (*) denote articles and monographs dealing with topics in Penobscot ethnology not covered in the present volume.

ALGER, A. L.—*In Indian Tents.* Boston, 1897.

BARRATT, JOSEPH.—*The Indian of New England, etc.* Middletown, Conn. (1851).

CONVERSE, HARRIET M., and PARKER, ARTHUR C.—*Myths and Legends of the New York State Iroquois.* Museum Bulletin, New York State Museum, No. 125. Albany, N. Y. (1908).

COOPER, J. M.—*Snares, Deadfalls and Other Traps of the Northern Algonquians and Northern Athapaskans.* Catholic University of America, Washington, D. C. Anthropological Series, No. 5, 1938.

COPWAY, G.—*The Traditional History . . . of the Ojibway Nation.* London, 1850.

CULIN, S.—*Games of the North American Indians.* 24th Annual Report, Bureau of American Ethnology. 1902–03, Washington, D. C.

DAVIDSON, D. S.—*Snowshoes.* American Philosophical Society Memoirs, Vol. VIII, 1936.

DELABARRE, E. B.—*Chief Big Thunder.* Rhode Island Historical Society Collections, Vol. XXVIII, Oct. 1935.

DILLINGHAM, C. A.—*The Penobscots.* Bangor, Me. N. D. 16 pp.

DAVIES, JAMES—"A Relation of the Voyage to Sagadahoc 1707–1608." Probably by James Davies. In *Early English and French Voyagers, 1534–1608.* Edited by H. S. Burrage, Scribners, N. Y. 1906.

ECKSTORM, FANNIE H.—1. *The Handicrafts of the Modern Indians of Maine.* Bulletin III, Abbe Museum, Bar Harbor, Maine, 1932.
2. "Katahdin Legends." *Appalachia,* December 1924.
3. "The Attack on Norridgewock." *The New England Quarterly,* Sept. 1934, pp. 541–78.
4. "Who Was Paugus?" *The New England Quarterly,* Vol. XII, No. 2, June 1939, pp. 203–26.

GANONG, W. F.—*Collections.* New Brunswick Historical Society, Vol. 2, 1905.

GODFREY, HON. J. E.—"The Ancient Penobscot or Panawanskik." *Historical Magazine,* Feb. 1872, Vol. I, No. II, Third Series, pp. 85–92.

HARRINGTON, M. R.—"Some Seneca Corn-Foods and Their Preparation." *American Anthropologist* (N.S.), Vol. 10, No. 4 (1908), pp. 575–590.

HALLOWELL, C. E.—*History of Thomaston, Rockland, and South Thomaston, Me.* 1865. 2 Vol.

HALLOWELL, A. I.—1. "Kinship Terms and Cross-Cousin Marriage of the Montagnais-Naskapi and the Cree." *American Anthropologist,* Vol. 34, No. 3, 1932, pp. 171–99.
2. *Recent Changes in the Kinship Terminology of the St. Francis Abenaki.* XXII Congress of Americanists, Rome, Sept. 1928, pp. 97–145.

HAGAR, STANSBURY—"The Celestial Bear." *Journal of American Folk-Lore,* Vol. 13, No. 49, pp. 92–103.

HOFFMAN, W. H.—1. *The Midewiwin or "Grand Medicine Society" of the Ojibway.* Seventh Annual Report, Bureau of American Ethnology (1865–86).
2. *The Menomini Indians.* 14th Annual Report, Bureau of American Ethnology (1892–93).

HUNTER, J. D.—*Manners and Customs of Several Indian Tribes Located West of the Mississippi.* Philadelphia, 1823.

KROEBER, A. L.—*Ethnology of the Gros Ventre.* Anthropological Papers, American Museum of Natural History. Vol. I, Part IV (1908).

LAURENT, JOS.—*New Familiar Abenakis and English Dialogues.* Quebec, 1884.

LEGER, MARY CELESTE—*The Catholic Indian Missions in Maine (1611–1820).* The Catholic University of America, Studies in American Church History, Vol. VIII, Washington, 1929.

LELAND, CHAS. G., AND PRINCE, J. D.—*Kuloskap—The Master and Other Algonkian Poems.* Funk and Wagnalls Company, N. Y. and London, 1902.

LELAND, CHAS. G.—*The Algonkian Legends of New England.* Boston, 1884.

LLOYD, T. G. B.—"On the Beothucs, a Tribe of Red Indians Supposed to be Extinct which Formerly Inhabited Newfoundland." *Journal of the Anthropological Institute of Great Britain and Ireland,* Vol. IV (1874–75), pp. 21–39.

LOWIE, ROBT. H.—1. *The Northern Shoshone.* Anthropological Papers, American Museum of Natural History, Vol. II, pp. 165–306 (N. Y. 1908).

2. *The Assiniboine.* Same Series, Vol. IV, Part I, pp. 1–270 (N. Y. 1909).

MAURAULT, ABBÉ—*Histoire des Abenakis.* Sorel (1866).

MOONEY, JAMES—*The Sacred Formulas of the Cherokee.* Seventh Annual Report, Bureau of American Ethnology (1885–86).

MOOREHEAD, W. K.—*A Report on the Archaeology of Maine.* Andover Press, 1922.

NICOLAR, JOSEPH—*The Life and Traditions of the Red Man.* Bangor, Me. C. H. Glass & Co. (1893).

ORCHARD, W. C.—1. "Notes on Penobscot Houses." *American Anthropologist*, Vol. II, No. 4 (1909), pp. 601–606.

2. *The Technique of Porcupine-Quill Decoration among the North American Indians.* Contributions, Museum of the American Indian, N. Y., Vol. IV, No. I, 1916.

PRINCE, J. DYNELEY—1. "The Passamaquoddy Wampum Records." *Proceedings* of the American Philosophical Society, Vol. XXXVI, No. 156, pp. 479–495 (1897).

2. "Some Passamaquoddy Documents." *Annals* of the New York Academy of Science, XI, No. 5, pp. 369–377 (1898).

3. "Notes on Passamaquoddy Literature." Same Series, XIII, No. 4, pp. 381–386 (1901).

PALMER, R. S.—"Late Records of Caribou in Maine." *Journal of Mammalogy*, Vol. 19, No. I, Feb. 1939, pp. 37–43.

PARKER, ARTHUR C.—1. "Snow Snake as Played by the Seneca-Iroquois." *American Anthropologist* (N.S.), Vol. II, No. 2, pp. 250–256 (1902).

2. "Iroquois Uses of Maize and Other Food Plants." *New York State Museum Bulletin*, 144 (Albany, 1910), pp. 1–119.

3. "Seneca Burden Strap in Process." N. Y. State Education Department, *Museum Bulletin*, 133 (1909), p. 65.

PENNYPACKER, S. W., II—"The Problem of the 'Plummet-stone' in New England." *American Antiquity*, Vol. IV, No. 2, October, 1938, pp. 142–146.

ROSIER, JAMES—"A True Relation of the Voyage of Captaine George Waymouth, 1605." *Early English and French Voyagers, 1534–1608*, edited by H. S. Burrage. Scribners, N. Y. 1906, pp. 353–394.

SKINNER, A. B.—*Notes on the Eastern Cree and Northern Saulteaux.* Anthropological Papers, American Museum of Natural History, 1910.

SPECK, F. G.—1. *Notes on the Mohegan and Niantic Indians.* Anthropological Papers, American Museum of Natural History, Vol. III, pp. 183–210, N. Y. (1909).

2. "A Modern Mohegan Pequot Text." *American Anthropologist* (N.S.), Vol. 6, No. 4 (1904).

3. "Huron Moose Hair Embroidery." *American Anthropologist* (N.S.), Vol. XIII, No. 1 (1911).

4. *Montagnais Art in Birch-Bark, A Circumpolar Trait.* Indian Notes and Monographs, Museum of the American Indian, Heye Foundation, N. Y., Vol. XI, No. 2, 1937, pp. 45–157, Pls. XXIV.

5. *The Double-Curve Motive in Northeastern Algonkian Art.* Memoire 42, Anthropological Series, No. 1, Geological Survey of Canada, 1914.

*6. "The Eastern Algonkian Wabanaki Confederacy." *American Anthropologist* (N.S.), Vol. XVII, No. 3, 1915.

*7. "Penobscot Tales." *Journal of American Folk-Lore*, Vol. XXVIII, No. 107, 1915.

*8. "Medicinal Practices of the Northeastern Algonquians." Fifteenth International Congress of Americanists, Washington, 1915.

9. "The Social Structure of the Northern Algonkian." Publications of the American Sociological Society, Vol. XII, 1917.

10. "Game Totems Among the Northeastern Algonkians." *American Anthropologist*, Vol. 19, No. 1, 1917.

*11. "Penobscot Transformer Texts" (dictated by Newell Lion). *International Journal of American Linguistics*, Vol. I, No. 3, 1918.

12. "Kinship Terms and the Family Band Among the Northeastern Algonkian." *American Anthropologist,* Vol. 20, No. 2, 1918.

*13. *The Functions of Wampum Among the Eastern Algonkian.* Memoirs, American Anthropological Association, Vol. IV, No. 1, 1919.

*14. *Penobscot Shamanism.* Ibid., Vol. VI, No. 3, 1920.

*15. *Bird-Lore of the Northern Indians.* Public Lectures of the University of Pennsylvania, Vol. VII, 1921.

*16. "Reptile-Lore of the Northern Indians." *Journal of American Folk-Lore*, Vol. 36, No. 141, 1923.

*17. *Symbolism in Penobscot Art.* Anthropological Papers, American Museum of Natural History, N. Y., Vol. XXIX, Part 2, 1927.

18. *Wawenock Myth Texts from Maine.* Forty-Third Annual Report, Bureau American Ethnology, Wash., 1928.

*19. "Penobscot Tales and Religious Beliefs." *Journal of American Folk-Lore*, Vol. 48, No. 187, 1935.

20. "The Penobscot Indians of Maine." *The General Magazine and Historical Chronicle*, University of Pennsylvania, July 1937, Vol. XXXIX, No. IIII, pp. 396–405.

21. "Mammoth or 'Stiff-legged Bear.'" *American Anthropologist*, Vol. 37, No. 1, 1935, pp. 159–63.

*22. "One of Caesar's Anecdotes among the Indians of Eastern North America." *The Alumni Register*, University of Pennsylvania, Vol. 19, No. 9, June, 1917, pp. 686–90.

STRONG, W. D.—"North American Traditions Suggesting a Knowledge of the Mammoth." *American Anthropologist*, Vol. 36, No. 1, 1934, pp. 81–8.

SULLIVAN, JAMES.—*The History of the District of Maine.* Boston, 1795.

TURNER, LUCIEN M.—*Ethnology of the Ungava District.* Eleventh Annual Report, Bureau of American Ethnology (1889–1890).

The Jesuit Relations and Allied Documents, Travels and Explorations of the Jesuit Missionaries in New France, 1610–1791, edited by Reuben Gold Thwaites. Cleveland, The Burrowes Bros. Co. 1896.

VETROMILE, REV. EUGENE—*The Abenakis and their History,* N. Y., 1866.

WISSLER, CLARK—*The Social Life of the Blackfoot Indians.* Anthropological Papers, American Museum of Natural History, Vol. VII. Part I, 1911, pp. 1–64.

WILLOUGHBY, C. C.—1. "Houses and Gardens of the New England Indians." *American Anthropologist* (N.S.), Vol. 8, No. I (1906), pp. 115–132.

2. "The Adze and the Ungrooved Axe of the New England Indians." *American Anthropologist* (N.S.), Vol. 9, No. 2 (1907), pp. 296–306.

3. "Dress and Ornaments of the New England Indians." *American Anthropologist* (N.S.), Vol. 7, No. 3 (1905), pp. 499–508.

4. *Prehistoric Burial Places in Maine.* Archeological and Ethnological Papers of the Peabody Museum. Harvard University, Vol. I, No. 6, Cambridge, Mass. (1898), pp. 1–52.

WILLIAMS, ROGER—*A Key into the Language of America.* London, 1643. (Reprinted by Narragansett Club.)

INDEX

Abenaki (see Indian tribes)

Acculturation, professional athletes among Penobscot, 182n; names, 92, 138, 154, 239

Acorns, 98

Adolescence, segregation of youths at, 247

Adoption of children, 237–38

Adze, of stone, 108–9

Age-groups, terms for, 251–53

Algonkian (see Indian tribes)

Algonquin (see Indian tribes)

Amusements (see Games), head rubbing, 181; blowgun (tag), 182; ice shinny, 182; canoe tilting, 182; foot racing, 182; wrestling, 182; modern sports, 182n; "roosters," 183; "little pines," 183; ogre, 183; marbles, 183; tag, 184; cat's cradle, 185; tobogganing, 185; anecdotes, 186–87

Androscoggin (see Rivers)

Animals (see Hunting), associated with family bands, 203, 211; emblems of family ("totemic") groups, 203–4; eponyms as boundary markers, 206, 207, as individuals' signatures, 206, as individual names, 206; Penobscot belief in human descent from, 211; characteristics shared by humans, 211; fluctuations in population, 12, 42; native classification of, 51; myths concerning, 52; designs, 161

Animal economic cycle, 26, 35–36

Armor, of bark, 147

Aroosaguntacook (see Indian tribes)

Art (see Beadwork; Birch bark; Carving; and Porcupine quill work), decorative, 155, 163; European influence, 155, 156, 163; double-curve motive, 155–56, 158, 160–61; see Bibliography (Speck, 5), 316; beadwork, 156; floral designs, 155, 156–57; geometrical designs, 161; space determination of designs, 160; carving, 161; porcupine-quill embroidery, 161; moose-hair embroidery, 162; bark etching, 163; decoration of bark vessels, 118; civil and political symbolism of, 159–60; symbolism, see Bibliography (Speck, 17), 316

Athapascan (see Indian tribes)

Avoidance, absence of mother-in-law, 206

Awl, 107

Babiche, 132–134

Bags, woven of basswood, 128

Bands, Penobscot (see Family), 203–4; assembly places of, 212; number of, 213; leadership of, 203

Bangor, 9

Basketry, 123–27

Basswood fiber, weaving of, 135–36, 137

Beadwork, 138, 140–42, 145, 147–48, 158, 160

Beaver castoreum, use of, 50–51

Beliefs connected with, hunting, 36, 43, 44; fishing, 82

Beothuk (see Indian tribes)

Berries, 92, 94

Bestiality, in myths, 221, 222

Birch-bark, 21, 27, 28; securing of, 122–23, 135; torch of, 31, 83; moose call of, 34–35, 38, 39, 306, 310; raincoat and hat, 76; pictographs on, 80–81; animal figures of, 81, 206; containers, 111, 116–22; use in tanning, 132

Bird-lore, see Bibliography (Speck, 15), 316

Bitsenagan, shoulder bag corresponding to Algonkian ceremonial pouch, 128

Blowgun, pellet, 182

Bone artifacts, 86, 109

Bow and arrows, 36, 113–16, 189; composite bow, 110, 113–14

Brother-sister relationship, 245

Burial, 259–60; preparation of corpse, 259; place of, 259; rites connected with, 259–60

Calendar (see Mensuration and counting)

Canoes, 41, 54, 108; of birch bark, 57–65; decoration of, 57; type, 57; construc-

319

Additional Photographs

The following photographs have been added to this University of Maine Press edition with permission from the University of Pennsylvania Museum Archives, Philadelphia. These undated photographs were taken or collected by Frank G. Speck.

Photographs are identified by their University of Pennsylvania Museum Archives negative numbers.

I. Clara Paul wearing clothing *circa* 1840;
cf. modified photograph, fig. 62, page 144 (#11587)

II. *left to right*: Penobscot Governor, Chief Big Thunder (Frank Loring)
with an unidentified Penobscot constable (#11913)

III. Theresa Sockalexes (#11924)

IV. Peter Nelson wearing tribal governor's ceremonial cape-collar and wrist-bands (#11927)

V. Nick Andrews (#11929)

VI. *left to right:* Francis Nicola and Myra Andrews (#11916)

VII. *left to right:* Elsie Paul Tomer and Marie Lewis Morris (#11915)

VIII. *back row, left to right:* Joe Solomon, Peter Nelson, Nicholas Solomon, Sr.
front: Nicholas Solomon, Jr. (#N6-11917)

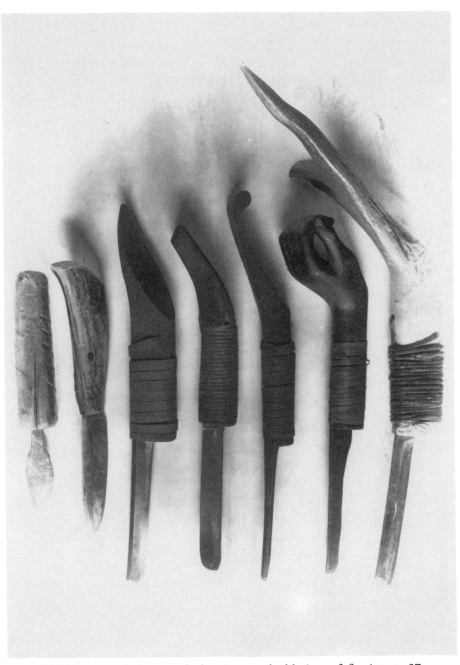

IX. Uncropped photograph showing crooked knives; cf. fig. 6, page 37
(#G6-11851)

X. Birch-bark moose call, covered basket and dish.
For line drawing and *in situ* photograph of similar moose call, see fig. 7, page 39
and fig. 8, page 40; for similar covered basket, see fig. 43-47, pages 119-21; for line
drawing of similar birch-bark dish, see fig. 41, page 117 (#11853)

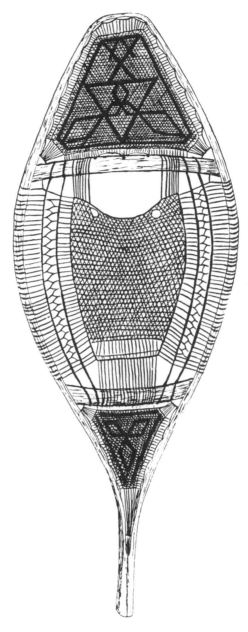

XI. Line drawing of snow shoe shown in photograph, fig. 19, page 69 (#13430)

XII. Another view of ornamented cradleboard shown in fig. 23, page 75 (#14279)

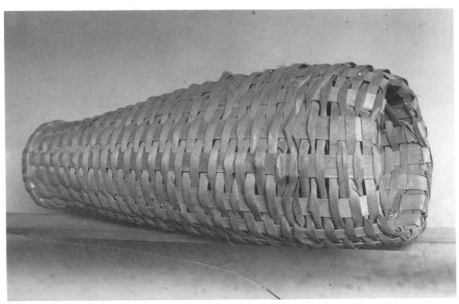

XIII. Splint basket trap set in streams for fish. Photograph used as basis for line drawing, fig. 32, page 88 (#14312)

XIV. Birch-bark seamless containers. Photograph used as basis for center and left line drawings, fig. 36, page 103 (#14283)

XV. Wooden and birch-bark spoons.
Photograph used as basis for line drawings, fig. 39, page 112 (#14289)

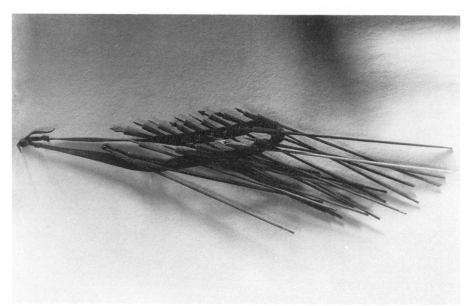

XVI. Arrows with leather holder for carrying arrows. Photograph used as basis for line drawing, fig. 40, page 115 (#14307)

XVII. Birch-bark dishes and pans.
Photograph used as basis for line drawing, fig. 41, page 117 (Neg #14285)

XIII. Birch-bark vessel with etched designs;
cf. vessel shown, fig. 42, page 118 (Neg #14316)

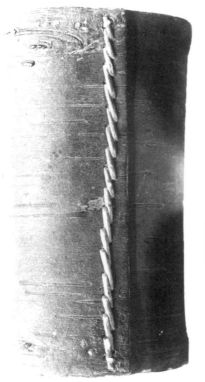

XIX. Birch-bark decorated baskets.
Two baskets at bottom shown in fig. 44, page 120; top basket not shown (Neg #13007)

XX. Wooden box and birch-bark baskets.

Wooden box shown in fig. 46, page 121. Bottom right basket
rendered in line drawing, fig. 45, page 120. Bottom left basket not shown (#14287)

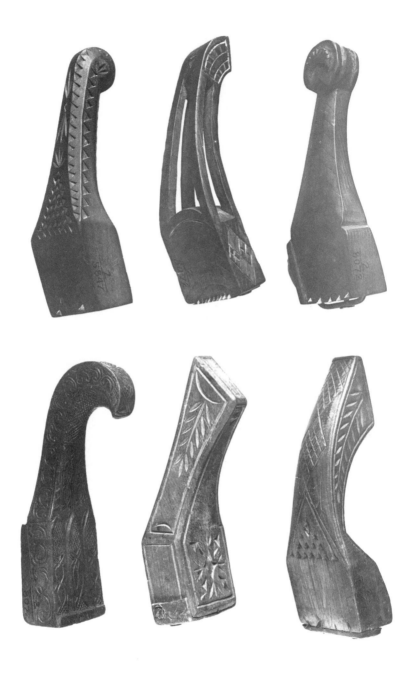

XXI. Basket splint-cutting gauge. The gauge lower left shown in fig. 49, page 126
(Neg #14318)

XXII. Woven basswood carrying bag and strap.
The basket shown in fig. 50, page 128; the strap not shown in original edition
(#13018)

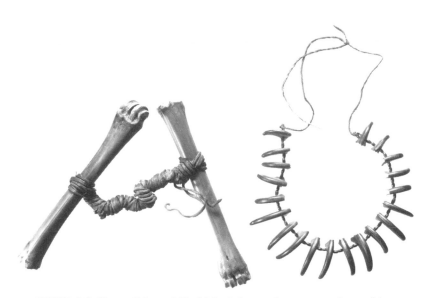

XXIII. *left:* Deer tibia and "babiche" thongs in process of stretching,
shown in fig. 57, page 133. Necklace at right not shown in original edition
(#13022)

XXIV. Chief Big Thunder (Frank Loring); cf. fig. 59, page 140 (#13024)

XXV. Tribal governor's ceremonial cape-collar and wrist-bands.
The collar shown in fig. 60, page 142; the wrist-bands not shown (#14304)

XXVI. Powder horns with incised designs.

The powder horn at bottom shown in fig. 67, page 159; the other two powder horns not shown in original edition (# 14288)

XXVII. Stone tobacco pipes.

The four pipes at top in fig. 69, page 161; pipes bowls at the bottom not shown in original edition (#14278)

XXVIII. "Dish game"; cf. line drawing, fig. 72, page 173 (#13009)

XXIX. Toss-pin-and-bundle games and corn-husk dolls, with related objects.
Photograph used as basis for line drawings, fig. 76, page 181 and fig. 77, page 185
(Neg #13014)

XXX. Wampum collars and belts; cf. fig. 78, page 200 and fig. 79, page 201 (# G6-14293)